An Israeli in Palestine

An Israeli in Palestine

Resisting Dispossession, Redeeming Israel

Jeff Halper

ICAHD-USA
P.O. Box 2565
Chapel Hill, NC 27515
www.icahdusa.org

Pluto Press

LONDON • ANN ARBOR, MI

in association with ICAHD

הוועד הישראלי נגד הריסת בתים
The Israeli Committee Against House Demolitions
الحركه الإسرائيليه ضد هدم البيوت

First published 2008 by Pluto Press
345 Archway Road, London N6 5AA
and 839 Greene Street, Ann Arbor, MI 48106

www.plutobooks.com

British Library Cataloguing in Publication Data
A catalogue record for this book is available from the British Library

ISBN   978 0 7453 2227 8   Hardback
ISBN   978 0 7453 2226 1   Paperback

Library of Congress Cataloging in Publication Data applied for

This book is printed on paper suitable for recycling and made from fully
managed and sustained forest sources. Logging, pulping and manufacturing
processes are expected to conform to the environmental regulations of the
country of origin.

10 9   8   7   6   5   4   3   2   1

Designed and produced for Pluto Press by
Chase Publishing Services Ltd, Fortescue, Sidmouth, EX10 9QG, England
Typeset from disk by Stanford DTP Services, Northampton
Printed and bound in the United States of America

Contents

Appendices

Rami and Micha, the Civil Society officials who carried
out the demolition of Salim and Arabiya's home.

The author resisting a demolition,
and being arrested.

The author resisting a demolition; here by chaining himself in a home.

The demolition of the Shawamrehs' home.

Salim, beaten for resisting demolition,
lies on the ground during the demolition of his home.

After Israeli, Palestinian and international activists poured the
concrete for the first rebuilt home. Here Salim is shaking hands
with Gush Shalom leader Uri Avneri.

Arabiya building her home with Israeli activists.

At the building site. *Left to right*: Arabiya and some of her children, the author, Uri Avneri, Salim, Ata Jabar (from the Baka Valley near Hebron, whose home was demolished twice and rebuilt each time by ICAHD), and Latif Dori of Meretz.

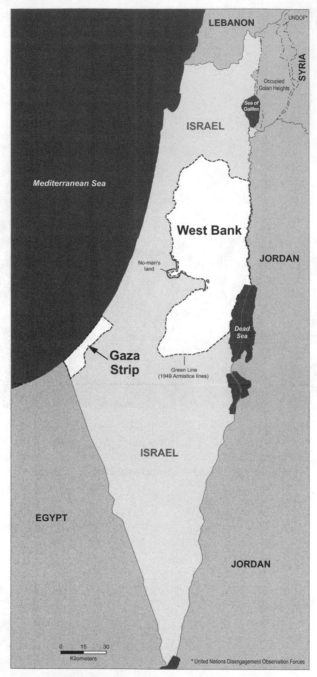

Map 1: Israel and the Occupied Territories/
the Full "Two-State Solution"

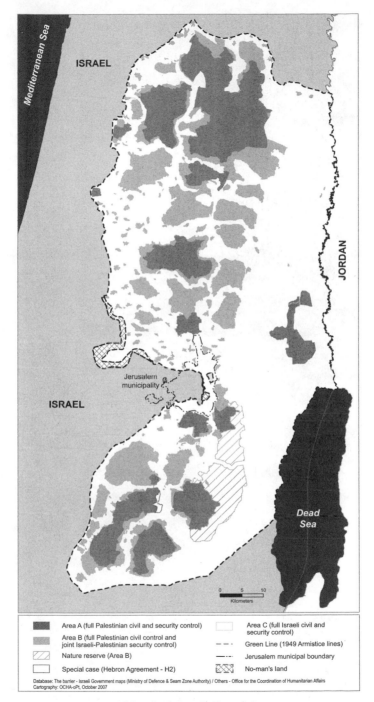

ISRAEL

Mediterranean Sea

JORDAN

Jerusalem
municipality

ISRAEL

Dead
Sea

0   5   10
Kilometers

Area A (full Palestinian civil and security control)

Area B (full Palestinian civil control and
joint Israeli-Palestinian security control)

Nature reserve (Area B)

Special case (Hebron Agreement - H2)

Area C (full Israeli civil and
security control)

Green Line (1949 Armistice lines)

Jerusalem municipal boundary

No-man's land

Database: The barrier - Israeli Government maps (Ministry of Defence & Seam Zone Authority) / Others - Office for the Coordination of Humanitarian Affairs
Cartography: OCHA-oPt, October 2007

Map 2: Areas A, B and C

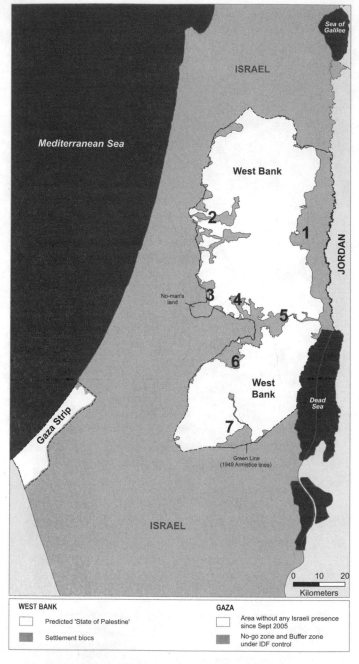

Map 3: Israel's Settlement Blocs: (1) Jordan valley, (2) Western
Samaria, (3) Modi'in, (4) Givat Ze'ev, (5) Ma'aleh Adumim,
(6) Gush Etzion, Efrat-Beitar, Illit, (7) Hebron

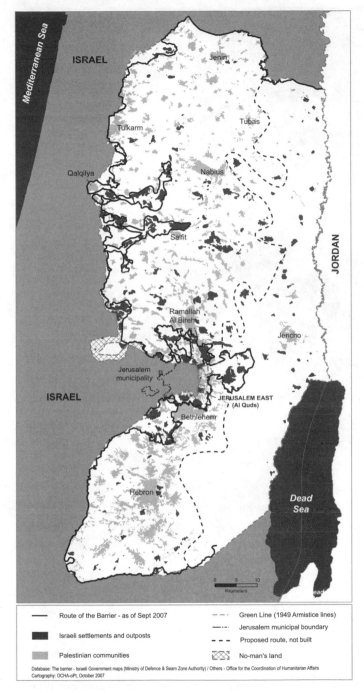

Map 4: Route of the Separation Barrier/Wall

Legend:

— Route of the Barrier - as of Sept 2007

■ Israeli settlements and outposts

▨ Palestinian communities

— - — Green Line (1949 Armistice lines)

— · — · Jerusalem municipal boundary

- - - Proposed route, not built

▨ No-man's land

Database: The barrier - Israeli Government maps (Ministry of Defence & Seam Zone Authority) / Others - Office for the Coordination of Humanitarian Affairs
Cartography: OCHA-oPt, October 2007

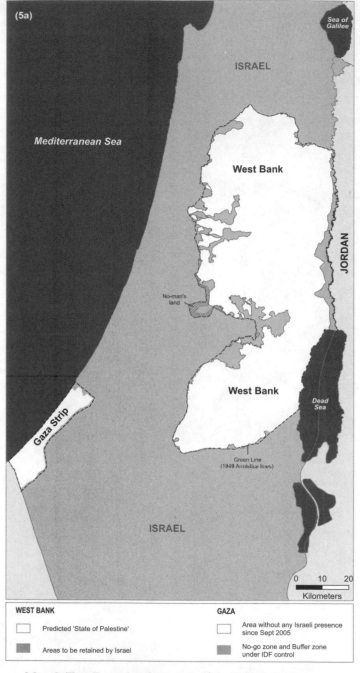

Map 5: Two Emerging Scenarios of the Palestinian Bantustan
(a) minimal areas Israel will retain

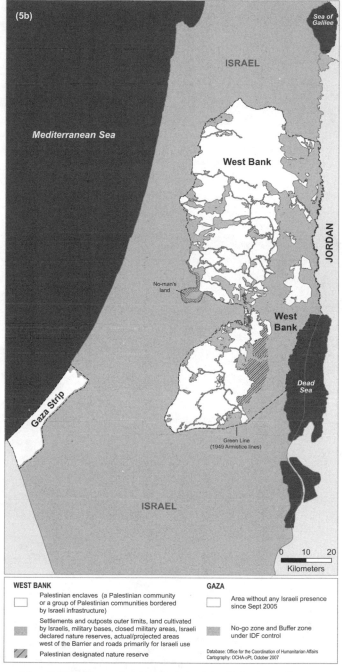

(5b)

Sea of Galilee

ISRAEL

Mediterranean Sea

West Bank

JORDAN

No-man's land

West Bank

Dead Sea

Gaza Strip

Green Line (1949 Armistice lines)

ISRAEL

0   10   20
Kilometers

WEST BANK

Palestinian enclaves (a Palestinian community or a group of Palestinian communities bordered by Israeli infrastructure)

Settlements and outposts outer limits, land cultivated by Israelis, military bases, closed military areas, Israeli declared nature reserves, actual/projected areas west of the Barrier and roads primarily for Israeli use

Palestinian designated nature reserve

GAZA

Area without any Israeli presence since Sept 2005

No-go zone and Buffer zone under IDF control

Database: Office for the Coordination of Humanitarian Affairs
Cartography: OCHA-oPt, October 2007

Map 5: Two Emerging Scenarios of the Palestinian Bantustan
(b) maximal areas Israel will retain

Introduction:
Getting It and Going There

One way of looking at the history of the human group is that it has been a continuing struggle against the veneration of "crap". Our intellectual history is a chronicle of the anguish and suffering of men who tried to help their contemporaries see that some part of their fondest beliefs were misconceptions, faulty assumptions, superstitions and even outright lies. We have in mind a new education that would set out to cultivate just such people—experts at "crap detecting"....We are talking about the schools cultivating in the young that most "subversive" intellectual instrument—the anthropological perspective. This perspective allows one to be part of his own culture and, at the same time, to be out of it.
—Neil Postman and Charles Weingarten,
Teaching as a Subversive Activity (1969)

When I began my career as an educator almost 40 years ago, I shared the simple, commonsensical and optimistic assumption of my fellow educators that people, when given sufficient information, will "learn." Indeed, education is based on the fundamental principle that if people are provided with the rudimentary tools of understanding—facts, context, concepts and an ability to figure things out for themselves—they can and will change their opinions and behavior. This does not mean they must easily give up the views and values they have been given by their society or which they have adopted themselves. It does mean, however, that they are capable of adapting their worldviews in light of issues or situations they might not have fully understood originally. Equally important—and this is the essence of learning—they are capable of modifying their worldviews even if the issues or situations at hand lead them

1

to conclusions contrary to what they have hitherto accepted as "right." As an anthropologist, an educator and a political activist, I still cling to that naïve idea. I am incapable of surrendering the belief that people are basically good and rational, the problem being that their deeply-held cultural identities, narratives, norms, experiences and interests often put them on a collision course with other equally good people whose own worldviews, practices and politics are diametrically opposed. It is this fundamental tension between the ability to learn and change, on the one hand, and, on the other, the fact that people are defined by the social and cultural templates they internalize and fiercely defend, that prevents us from transcending our ethnocentrism and finding ways to deal fairly with those we define as our "enemies."

This tension explodes into full-blown xenophobia when we add other elements characteristic of our global village. Rapid technological and political change keeps us in a constant state of confusion, tension and defensivity as the very values, views and lifestyles we grew up with are thrown into question. "Future-shock" as Alvin Toffler called it. Conflict rises, but a new and more threatening type of conflict, not traditional wars between ideological enemies but seeming "clashes of civilizations." Given, however, the unsustainable lifestyle of ours, the privileged portion of humanity, civilizational "clashes" are but a self-serving way of concealing a brutal reality: that in order to maintain our lifestyles we must control the increasingly scarce resources found, for the most part, in lands of marginalized peoples. Our standard of living depends upon domination and oppression. "How did our oil get under their sand?" as the American bumper-sticker has it. No wonder the defensive mechanisms go up and the good and privileged ones—everyone reading this book—stop listening and circle the wagons.

This is always disappointing to educators, but it does not contradict our conviction that rationality will eventually prevail if people have genuine opportunities to understand and act. Contrary to popular views, this is something permitted by all cultures, all of whom contain both conservative and liberal elements. When cultures close down and appear to become xenophobic or oppressive, it is invariably because of adverse external circumstances rather than anything deriving from the culture itself. The problem of good, intelligent, rational people tolerating and even supporting oppression, intolerance, chauvinism and conflict has, therefore, little to do with "human nature" or "clashes of civilizations." It arises, instead, because people are disempowered by their society's power elite and their cronies, "opinion-makers." Parents, teachers, political and community leaders, clergy, celebrities and the media—all play their role in confining us to the "box," a narrow set of behaviors and opinions that define us as "normal." Since boxes can be confining and supremely boring, the most effective way of keeping us in them is, as the American educator John Taylor Gatto has persuasively argued, to "dumb them down." Assigned to teach "average" kids from whom nothing in particular was expected, Gatto (1992:xi–xii) noticed over the years that

> the unlikeliest kids kept demonstrating to me at random moments so many of the hallmarks of human excellence—insight, wisdom, justice, resourcefulness, courage, originality—that I became confused. They…did it often enough that I began to wonder, reluctantly, whether it was possible that being in school itself was what was dumbing them down. Was it possible I had been hired not to enlarge children's power, but to diminish it?

The great task of any educator, therefore, is to break people out of The Box, to enable them to transcend the confines imposed upon them and to re-link their innate capacity to understand with those elements of their cultures that allow them to reach out rather than close in. This is not an easy task. Liberating ourselves from The Box means bucking those very "gatekeepers"—gatekeepers who possess significant power and sanctions—who constructed it and who work so diligently to keep us inside. If holes can be punched in The Box most people will do what comes naturally: they will peek outside. Now the powers-that-be know this, and so to prevent people from looking out, they demonize the hole-punchers. When critical individuals found in every culture succeed, then, in opening a new window on "reality," the very act has already been so discredited that the gatekeepers often need do nothing; the "average people" themselves quickly paper it over.

Now the modern media—newspapers, television, radio, the internet, satellite dishes, cell phones, mass transportation, plus libraries and so much more—have themselves punched holes in The Box; they have even given people in liberal societies the impression that there *is* no box. Dumbing down, then, has another function: preventing people from "getting it" even if they do manage to glimpse a world outside The Box. "I began to realize," writes Gatto (1992:xii), " that the bells and the confinement, the crazy sequences, the age-segregation, the lack of privacy, the constant surveillance, and all the rest... were designed exactly as if someone had set out to *prevent* children from learning how to think and act, to coax them into addiction and dependent behavior." Although some people "get it" without any outside intervention, it usually requires the development of critical thinking, something the gatekeepers in every society and culture oppose. Only limited forms of critical thinking are tolerated, mainly in the rarified worlds of art and literature, but in general critical thinkers are considered subversive. What exactly are those "critical" elements of thinking that, without them, we can't really "get it"? Among others, they include control over one's thinking processes, enabling one to detect elements of irrationality, prejudice, fear, peer pressure and social conditioning; an intellectual readiness to consider new ideas and ways of doing things; a problem-posing rather than formulaic approach to the world, fostering problem-solving skills; and an ability to contextualize oneself.

Experience in other cultures also helps, since it nurtures an ability to see things from multiple perspectives. In the end, because of their exposure to the world and their ease with other points of view, critical thinkers tend to have a heightened sense of social responsibility and an ability to criticize their own societies.

Why am I getting into all this? Because it is crucial for peace-making. Our problem in Israel-Palestine is not how to make peace—there are a number of viable solutions and an overwhelming will for peace is present among both the Israeli and Palestinian publics—but how to overcome the fear and obfuscation by which Israel's gatekeepers deflect all attempts to arrive at a just peace, manipulating the thought and feelings of peoples and governments that don't, or won't, "get it." Because of both the emotionalism involved and the "clash of civilizations" framing, the struggle to articulate an approach to the conflict that will lead towards its resolution rather than blind support for one "side" over the other is virtually impossible. Effective peace-making requires that uncritical "support" for Israel, one expression of gatekeeper-controlled thought, be replaced by a more nuanced, critical approach to this complex issue, one that encompasses both "sides." I don't ask you to take "sides"; in fact, a chief claim of this book is that there *are* no sides. My job is to generate critical political discussion and effective action that will help us all—Israelis, Palestinians, peoples of the wider Arab and Muslim world and, indeed, people everywhere affected by this conflict—get out of this mess we share and suffer from.

If, on the way, engaging in this conflict nurtures critical thinking, that is only for the good. But this is not a course in critical thinking. How, then, do you move people willing at least to think out of The Box but lacking the knowledge and the skills to do so? One method employed in this book is reframing. If I can offer an alternative way of looking at the conflict, one which opens possibilities for resolution foreclosed

by Israel's "security" framing, I can empower the reader to
critically reframe other issues that apply to other peoples and
places as well. My task is to problematize, to break down the
accepted categories and terms that block fresh, constructive,
approaches to peace, and then to reframe the conflict in a
way that offers new ways of thinking, new possibilities of
resolution. The very title of this book, *An Israeli in Palestine*,
highlights the holistic, out-of-The-Box, fluid, contradictory
reality in which we all live, and nowhere more so than in
the Middle East. The phrase *An Israeli in Palestine* makes
sense and is useful only if we break down the seemingly self-
evident us-and-them dichotomy that typifies ossified political
discussion in and about Israel-Palestine, as elsewhere.

There is one other important element in my approach: Going
there. I am, after all, an activist. I like to call myself an *engaged*
anthropologist, one who combines his personal, professional
and political lives. Acquiring a critical consciousness, being
able to think "out of The Box," is a crucial first step. But what
good is it unless one actually *steps out* of The Box. Only by
bringing coherency and justice to that liminal space between
the Boxes can Boxes themselves be eliminated and a truly
global reality, a *good* reality within which cultural differences
flourish without defensivity and conflict, be forged. This is the
job of us, the people, not of the gatekeepers who jealously
(and violently) guard the Boxes and keep us imprisoned.
This is a book with a clear, empowering message: if we, the
people, lead, our governments will follow. But we have to
empower ourselves.

ISRAEL/PALESTINE: THE TEST-CASE

This book, then, has several agendas and can be read on several
levels (and, again, I hope it will be of value to readers who are
not Middle East "wonks"). At its most basic level, this book
seeks to present a more critical view of the Israeli-Palestinian

conflict than is often offered. It is based upon what we anthro-pologists call "grounded analysis," an intimate knowledge of the local landscape—the physical landscape of Palestine under occupation as well as the political landscape of Israel—where I have lived as an Israeli citizen for the past 35 years. It also incorporates, as I have been trained to do, relevant academic research and concepts.

But since I am interested not only in enlightening but also in galvanizing to action, this book has a point of view as well. It *advocates* for a just, win–win peace in which the concerns and needs of *all* the parties are addressed, the only approach I can see to a genuine solution to this century-long conflict. It also advocates for human rights. The world today is at an intersection. Either we continue along the well-worn path of power, militarism, realpolitik and domination that has led us to our sorry state, or we will begin forging a new one of inclusion, equality, human rights, international law, justice, peace and development. Which way we will go will be determined in large part by the Israeli-Palestinian conflict. This is undoubtedly the most documented and transparent conflict in history, with the possible exception of the current war in Iraq. If Israel can continue as a respected member of the international community and yet maintain a violent occupation for 40 years and more that denied another people its fundamental rights, then what can be said for accountability to norms of human rights? And if accountability is removed as an international mechanism, we condemn ourselves to the unrestrained reign of power politics, with all the injustice and inequality that implies. The failure of the international community to bring this most transparent of conflicts to a just conclusion renders hollow all those values embodied in human rights. In addition to its power to destabilize the international system, this concern is what elevates the Israeli-Palestinian conflict from a local to a global one, with enormous stakes for all of us.

The point of view put forward in this book is that of a critical Israeli Jew who knows that a "balanced" approach to the conflict is based on a false symmetry; holding "both sides" equally accountable and ignoring the enormous power differentials between Israelis and Palestinians fundamentally distorts the picture. There is, after all, only one state with one army involved in this conflict, Israel; the Palestinians have no state, no territory or borders, no sovereign government and certainly no army. And there is only one Occupying Power; Israeli troops sit in the West Bank and invade cities and villages throughout the West Bank, East Jerusalem and Gaza at will; the Palestinians are not occupying Tel Aviv. This is not to say that the Palestinians cannot be held accountable for human rights violations—deliberate attacks on Israeli civilians, for example—or are exempt from political mistakes. It is to say, however, that the lion's share of responsibility for causing the conflict, perpetuating it and preventing its just resolution falls on Israel.

THE BOOK'S STRUCTURE

I have organized the chapters into four parts, each dealing with a different facet of oppression. Why "oppression"? Why not "nationalism," "conflict," "occupation," "peace-making," "human rights," "critical analysis" or any one of the many other key concepts upon which this book rests? Because oppression seems to me the most generic term for what we're talking about, the one which encompasses all the others. "Oppression" cuts through the various ideologies and pretexts, the myriad and diverse ways by which one group seeks to dominate or eliminate others, and gets to the heart of the matter: an inhumane, unsustainable and intolerable situation which must be ended as quickly as possible, period. No "ifs, or buts" about it, no self-serving rationalizations, no blaming the victim. "Oppression" names the situation and names the oppressor as well, in this case Israel and the Zionist movement that preceded it. The book progresses through the various manifestations of oppression that I have identified both academically and through my own consciousness-raising activities, primarily as a peace activist. The structure is much more linear than the process by which I came to understand Israel's oppression of the Palestinians, but such a progression will hopefully make the journey more comprehensible.

In Part I, "Comprehending Oppression," I begin by defining the "Israeli" part, especially as it has played itself out in my own life. Chapter 1, "The Making of a Critical Israeli," is a kind of intellectual introduction of myself. By focusing on the dual process of my progression toward becoming an Israeli yet one with a critical approach to the Israel-Palestine conflict, I try to bring you into the inner dilemmas, processes and struggles that go beyond easy categorizing. Israel is a real place, and its people are not cardboard figures. In the second chapter, "The Message of the Bulldozers," I also introduce you to the transformative experience of witnessing and resisting Israel's policy of demolishing Palestinian homes, and the question underlying my entire analysis: Why in the hell did Israel destroy the Shawamreh family's home? It is through this experience leading to that question which, more than any internal intellectual process, enabled me to comprehend oppression.

Part II, "The Sources of Oppression," delves into the ideological and historical background behind the current conflict. It explores the roots in the proto-Zionist and Zionist movements in the "tribal nationalism" of Eastern and Central Europe of the late nineteenth and early twentieth centuries, which eventually gave rise to an exclusive Jewish ethnocracy in 1948, accompanied by an unavoidable process of dispossession that has continued these past 60 years. How oppression is "packaged" to make it palpable and even admirable, how it is "framed," is the subject of the chapter "The Narrative of Exodus."

How oppression is structured, focusing on Israel's 40-year-plus Occupation in particular, is the subject of Part III. It surveys Israel's attempts to transform its occupation into a permanent regime of control over the entire Land of Israel. It looks at both the ideologies and policies guiding Israeli actions on the ground and the structures they produced which, in turn, determine the parameters of what can be negotiated.

Part IV, "Overcoming Oppression," suggests solutions to the conflict based on a human rights-based and regional approach, solutions that require of Israel to reconceptualize itself if it is to be redeemed from its colonial past and present. It also confronts, as it must, the question of terrorism that underlies and distorts so much of the discourse around the conflict. Finally, since this book will hopefully advance efforts to resolve our century-long conflict, it offers practical ways for getting out of the mess. The program of grassroots resistance, organization and advocacy, both local and international, which I describe in the final chapter may offer an outline of how grassroots campaigns can be organized in other parts of the world.

I hope you will find something of value here, whether you care about Israel and/or Palestine or are engaged in some other struggle and are searching for useful approaches, concepts and models. This book, I also have to say, is somewhat unfinished. One of the problems of a full-time peace-maker on the front lines of a chronic conflict is that you have no space of your own, have little control of your time and schedule which are overtaken by events, and are constantly on-call, whether at home or abroad. A peace-maker has to be multi-tasked; the vast majority of this book I wrote literally at airports (I know where to find the hard-to-find electrical outlets for my battered computer in airports throughout the world), on trains (the last draft I finished as I traveled to twelve German cities in eleven days) or in hotel rooms. Besides working on this book, I do an enormous amount of writing, but most of it consists of urgent articles, position papers and funding proposals, only a small part of which finds itself into these pages. My most personally pressing project, the book you are now holding, was often laid aside for weeks at a time. The manuscript has taken four years longer than anticipated due to the difficulties faced in trying to find the time and space to write in between peace-making activities. But it had to be done. If I hadn't sent it when I did, its publication would have been delayed another year or so. But I have missed the final polishing, filling in the last holes, the feedback of readers who have more distance on the manuscript than I do. I envy my friends at universities who have research assistants, time, quiet, financial support and academic retreats. There are no sabbaticals for peace-makers, certainly not for me who feels a responsibility to "be there" and who must also run an office. The Occupation takes no summer breaks.

In fact, I'm completing the manuscript in Birmingham, Alabama, where I'm attending a conference organized by Sabeel, the Palestinian Christian liberation theology organization. I did take a couple hours to visit the Civil Rights Museum here, where the door of the cell in which Martin Luther King wrote his famous *Letter from Birmingham Jail* in 1963 is displayed. That was the letter in which he reminded us that "Injustice anywhere is a threat to justice everywhere." The Israel-Palestine conflict is not a localized one in some far-off land. Like all other conflicts, it ultimately touches the lives of all of us, especially since the Occupation and Israel's expansionist policies could not be maintained for a month without the active complicity of your government, wherever you are. Reverend King also wrote in that letter: "We know through painful experience that freedom is never voluntarily given by the oppressor; it must be demanded by the oppressed." As I did when I was involved in the civil rights and anti-war movements in the US in the 1960s, I today stand with the oppressed, the Palestinians, in a struggle for freedom, justice and human rights that is truly global. It is to them, and to my comrades in the Israeli peace movement, as well as to our supporters everywhere, that I dedicate this book. And to others without whom even this unfinished manuscript would not have been completed: the Israeli Committee Against House Demolitions (ICAHD) staff; Linda Ramsden, the Director of ICAHD UK, and the writer Kim James, both of whom gave me valuable feedback on the draft; my publisher; and, of course, my family. In particular I dedicate this book to my granddaughter Zohar, who adds special urgency to my quest for a just peace.

Part I

Comprehending Oppression

1
The Making of a Critical Israeli

The Jews made a religion of Justice.
　　—Leon Blum, Prime Minister of France, quoted in Joel Cotton,
　　　　　　　　　Leon Blum: Humanist in Politics (1987:7)

I first became aware of being an "Israeli in Palestine" on July 9, 1998, the day my friend Salim Shawamreh calls "the black day in my life and in the life of my family." On that day the bulldozers of Israel's Civil Administration, its military government in the West Bank, demolished his home for the first time. It was an act so unjust, so brutal, so at odds with the ethos of the benign, democratic, Jewish Israel fighting for its survival I had absorbed on "my side" of the Green Line that it was inexplicable in any terms I could fathom. It had nothing to do with terrorism or security. It was not an act of defense or even keeping Palestinians away from Israeli settlements or roads. It was purely unjust and brutal. As the bulldozer pushed through the walls of Salim's home, it pushed me through all the ideological rationalizations, the pretexts, the lies and the bullshit that my country had erected to prevent us from seeing the truth: that oppression must accompany an attempt to deny the existence and claims of another people in order to establish an ethnically pure state for yourself.

The very fact that I found myself resisting my government's demolition of Palestinian homes did not necessarily remove me from the liberal Zionist Israeli peace camp. Over the past 40 years of the Occupation, dozens of peace-minded

organizations have arisen. Perhaps the best known is Peace
Now, founded in 1978 by reserve army officers who feared
that the Begin government would fail to seize the chance for
peace extended by Anwar Sadat on his recent visit to Israel. In
a letter addressed to Menachem Begin, 348 officers wrote of
the "deep anxiety [that the] government...prefers the existence
of the State of Israel within the borders of 'Greater Israel'
to its existence in peace with good neighborliness," a policy
"that will cause a continuation of control over millions Arabs
and will hurt the Jewish-democratic character of the state"
(<www.peacenow.org>).

Peace Now defines itself as a "Zionist" organization
in that it supports the continued existence of Israel as a
Jewish state—or a "Jewish democracy," a fine-sounding but
problematic concept to say the least. In order to support both
the Jewish state of Israel and the Palestinian people's right to
self-determination, Peace Now can accept only one solution to
the conflict: a two-state solution in which a Palestinian state
emerges in the territories conquered by Israel in 1967: the West
Bank, Gaza and a shared Jerusalem. It also opposes the return
of Palestinian refugees to Israel. Many other peace groups have
also arisen within this Zionist framework. "Courage to Refuse"
was launched with a letter to Sharon's government in 2002
signed by more than 635 reservist soldiers (another 1,000 have
signed on since) declaring their refusal to serve in the Occupied
Territories. It begins with this self-presentation: "We, reserve
combat officers and soldiers of the Israel Defense Forces, who
were raised upon the principles of Zionism, sacrifice and giving
to the people of Israel and to the State of Israel, who have
always served in the front lines, and who were the first to carry
out any mission, light or heavy, in order to protect the State of
Israel and strengthen it." It then goes on to state:

> We, combat officers and soldiers who have served the State of
> Israel for long weeks every year, in spite of the dear cost to our
> personal lives, have been on reserve duty all over the Occupied

Territories, and were issued commands and directives that had nothing to do with the security of our country, and that had the sole purpose of perpetuating our control over the Palestinian people....The missions of occupation and oppression do not serve this purpose [of Israel's defense]—and we shall take no part in them.

Bat Shalom, the Israeli women's peace organization, Uri Avneri's Gush Shalom, Rabbis for Human Rights, the Peres Center for Peace, the Council for Peace and Security, an "association of national security experts in Israel," Yesh Gvul, an organization of reservists who refuse to serve in the Occupied Territories— these are only a few of the peace groups that exist within a Zionist framework. Add to that prominent human rights organizations such as B'tselem and ACRI, the Association of Civil Rights in Israel, plus political parties like Meretz and even parts of the Labor Party, and there are many other Israeli Jews who, like me, could have been in the West Bank protesting our government's policy of demolishing Palestinian homes—18,000 in the Occupied Territories since 1967.

They wouldn't have been found, however, sitting on the ground blocking an Israeli army bulldozer. It is the fine line between protest and resistance that creates the divide, the chasm, between mainstream Zionist and what I call critical Israeli peace groups. I didn't always realize that. For many years I was active in organizations that could have been described as "Zionist," from Siakh, the Israeli New Left in the early 1970s through "The 21st Year" to various ad hoc coalitions, although they always pushed the "left" side of The Box. (I was an active member, for example, of the Committee for the Support of Beir Zeit University, a Palestinian university that had been placed under severe constraints, including prolonged closures, censorship of books and mass arrests of students and teachers, an activist group far beyond the Israeli mainstream.) Even the founding of the Israeli Committee Against House Demolitions (ICAHD) in 1997, in which I took a leading role, did not signal the crossing of any particular ideological line. It was merely another activist group protesting another particular element of the Occupation and included members of Peace Now, Meretz and Rabbis for Human Rights.

What pushed me beyond Zionism into a much more critical but contested and prickly political space was the demolition of Salim's house. If, as the popular saying has it, a conservative is a liberal who has been mugged, then a post-Zionist is a Zionist who has witnessed a house demolition. The conversion experience was unplanned. ICAHD had been in existence a full year but we had not yet actually seen a demolition. Demolitions are normally done early in the morning, just after the men have left for work, and with no prior warning. It was only through an unusual constellation of elements that day that I happened to be on the scene. The Civil Administration officials, who had already demolished five homes in the Anata area, thought they could squeeze in one more. They did not begin on Salim's house, then, until late morning. Salim's resistance—he had rushed home when he heard of the demolitions taking place— delayed things even longer. At noon he heard the dreaded knock on his door. Opening it, he saw his house surrounded by dozens of soldiers and Border Police. Micha Yakhin, a heavily armed inspector of the Civil Administration, stood menacingly before him. "Is this your house?" Yakhin asked brusquely. "Yes, it's my house," Salim replied. "No it isn't," said Yakhin, "it is our house now. You have fifteen minutes to remove all your belongings, we are going to destroy it."

As Micha and the soldiers pushed their way into the home, Salim argued and pleaded with them. When, however, he touched Micha as the latter advanced on him in a threatening way, Salim's protestations turned instantly into "resistance," triggering a full military response. Salim was beaten, handcuffed and thrown out of the house. In the pandemonium, Arabiya, Salim's wife, managed to quickly slam the door shut and lock it with her and her six children inside. She then began calling frantically for help; one of the numbers she called was ours. By chance I happened to be close by preparing for a demonstration against Israel's demolition policy in front of the Civil Administration offices in the nearby settlement of Beit El. As I rushed to the site, I crossed the membrane few Israeli Jews ever cross, running right through the lines of Israeli troops that surrounded the house. It was so unheard of that any outsider would show up on the scene, let alone an Israeli, that I took them by surprise and ended up at Salim and Arabiya's door before they could stop me.

I arrived just after the soldiers had thrown canisters of tear gas through the windows of the house to flush Arabiya and the children out and had broken down the door. I saw Arabiya being carried out unconscious, her young children running and screaming in all directions. (I later found several of the tear gas canisters. They were made in the Federal Laboratories in Philadelphia and were clearly marked with the warning: "For outdoor use only.") Micha then ordered the owner of the commercial wrecking company sub-contracted by the Civil Administration to demolish Palestinian homes to send his workers—foreign guest workers from Romania—into the home to remove the furniture. Given only a few minutes to do so, the workers tore out the bedroom and living room sets, ripped out the kitchen appliances and, in a kind of a chain, jettisoned all the sundry "disposable" items: pictures that had hung on the wall, the children's toys, kitchen cutlery, tables and chairs, the TV, books and schoolbooks. The family's papers, photos and the kid's homework littered the landscape, trampled underfoot by soldiers and neighbors alike.

In the very midst of the tumult, Micha noticed me standing nearby, not knowing what to do. He asked who I was and I told him I was an ICAHD activist. In an almost surrealistic scene, he pulled maps out his bag and began explaining to me why Palestinian homes had to be destroyed. Just then he got word that the house had been cleared. He ordered the bulldozer, which had been waiting down the hill, to come up and finish the job. As it passed by me, I did almost instinctively what I have done many times since: I threw myself in front of it to stop the demolition. This was the first time anyone had ever done anything like that. No one knew what to do. It was clear, however, that I was an Israeli Jew, so no one was ready to shoot me. After trying to coax me to get out of the way, the soldiers brusquely (but not too roughly) pushed me down the hill, where I found myself lying in the dirt and dust next to Salim.

As we lay together on the ground, guarded by soldiers whose guns pointed at us menacingly, watching helplessly as the bulldozer proceeded to systematically demolish his home, I watched Salim's face contort in pain and disbelief. "But I didn't do anything wrong," he kept saying. "I'm not a criminal. I'm not a terrorist. I tried to get a permit for the house. Why are they doing this to me?" Occasionally I heard him gasp and sob, as when the antenna and water tanks on the roof collapsed, these poignant moments bringing home to him the reality of what was happening. At one point, when the bulldozer emerged from the ruins of his home through his children's bedroom, I saw him raise his arms high as if beseeching someone to intervene. Wiping the perspiration from his pained face, trying to find words of awkward consolation, I promised him that the world would hear his story.

On that day, lying on the ground at gunpoint with a Palestinian innocent of any wrongdoing witnessing one of the most wrenching experiences that can ever happen to a person, I found myself in another country I thought no longer existed, Palestine, amongst people who were supposed to be my enemies yet who shared their suffering with me at the hands of what could only be called Israeli state terrorism. Nothing could reconcile what I was witnessing and experiencing with the Zionist narrative I had learned. No, something else was going on here, something of fundamental importance that I had to understand and grapple with. I could not go home as if nothing had happened except yet another atrocity of the Occupation. Only by understanding what had transpired that day would I truly grasp the nature of the Israeli-Palestinian conflict and, perhaps, how to get out of it.

FROM ETHNIC JEW TO JEWISH NATIONAL TO ISRAELI

Until that July day in Anata I suppose you could have called me a "Zionist." I was a Jew who had emigrated to Israel from the United States 25 years earlier, and I generally subscribed to what may be described as Zionist principles, if not to the full-blown ideology. I accepted the idea, fundamental to Zionism, that the Jews constitute a nation in the political sense of the term, based upon their national existence in biblical times, on a kind of religio-nationality maintained throughout the centuries of Exile/Diaspora, and on a revived national existence emerging with other national movements in nineteenth-century Europe. As a nation the Jews possess the right of self-determination in their historic homeland, just as any other nation does, and it seemed to me self-evident that that homeland was the Land of Israel. As a liberal-left Zionist I, of course, accepted the Palestinians' right to self-determination as well, but only in a state *alongside* the State of Israel. When pressed, even by own doubts, I would invariably fall back upon a conviction that, for me, trumped all the problematics of Zionist claims and excesses: the Jews were truly a persecuted people who needed, as well as had a right to, a state of their own. I took umbrage in Mazzini's famous dictum: "Without Country you are the bastards of Humanity." That alone seemed enough to justify the existence of Israel as a Jewish state while subordinating Palestinian claims to the historical necessity of the Jews to control their own destiny. The Palestinians had to fit into the nooks and crannies of my national existence in "my"

country. I did not press the issue any further. I believe that
this position, flexible, short of an actual ideology and capable
of accommodating a variety of political solutions, typifies the
stance of most Israeli Jews.

Why did this speak to me? What led me, a normal secular
middle-class Jewish-American from a small town in the
Midwest, to adopt a radically different identity, that of a Jew in
the primary, national sense—the first step towards becoming an
Israeli—instead of the ethnic Judaism characteristic of the Jews
among whom I lived? (Only 1 percent of American Jews ever
emigrated to Israel, and most of those did so out of religious
rather than national reasons.)

In fact, I came to my Israeliness easily, almost naturally,
without any need of a Zionist ideology or even close contact
to a Jewish community. A third-generation American, I grew
up in a small town in northern Minnesota—Hibbing—where
the immigration experience was still strong. Hibbing was
still populated by immigrants from Scandinavia, Croatia,
Serbia, Poland and Italy and their children, my friends.
The immigrants' languages were still fresh, their foods and
traditions still permeated local life rather than being packaged
into ethnic "fairs." Hibbing had been founded by companies
seeking to mine the rich strata of ore that underlie the Mesabi
iron range, but the bosses, the mining company executives,
stayed far away from this seemingly barren stretch of the sub-
zero Northern Woods. Hibbing therefore lacked a dominant
"host" population of White Anglo-Saxon Protestants. As a
result, immigrant Hibbingites and their offspring were free
of pressures to "Americanize"; they felt no need to hide their
ethnicity in the privacy of their homes or churches.

This was true of the small Jewish community as well.
Composed of about 15 families, it had a small wooden synagogue
but no rabbi. My parents, despite their thoroughly secular
Americanism, very much wanted their children to "remain
Jewish" or at least to preserve a modicum of "Jewish identity."

Yet the Judaism we observed was casual and unobtrusive, as perhaps it had to be in a small town. Although my father served as president of the synagogue, nothing Jewish ever interfered with our "normal" American life, except the High Holidays. As if cramming an entire year of worship into an excruciating three days, we were forced to spend the entire two days of Rosh Hashana from morning to night and the entire day of Yom Kippur, on which we fasted diligently, in synagogue. A rabbi was imported and the mind-numbing tediousness of those three grueling days of standing and sitting to recite in unison meaningless prayers in English and Hebrew was made tolerable only by the constant undertone, like low background noise, of the menfolk sharing their fishing news to the consternation of the rabbi and the women.

Lacking any relation to a belief in God and pursuing effortlessly a quintessentially "American" lifestyle, yet proud of its heritage which melded well into Hibbing's mix of ethnicity and small-town America, the Judaism I grew up with was defined by its ethics. I am still guided by the definition of Judaism propagated by the official textbooks of the Conservative Movement, which I used in my Sunday school teaching: "ethical monotheism." Perhaps that spoke to me because of the general ethos which I absorbed in Hibbing, plain old Midwestern fairness. The Midwest is famous for its flatness: its geographical flatness, a flatness of its spoken language (celebrated in the film *Fargo*), even a flatness of lifestyle exhibited in Jimmy Stewart movies. It was a kind of easygoing casualness that we locally called "Minnesota Nice." My moral position in the world was defined by that down-to-earth, rock-solid sense that if the people are simply fair and nice, we'll all get along fine with each other. I remember watching accounts of the terrible Chinese crackdown on Tibet in the late 1950s and hearing my mother comment: "It's just not right. Those poor people. It's not fair what is happening to them." When pictures of refugees appeared on the screen she said: "What a shame. People only live once. What a waste." This corny philosophy, which still informs my thought and actions, no matter how critical or "intellectual" I become, finds expression in Robert Fulghum's *All I Really Need to Know I Learned in Kindergarten* (1988). The essential rules of life, he says, are those we all learned in kindergarten: play fair, share, don't hit other kids, say you're sorry when you hurt someone, clean up after yourself, don't take things that don't belong to you....I'm not sure if they are universal—I'm not even sure those are rules followed by Jews in Brooklyn—but they do define the values that until today shape my political views and analyses. It was that deep sense of unfairness and outrage which welled up in me as I witnessed the demolition of Salim's house and propelled me in front of the bulldozer. Elemental outrage at simple unfairness is what underlies much the bigger concept of justice.

Hibbing also provided an almost radical ambience in which concerns of social justice were in the air. At its center, geographically and socially, stood a magnificent castle of a school, an intellectual center spanning first grade through junior college where everyone in town met and mingled: students, teachers, the entire community. Adorning its walls were Hibbing's version of Diego Rivera murals, gigantic oil portraits of local life, of farmers and miners, pioneers, Native Americans and immigrants, painted in the 1910s, commemorating labor depicted in heroic scenes and in stirring poetry:

> *They force the blunt and yet unbloodied steel to do their will—*
> Couper

> *Lifting the hidden iron that glimpses in labored mines undrainable of ore*—Tennyson

I remember being particularly moved by "The Ploughman" painted on the wall in the main corridor. I went back to visit while I was writing this book; I wanted to recall why it impacted on me so deeply, and what words still stirred in me but which I had forgotten. "The Ploughman homeward plods his weary way" is inscribed beneath a portrait of the stout ploughman with his Romanesque horse evincing, indeed, the strain, sweat and weariness that were his lot. Hibbing was perhaps the closest America has ever got to a classless society. Labor was glorified—most of the town's breadwinners still earned their decent wages as skilled miners in the vast open-pit mines—and two of its finest sons were Gus Hall, long the head of the American Communist Party, and Woody Guthrie's protégé, Bob Dylan.

In the thick ethnic environment of Hibbing in the 1950s and 1960s, Americanness was thin and unfulfilling. Like many third-generation Americans, I sought a return to my ethnic roots, but Jewish life in the Midwest resembled nothing more than warmed-over Protestantism. I even enrolled in the Hebrew Union College, the Reform rabbinical seminary in Cincinnati, but to no avail. The only meaningful connection I could forge between my Jewish identity and American life took the form of my involvement, *as a Jew*, in the civil rights and anti-Vietnam War movements, which I associated with the value Jews placed on social justice. I wore a skull cap in demonstrations and meetings, and noted with pride the disproportionate number of Jews likewise involved. Over the years my Jewish identity gradually took over, displacing my ethnic one. Unbeknownst to me at the time, I was moving beyond Jewish ethnicity towards a kind of proto-Israeliness, with Israel itself entering the equation unintentionally, almost accidentally.

In 1966, as an undergraduate student at Macalester College in St. Paul, I won a scholarship to study the Falashas, the Jews of Ethiopia. As I was booking my ticket I found out that going through Tel Aviv was as cheap as any other route. So I decided to make a brief stop-over. Landing in Tel Aviv that summer, I found my way to a youth hostel run by an old man named Joseph, who took a liking to me. Soon after I arrived he

invited me to travel with him to Jerusalem for the day. About
the only thing I remember clearly is standing in an observation
tower looking out over the Old City, which was still under
Jordanian rule.

That was it. On the surface nothing dramatic had happened.
I did not change my views in any way; I was not "transformed"
and still knew nothing about Zionism. But those few days in
Israel had touched me. The fact that my initial contact with
Israel was not through some official agency peddling *aliya*
(immigration) but rather through Joseph, a "real" Israeli who
took me into the lives of other "real" Israelis for a couple
days, probably made all the difference. Though I was feeling
increasingly "Jewish," I would have resisted the nativism
inherent in Zionism, the erection of national walls between
me and the other peoples of the world, including Arabs. My
Judaism was still progressive and based in Jewish ethics which
I considered inclusive and global. Joseph, that wizened, smiling
old man, was certainly no Ari Ben Canaan. He did not fit the
mold of the heroic Israeli, "reborn" out of war as portrayed by
Leon Uris in his epic Zionist paean *Exodus*. But he provided
the perfect entrée to Israel. In hindsight, it was Joseph who not
only led me into a "real" Israel that offered me a next natural
stage in my evolution as a Jewish national, but who allowed
me, at that early stage, to bypass the tension contained in my
view of myself as "an Israeli in Palestine." I was able to take
on "Israeliness" as my primary identity while, on a political
level, retaining my loathing of Israeli policies, deriving as they
are from a racist and insular national narrative.

FROM ISRAELI TO CRITICAL ISRAELI

By the summer of 1973, at the age of 27, I was ensconced
finally in Israel. My transition to life there was very smooth and
happy. As a Ph.D. student in anthropology, I had a professional
agenda. My fieldwork, for which I had a generous fellowship,

involved research into the ethnic identities of working-class Kurdish Jews in the inner-city neighborhood of Jerusalem, which I had come to know as a volunteer when I was at HUC and where I still live. In Nakhlaot I found a community where I felt welcomed and accepted. My Hebrew was passable and getting better, and I enjoyed interviewing elderly Jews from the Kurdish areas of Turkey, Iraq and Iran, as well as from Yemen, and their children. I had reconnected to the "real" Israel without official intermediaries and was being socialized, rather than indoctrinated, by my neighbors and friends. And I was finally free of the dilemma that had come to preoccupy my life in the US: how to integrate a Jewish identity into my daily life. The "Jewish" part of my identity melted away in favor of an Israeli one upon my arrival in Israel, and it has never returned.

My work among *Mizrahi* Jews (that is, Jews from Muslim countries) grounded me solidly in Israeli society. The other community with which I was involved, the Israeli peace camp, remained important to me. No sooner had I landed in Jerusalem than I attended a meeting of *Siakh*, the Israeli New Left, where I met my future wife and partner-in-crime, Shoshana. I was critical of Israeli policies towards both the Palestinians and the *Mizrahi* Jews, but my romance with Israel continued to dominate my personal and professional life. I was fascinated by the Israeli culture that had emerged over the past century. I wrote a book about the Jewish community of Jerusalem in the nineteenth century, and intended to write another on the development of the two national cultures, a "Hebrew" one emerging in the pre-state Jewish community from the turn of the century into the 1960s, and its successor, the contemporary Israeli one. I did activist peace work over the years, but it was by no means my main preoccupation. I even mentioned to Shosh a few times that we should try to have more Arab friends, but like other Israelis we had few opportunities to even meet Arabs, let alone socialize with them.

The Arab-Palestinian element of Israeli life started to break through only when I took over the Middle East Center of Friends World College, an American college based on experiential learning, and hired as a co-faculty Nabila Espanioli, a Palestinian citizen of Israel who lived in Nazareth. As we traveled with the students through Israel, the Occupied Palestinian Territories, Jordan and Egypt, Nabila, the first Palestinian I had really spent time with and a keen critical thinker, opened my eyes to Palestinian realities. I remember in particular one of our first study trips together, when Nabila took the students and me into a Jewish National Fund forest planted over the remains of the Palestinian village of Saffuriyya. She began to explain the history of the village of 4,000 inhabitants, their expulsion in 1948, the "ethnic cleansing" of the Galilee by Israeli troops, massacres that had occurred and how Jews had been allowed to take over Arab lands; as in Saffuriyya, which has been replaced by a Jewish town called by the Roman-era name Tzipori.

When we returned to the minibus I began to gently "correct" Nabila. Not that the facts weren't true, mind you, but that the tone was one-sided; as an Israeli Jew I didn't feel that "my side" had been fairly presented: that Tzipori had once been a famous city where part of the Jewish Talmud was codified; that the city had been taken in 1948 in the context of a war; that Jews had "returned" to the city as part of their own national revival. The more Nabila insisted on her version, the more defensive I became. Our voices rose to a shouting match. I told Nabila that as educators we had a responsibility to present our facts in a balanced way, that as an anthropologist I wanted to understand both sides, that we couldn't just propagandize our students. And here's where the students stepped in. "Wait a minute," they told me. "Why are you getting defensive? We haven't heard anything from you that contradicts what Nabila said. 'Tone?!' What do you expect from a Palestinian standing at the site of a demolished village? How many times did you talk about persecution of Jews in your lectures to us—and with a definite 'tone' of sympathy? Why should your voice, your narrative, your 'tone' be privileged over Nabila's? Don't bullshit us about critical thinking and then pull rank as a professor and Jew. And a man! We resent your using your louder male voice to drown out Nabila's."

They were perfectly right, of course. That interaction was a turning point in my life. I confronted for the first time the hidden reality on the "other side" of the Israeli-Palestinian membrane, that porous, transparent filter which defines and envelops Jewish space and turns everything "Arab" into mere background, which separates "us" from "them." But I also confronted the uncompromising demands of intellectual honesty. Without the benefit of a classroom where I controlled the discussion, without the safe distance between teacher and pupil, my students compelled me to adhere to the very intellectual standards I had been asking of them. I learned that defensiveness is not an honest intellectual position. Quite the opposite, it obfuscates; it is employed when a strong argument is lacking, or when you know the other side has a point. Nabila and the students did not give me the luxury of staying comfortably within self-imposed parameters, using sophistic intellectual devices to avoid going where I didn't want to go. What I learned that day proved crucial to my ability to deal with such a charged, emotionally-laden issue like Israel-Palestine. One of the hardest parts of critical thinking is the ability to detect in yourself elements of irrationality, prejudice, fear, peer pressure and social conditioning—and to confront them.

In 1997, in the wake of Benjamin Netanyahu's election, a number of us in the Israeli peace movement met and decided it was time to re-engage in resisting the Occupation. The Oslo "peace process" was in an obvious state of collapse, the Occupation was brutally reasserting itself, and the peace movement had become dormant during the years of Rabin and Peres. But what to do? We sought the views of Palestinians whom we knew, asking them: What issues do you consider of greatest priority? In what ways could we best work together? The bottom line, of course, was—and is—bringing about a total end of the Occupation. On the way, one issue arose repeatedly: Israel's constant demolition of Palestinian homes. Several members of our political circle had become involved in efforts to save the home of Ata Jabar and his family near Hebron which the Israeli authorities threatened to demolish due to the lack of a building permit, but we did not really know much about the phenomenon.

One day in July, 1997, Amos Gvirtz, a long-time peace activist and Israel's foremost proponent of non-violent resistance, received a phone call from Ismail Shawamreh, Salim's cousin and neighbor in the village of Anata, on the northeast border of Jerusalem. Ismail, a father of ten, had just received a demolition order from the Israeli authorities and feared for his home. Galvanized into action around this issue, ICAHD, the Israeli Committee Against House Demolitions, was created at a meeting attended by eight people representing different peace groups: Bat Shalom, Yesh Gvul, Rabbis for Human Rights, Palestinians and Israelis for Non-Violence, and the Public Committee Against Torture, as well as several members of the Meretz party and Peace Now.

I wish I could say that when we decided to form ICAHD we chose the issue of house demolitions consciously and strategically, out of a well-informed assessment of the political situation and a clear notion of where we were going as a political action group. We didn't. We backed into it without fully appreciating how powerful a vehicle of resistance the issue of house demolitions would turn out to be. Only gradually did we discover that Israel's policy of house demolitions constituted the very essence of the conflict: Zionism's program of dispossessing the Palestinians altogether.

After decades of life in Israel, raising a family here, going to the army (which I did do, my only saving grace being that all three of my children are conscientious objectors, one having spent a significant amount of time in prison for it), involving myself deeply in academic work, in teaching, in political activity with both the *Mizrahi* and Ethiopian communities, as well as in the peace movement, having run (unsuccessfully) for the Jerusalem city council and participating in all the myriad experiences of daily life that are part and parcel of who we are, I can say that I had become an Israeli. My "Israeliness" had completely supplanted the ethnic Jewish identity I had grown up with, but it also superseded Zionism. My relationship with Zionism had always been tangential; I managed to bypass ideology and Zionist institutions on my way to becoming an Israeli. Now, as I became involved in ICAHD activities with the Palestinians in the Occupied Territories, I saw how important it was to go beyond Zionism—which has become quite destructive and racist, as we'll see—and do what I have been doing all these years: relating to Israel as a real country and not as some ideological construct.

Are you a Zionist? I'm often asked. Or a post-Zionist, a neo-Zionist, an anti-Zionist? The question, for me, is irrelevant. I am an Israeli living in a real country called Israel. That means, for me, that Israel is a fact of life. No matter whether Israel should have been established, the crimes committed in 1948, Israel's deplorable 40-year Occupation and its ongoing persecution of the Palestinians—Israel is a political fact that cannot be simply erased, even if one feels all the moral justification to do so. This is the starting point of my political work. But only the starting point. Israel, like all colonial regimes who managed in the end to redeem themselves from their oppressive pasts, must transverse a long and painful trail from de-colonization through reconciliation to a new form of political life that is just and inclusive of all the country's inhabitants *before* it can expect security and normalization.

Israel did not have to become a colonial state. Unlike, say, British farmers who woke up one morning and decided to move to Kenya where they could get 1,000 acres and cheap African labor, Jews did feel a genuine connection to the country arising out of the sincere belief that they were, in fact, returning to their ancient homeland, the Land of Israel. *I* felt that sense of "return," of belonging. Had Zionism only acknowledged the existence and claims of the other indigenous people living in a land, the Palestinians, I believe an accommodation could have been worked out. The Arab-Israeli conflict was not inevitable. In fact, the Zionist movement contained many progressive figures, institutions and even political parties, many if not most of them overtly Socialist in outlook. The combination, however, of an exclusivist nationalism with a small circle of highly ideological decision-makers led the pre-State Zionist community (the *Yishuv*) to adopt a confrontational rather than conciliatory approach to the Arabs. The results, as we see today, were disastrous. The denial of the national existence and rights of the Palestinians, often their very humanity, resembled that of other colonial regimes. Native resistance to colonizers was routinely labeled "terrorism." But the establishment of a state which set out to systematically drive the indigenous population from the country altogether and then "cleanse it" of any trace of that people is something else.

In this Israel falls squarely into the colonial camp, and I think all of us would agree that a *colonial* state clearly has no right to exist—or, to put it another way, a colonial situation must be totally ended before any state can expect acceptance and normalcy. OK, you may say, but that is true of other countries as well, including the US and all the colonial powers of Europe. Well, they, too, had to undergo a process of de-colonization and reconciliation of one kind or another before normalization. There are colonial societies that have redeemed themselves, to a greater or less degree, by both ending their colonial regimes and making amends with peoples they exploited and oppressed. Countries like France, Britain, Belgium, Portugal and Russia (to name but a few) left their colonies, though they tend to accept their ongoing obligations towards them both by extending economic assistance and accepting their emigrants, even if reluctantly. Indeed, former colonial states have reconceptualized themselves as pluralistic and democratic societies. Canada recognizes its native peoples as First Nations and, with the US, granted its Native Americans both citizenship and recognition as nations with certain extra-territorial rights. Modern New Zealand is founded on the Treaty of Waitangi, proudly displayed in the center of its national museum, a pact entered into with its Maori population in 1840, though being implemented only in the past two decades. And when South Africa repudiated apartheid, it did far more than merely give its black citizens the vote; it adopted an entirely new constitution, reconstituted itself as a country for all its citizens and even instituted a Truth and Reconciliation Commission.

This is not to say that decolonization has resolved all the issues extant between the former colonial regimes and their victims. It is a process, a continual struggle. But it is a necessary step towards redeeming an unjust past, underpinned by notions of restorative and transformational justice, and, of course, human rights. Only through such a restorative process can normalization be achieved. The issue for me, then, is not whether Israel started out as a colonial enterprise, but whether it has taken effective measures to de-colonize and enter into a new relationship with the Palestinians. And here is where we enter into great difficulty. Sixty years after its establishment, accompanied by what only can be described as a campaign of ethnic cleansing against the Palestinian population (Pappe 2006), Israel is still deeply entrenched in its colonial enterprise. Not only have the remnants of the Palestinian people inside Israel been reduced to second-class citizenship at best, excluded from living on a full 93 percent of the country, but the Occupation under which almost 4 million other Palestinians live confined to tiny enclaves by massive

Israeli settlements and now the "Separation Barrier" grows only stronger. If history and justice have anything to do with it, Israel's expansionist form of Zionism is doomed to the same fate as other systems of colonialism. As an Israeli, my task is to bring Israel's Occupation to as quick an end as possible, thereby releasing a dynamic whereby Israel is able to reconceptualize itself and, in the end, normalize its position both in the Middle East and internationally.

As an Israeli rather than a Zionist, I can go there. I don't know what form Israel will eventually assume. It may stay a Jewish country in the way Britain is British, a pluralistic society belonging eventually to all its citizens but with Hebrew as a main language and an "Israeli" core. Or it may morph into something entirely different: a bi-national state, a member of a wider Middle Eastern confederation, or something we cannot today imagine. I do know, however, that the present situation is untenable and that Israel will transcend Zionism, even if the latter remains an important element of Israeli history and mythology. A country, which evolves in ways completely unpredictable, cannot be forcibly contained within the narrow, constricting confines of an ideology.

In the meantime, the task I have set before me is to hasten a just peace and, in the process, help Israel redeem itself from the worse-than-colonial situation in which it is mired. Since I am now an Israeli and since Israel, in my view, carries the lion's share of responsibility for the conflict as the strong party in the region and an Occupying Power, my modest approach to peace-making begins at home: trying to understand where Israel is coming from as a country and a people dedicated to an expansionist national ideology, and therefore where it is going—indeed, where it can or cannot go given the massive "facts on the ground" it has established both in the Occupied Territories and at home. And since anthropologists read the world from the ground up, it is entirely appropriate that I begin with the act of demolition that brought me to Anata on that "black day" in Salim's life, when I finally realized that I was not only an Israeli, but an Israeli in Palestine, a condition I would have to address if I was to reconcile my values and commitments with my personal life. So the journey to discover what Israel wants and how I can contribute to the struggle to normalize its existence begins with a single question: Why in the hell did they demolish this family's home?

2
The Message of the Bulldozers

On 21 August 2003, on the morning of his wedding, As'ad Mu'yin
had his house demolished; the house of his cousin Ziad As'ad, who
had married a week earlier, was demolished at the same time. The two
adjacent houses were in the West Bank town of Nazla 'Issa. As'ad Mu'yin
had been living on the ground floor of the house with his parents and
three brothers and had furnished and prepared the second floor to move
in with his wife. The house was demolished before he could do so.
The new furniture and the wedding gifts disappeared under the rubble,
along with the content of the family home on the ground floor. He told
Amnesty International: *"The army came early in the morning, at about
7am. I was getting ready for the wedding, for a very happy day. They
had bulldozers...they gave us 15 minutes to leave the house. We had
no time to salvage anything. They said that we did not have building
permits....But everyone knows that Israel does not give building permits
to Palestinians in Area C."*
    —Amnesty International, *Under the Rubble* (2004:4)

Lying in the dirt with Salim as the bulldozer tore through
his home, I struggled to comprehend what was happening.
Nothing in my Israeli experience could make sense of it.
As a long-time peace activist, I wasn't naïve. I knew Israel's
occupation policies had little to do with security, that they were
in fact proactive claims to the entire country, but pursuing my
own affairs, I did what other Israelis do: I didn't inquire too
closely, I didn't cross the membrane.

As dramatic as the events surrounding their home turned
out to be—hundreds of soldiers, Border Police, Israeli officials
and demolition workers beating and threatening and shooting,
throwing out furniture, yelling, giving orders and, in the end,

leaving a demolished family in the dust and ruins of their home—Salim, his wife Arabiya, and their six children were also doing nothing more than living their ordinary lives, albeit under occupation. Cousins, both came from families made refugees in 1948. Their native village, located in the well-watered, grape-growing area of southern Judean Hills just across from the southern West Bank of today, was named Amishagav. Its ruined houses and terraces still remain; they are found, however, in a closed military area close to the Separation Barrier, and thus cannot be visited. Amishagav's fields have been parceled out among the members of Shekef, an Israeli farming community built on Amishagav land. During the war Arabiya's family emigrated to Jordan, where she grew up. Salim's family moved to Jerusalem, first to the Old City, then to the Shua'fat refugee camp outside the Old City (known as "East" Jerusalem since it was conquered and annexed by Israel in 1967), where he graduated from the local United Nations Relief and Works Agency (UNRWA) vocational high school as a construction engineer. In the early 1980s he and Arabiya married, then spent almost ten years in Saudi Arabia where Salim worked, accumulating a nest egg for when they returned home to Palestine.

In the early 1990s, Salim brought his growing family back to Jerusalem. Since the refugee camp was chronically overcrowded, he used his savings to purchase a small plot of land on the outskirts of the nearby village of Anata, which he duly registered with the Civil Administration. He then applied for a permit to build a modest home, not knowing that Israel had zoned almost all the West Bank as "agricultural land." Although Salim's plot was dry and rocky—"never farmed since the time of Adam," as he often says—it didn't matter. After all, since the late 1960s Israel has built more than 200 settlements accommodating 500,000 Jewish settlers in some 150,000 housing units on that same "agricultural" land where Palestinians were denied building permits. Zoning

Salim's property as agricultural only provided the pretext for legally denying him a permit without appearing discriminatory against Arabs. After paying $5,000 in fees and waiting for more than a year, Salim received word that his application had been denied.

Having nowhere else to live, Salim, an outgoing person who believes that people are innately good and reasonable, applied again—actually another three times, each time encouraged to do so by the good cops/bad cops of the Civil Administration. One would suggest helpfully that he apply for a permit to build on agricultural land, another would deny the permit because his plot wasn't big enough to be considered agricultural. Another seemingly friendly official told Salim that he was missing two signatures on his deed of ownership, and if he supplied them he would surely be given a permit. When asked whose signatures were missing, a less friendly head of the planning department informed him that they had no idea, since his file had been lost. Each application cost some $5,000 in fees, surveying and legal expenses, and his request was repeatedly denied, each time for a different reason. The slope leading to his property was too steep he was told ("but Jerusalem is built on mountains," Salim comments dryly, "and every mountain has to have a slope"), and besides, his plot lay too close to a planned "bypass" road.

By now desperate for a place to live, understanding that he would never be granted a permit yet encouraged by the expectation that his land would be returned to the Palestinians in the course of the just-launched Oslo peace process, Salim went ahead and constructed a modest home for his family without the permit. He was immediately issued a demolition order by the Civil Administration. Salim appealed all the way to the Supreme Court, paying out thousands of additional dollars in legal fees although, like other Palestinians in similar situations, he knew he would eventually lose. "You hope they won't actually come to demolish," he explained. "Or you hope that peace will come before they do. Or you hope that with all the houses they have to demolish they'll skip yours, at least for a few years, and in the meantime maybe something will happen to change the situation." And, indeed, Salim, Arabiyah and their children lived in their home for almost five years, suffering the daily fear that the bulldozers might suddenly appear. They finally did following Micha's knock on the door.

Salim's neighbors, all of whom had demolition orders themselves, tried to resist the demolition that July day, throwing rocks at the bulldozer and the soldiers. They were met with tear gas, percussion grenades and rubber bullets. A 16-year-old boy was shot in the area of the stomach, losing a kidney. In the meantime, and completely by chance, two busloads of Israelis who had been traveling to the demonstration we had been organizing in front of the Civil Administration in nearby Beit El were diverted to the site. Witnessing the demolition from the crest of a hill provided Israelis with a rare glimpse of an actual demolition. Even more, many of the Israelis who stood on that hilltop were parents of soldiers who that day saw their children—or soldiers who could have been their children—in "action" for the first time. For Israeli parents, even liberal ones who also had served in their day, the army experience is considered a positive thing, a rite of passage to becoming an adult and truly "Israeli." They expect their children to choose something "meaningful" to do—combat units (and in particular "elite" combat units) or intelligence—rather than passing their army service as mere "jobniks."

When their kids—the same soldiers who beat Salim and tear gassed his family—come home on weekends looking "cute" in their uniforms, Mom prepares their favorite dishes and happily washes their dirty clothes. In the evening the soldiers revert to being teenagers, meeting up with their friends and going out to the local disco or partying place. On Sunday morning, the beginning of the week in Israel, the kids, once again dressed in their now-clean uniforms, M-16s strapped around their shoulders, are driven to the bus station by Dad. Quick kisses, and the boys and girls hurry off to their buses. It is the transformation of their children back into soldiers that the parents never see: the hard, cold looks when encountering Arabs, the aggressive posture, the callousness. Parents would have difficulty even recognizing their kids. This is what dismayed the Israelis who observed the demolition: they saw their own children shooting into the crowd, almost hitting *them*. The boy who was shot was standing next to 80-year-old Rabbi Max Warschawski, a former Chief Rabbi of Strasburg and a member of Rabbis for Human Rights. "While in the French Resistance in World War II I was shot at several times," he later said. "But I never came so close to actually being shot as I did in Israel, that day in Anata, and *by Jews*."

Many of those on the hilltop even tried yelling at the soldiers, just as parents would yell at their kids. Being ignored or stared at in the cold, impersonal, disparaging, threatening way that soldiers do, being pushed back with rifles and even shot at, shook them to the core.

Every demolition is a microcosm of the Occupation, and every one contains its own tragic twists. The driver of the bulldozer, we learned later, was himself a Palestinian, employed by the Israeli wrecking company. He came from a village near Jerusalem that had been demolished after the 1948 war—and, it turned out, he knew Salim. Compelled to drive by his Israeli employer and unable to risk losing his job, he found himself dodging stones thrown by other Palestinians. When, after demolishing only half of the house, he tried to drive away, Micha and the soldiers ran after him and forced him to return until the home was reduced to rubble.

A NATIONAL OBSESSION

Dramatic and tragic as it was to us, the demolition of Salim and Arabiya's home was actually quite routine. In fact, Salim's was the fifth house demolished that very day in Anata; on other days the Civil Administration has destroyed 150 or more homes and shops in one fell swoop. Piecing together the details, I discovered that Israel had demolished more than 9,000 Palestinian homes in the Occupied Territories (the figure at this writing, early 2007, now stands at 18,000; see Appendix 1). And, as in the case of the Shawamreh family, in 95 percent of the cases the demolition had nothing to do with terrorism or security. To make matters worse, in most cases these were homes of Palestinian refugees whose original homes inside Israel were systematically demolished as well.

The policy of demolitions did not begin, of course, in 1967. The British, realizing how painful the loss of their homes was to Palestinians, employed it as a "deterrent," though never used it against Jews. Between 1948 and into the 1960s, Israel systematically demolished between 417 and 536 Palestinian villages inside of what became the State of Israel, fully half the villages of Palestine, in an attempt to "cleanse" the country of the Arabs and their presence (Khalidi 1992, Pappe 2006:9). And here appears a fact that arises time after time to this day: this massive campaign to de-Arabize Palestine was initiated not in the heat of battle, not for security reasons, but as a proactive policy to create "facts on the ground." Organized attacks on Arab communities began as early as December 1947, six months before the State of Israel was established and the war began, at Israel's initiative and lasting *years* after their residents had fled or were driven out (Morris 2004, Pappe 2006).

That pattern continued in the wake of the 1967 war—and even before. The very first act of the Israeli Occupation, carried out even as the war was proceeding, involved the demolition of hundreds of homes in the Old City of Jerusalem. On July 11, with no connection to wartime activities or any security concerns, more than 135 Palestinian families in the historic Muslim Mughrabi Quarter of Jerusalem's Old City were roused from their beds in the dead of night. They watched in horror as Israeli bulldozers summarily destroyed their homes and the quarter's two mosques to create a plaza for Jewish worshippers in front of the Western Wall. So rushed was the job—another characteristic of house demolitions—that an elderly Palestinian woman, Hajja Rasmia Tabaki, was killed when her home was demolished on top of her. She became the Occupation's first victim (Gorenberg 2006:42–45).

In addition to the Mughrabi Quarter, four entire villages, at least 2,000 houses, were razed in the Latrun area west of Jerusalem immediately after the war; their ruins have since been covered over by what is known as "Canada Park," a popular picnic spot for Israeli families. Another 2,000 or so were demolished in other parts of the Occupied Territories; a third of the city of Qalqilya, for example. A couple years later, in 1971, Ariel Sharon, then Commander of the Southern Command, cleared 2,000 houses in the Gaza refugee camps so as to facilitate the movement of military vehicles, including tanks, in the crowded camps. (In his five years as Prime Minister, 2001–06, Sharon oversaw the demolition of at least 1,500 homes in Gaza.)

As the years progressed it seemed as if the demolition of Palestinian homes had become a national obsession. Two thousand houses were destroyed in the Occupied Territories in the course of quelling the first Intifada in the late 1980s and early 1990s. Another 1,700 were demolished by the Civil Administration *during the course of the Oslo peace process* (1993–2000). Most of the demolitions had nothing to do with security but were carried out as a form of collective punishment, illegal under international law, to "bring a message to the Arabs." No formal legal or administrative process accompanies those demolitions: no formal demolition orders, no warning, no time to remove furniture or personal belongings. You often have barely time to escape before the house is brought down around your ears. Since 2004 the army has gone so far as to enact a policy of demolishing homes on top of their residents if "wanted" persons are suspected of being inside and do not surrender. Indeed, your home may become "collateral damage" to that of a neighbor whom the Israeli authorities have targeted. Nuha Maqqdmeh Sweidan, a Gazan mother of ten and nine months pregnant, was killed when the house next to hers was dynamited by Israeli troops. "We were in bed, the children were asleep," her husband related to Amnesty International (2004:3). "There was an explosion and walls collapsed on top of us. I pulled myself from under the rubble....I started to dig in the rubble with my hands. First I found my two little boys and my three-year-old girl....One by one we found the other children, but my wife remained trapped under the rubble with our youngest daughter, who is two. She was holding her when the wall fell on her...."

Writes Amnesty in its report *Under the Rubble* (2004:3):

> The Israeli authorities claim that these demolitions are not intended as punishment, but rather to "deter" Palestinians from getting involved in attacks. Israel has never destroyed the homes of Israeli Jews who committed serious attacks, such as the murder of Prime Minister Rabin, or bomb attacks against Palestinians or Israeli Arabs. These punitive forced evictions and house demolitions are a flagrant form of collective punishment and violate a fundamental principle of international law, which stipulates that collective punishment is never permissible under any circumstances.

At times it seemed the easiest, most direct, most painful way to simply "get" the Palestinians. Here is the volunteered testimony of reservist Moshe Nissim, a bulldozer driver and self-described "average Israeli," who spent three "satisfying" days and nights of action as he used his massive D-9 Caterpillar bulldozer to demolish homes in the densely packed Jenin refugee camp at the onset of Operation Defensive Shield, in March 2002.

> For three days I just erased and erased. The entire area. I took down any house from which there was shooting. To take it down, I would take down several more. The soldiers warned with a speaker, that the tenants must leave before I come in, but I did

not give anyone a chance. I did not wait. I didn't give one blow, and wait for them to come out. I would just ram the house with full power, to bring it down as fast as possible. I wanted to get to the other houses. To get as many as possible....I didn't give a damn about the Palestinians, but I didn't just ruin with no reason. It was all under orders.

Many people were inside houses we set to demolish. They would come out of the houses we were working on. I didn't see, with my own eyes, people dying under the blade of the D-9. And I didn't see houses falling down on live people. But if there were any, I wouldn't care at all. I am sure people died inside these houses, but it was difficult to see, there was lots of dust everywhere, and we worked a lot at night. I found joy with every house that came down, because I knew they didn't mind dying, but they cared for their homes. If you knocked down a house, you buried 40 or 50 people for generations. If I am sorry for anything, it is for not tearing the whole camp down.

I didn't stop for a moment. Even when we had a two-hour break, I insisted on going on....I had plenty of satisfaction. I really enjoyed it. I remember pulling down a wall of a four-story building....If the job was to hard, we would ask for a tank shell. I couldn't stop. I wanted to work and work....On Sunday, after the fighting was over, we got orders to pull our D-9s out of the area, and stop working on our "football stadium", because the army didn't want the cameras and press to see us working....

I had lots of satisfaction in Jenin, lots of satisfaction. I kept thinking of our soldiers. I didn't feel sorry for all those Palestinians who were left homeless. I just felt sorry for their children, who were not guilty.... (quoted in "7 Days," *Yedioth Ahronoth* Supplement, May 31, 2002)

Moshe Nissim earned a medal of valor from the army command and was hailed as the "hero" of the Operation. What can you say when one becomes a hero for demolishing the homes of people innocent of any crime? Amnesty International did find something to say. In its report *Under the Rubble: House Demolition and Destruction of Land and Property* (2004), it comments:

The largest single wave of destruction carried out by the Israeli army was in the Jenin refugee camp in April 2002. The army completely destroyed the al-Hawashin quarter and partially destroyed two additional quarters of the refugee camp, leaving more than 800 families, totaling some 4000 people, homeless. Aerial photographs and other evidence show that much of the house destruction was carried out after clashes between Israeli soldiers and Palestinian gunmen had ended and Palestinian gunmen had been arrested or had surrendered.

Thousands of other demolitions carried out over years, "administrative demolitions" such as those suffered by Salim and Arabiya, are carried out by government bureaucracies according to dry planning codes which effectively conceal the political agendas lying behind them. No less than *five* Israeli government bodies, all with semi-autonomous branches, actively demolish Arab homes on both sides of the Green Line. The Civil Administration, under the aegis of the Ministry of Defense, has jurisdiction over the West Bank (and formally Gaza). In Jerusalem demolitions are carried out by both the Ministry of Interior and the Jerusalem municipality. Inside Israel, the Ministry of Interior, the Israel Lands Authority and the Ministry of Agriculture both demolish Palestinian and Bedouin homes, together with the Jewish-dominated municipalities in "mixed" cities such as Lod, Ramle and Jaffa.

The overall process is similar, and since it is designed to de-Arabize lands and confine Arabs to small enclaves, it is never directed at Jewish homes. The purpose is to confine the 3.7 million Palestinians of the Occupied Territories, together with the 1.3 million Palestinian citizens of Israel, to small, disconnected enclaves (referred to by Sharon as "cantons") on about 15 percent of the entire country—Areas A and B (70 islands on 42 percent of the West Bank), the 3.5 percent of Israel to which its Arab citizens are confined by zoning and social pressure, plus fragmented enclaves in "east" Jerusalem that account for another 1 percent (see Map 2, p. xiii). It's clear that the demolition policy is part and parcel of *nishul*, dispossession; turning the Land of Israel into an exclusively

Jewish space—or at least a Jewish-controlled space; a sustained 60 year process of de-Arabization and Judaization.

So as to preserve Israel's image as a law-abiding, democratic country, demolitions are carefully couched within dry, technical, seemingly neutral master plans and zoning regulations. In this way the authorities in Israel can deny building permits to Palestinians without appearing discriminatory. So Palestinian Arab citizens of Israel are barred from 95 percent of the land of their own country, since 93 percent—state lands as well as those of the Jewish National Fund—is reserved for Jews only, while almost half the lands privately owned by Israeli Arab citizens has been taken or frozen for "public purposes" (Abu Hussein and McKay 2003, Davis 2003). In "East" Jerusalem, where some 220,000 Palestinians reside, all urban policy has been directed towards maintaining an artificial 72–28 percent majority of Jews over Arabs, the proportion that existed when the two sides of the city were unilaterally "united" in 1967. A complex system involving the partisan use of planning and zoning mechanisms, land expropriation and house demolitions, combined with bureaucratic policies of revoking Palestinians' Jerusalem residency for a myriad of reasons, ensures the "Jewish character" of the city. In Jerusalem, explains Amir Cheshin, the long-serving Advisor on Arab Affairs for the Jerusalem Municipality under Teddy Kollek and, for a time, under Ehud Olmert,

> Israel turned urban planning into a tool of the government, to be used to help prevent the expansion of the city's non-Jewish population. It was a ruthless policy, if only for the fact that the needs (to say nothing of the rights) of Palestinian residents were ignored. Israel saw the adoption of strict zoning plans as a way of limiting the number of new homes built in Arab neighborhoods, and thereby ensuring that the Arab percentage of the city's population—28.8% in 1967—did not grow beyond this level. [Despite this, the Jewish majority has today dwindled to about 66 percent—JH.] Allowing "too many" new homes in Arab neighborhoods would mean "too many" Arab residents in

the city. The idea was to move as many Jews as possible into East
Jerusalem, and move as many Arabs as possible out of the city
entirely. Israeli housing policy in East Jerusalem was all about
this numbers game. (Cheshin et al. 1999:10, 31–32)

While Palestinian residents of "East" Jerusalem are confined
to highly circumscribed enclaves, 35 percent of their land has
been expropriated for Israeli settlements, roads and other
Israeli facilities since 1967, while the rest of their unbuilt-upon
land, a full 54 percent of East Jerusalem, has been designated
as "open green space." Palestinians may own their land but
are denied the right to build upon it. "Planners with the city
engineer's office," writes Cheshin (Cheshin et al. 1999:37),

> when drawing the zoning boundaries for the Arab neighborhoods,
> limited them to already built-up areas. Adjoining open areas
> were either zoned "green," to signify they were off-limits to
> development, or left unzoned until they were needed for the
> construction of Jewish housing projects. The 1970 Kollek plan
> contains the principles upon which Israeli housing policy is based
> to this day—expropriation of Arab-owned land, development of
> large Jewish neighborhoods in East Jerusalem, and limitations on
> development in Arab neighborhoods.

As a result of these discriminatory policies, only 11 percent of
East Jerusalem land is available for Palestinian housing and
communal needs, only 7 percent of the city's total urban space
(since Palestinians are prohibited, by social pressures if not by
law, from residing in Jewish West Jerusalem). In other words,
93 percent of municipal Jerusalem is off-limits to Palestinians
(Bimkom 2005, Bollens 2000, Cheshin et al. 1999, Margalit
2006a). The overall goal, which in Israel is known as the
"Quiet Transfer," is to confine Palestinians to small enclaves
of "East" Jerusalem or to remove them from the city altogether.
Ultimately, of course, it is to induce their emigration from the
country altogether. The system works like this:

- Since Palestinian residents of Jerusalem cannot acquire
  building permits (and the government certainly does not

construct housing for them, as it does for low-income Jews), an artificial, induced and deliberate shortage of about 25,000 housing units has been created in the Palestinian sector.

- The housing shortage causes a rise of prices to unaffordable levels. Since 70 percent of the Palestinian residents of East Jerusalem live below the poverty line, they are forced to find less expensive accommodations in Palestinian villages excluded from the city by the Israeli-gerrymandered municipal borders.

- Unlike Jewish residents of the city, Palestinians wishing to retain their Jerusalem residency must continually prove to the Ministry of Interior that their "center of life" is Jerusalem. Moving to affordable housing just beyond the municipal border invalidates that status, allowing the Interior Ministry to revoke the residency of those "emigrants." It is estimated that since 1967 about 6,000 Jerusalem ID cards have been confiscated, forcing some 25,000 Palestinian Jerusalemites into exile or illegal residency in their own homes. Thousands of other Palestinian Jerusalemites cannot obtain permission for their spouses coming from other places to reside in the city. "The Jerusalem Municipality expropriates land, prevents preparation of a town planning scheme for Palestinian neighborhoods, and refuses to grant building permits," according to B'tselem (1998),

  > CAUSING a severe housing shortage, FORCING residents to build without a permit, AFTER WHICH the Ministry of Interior and the Municipality demolish the houses, SO the residents move into homes outside the city, AND THEN the Ministry of Interior revokes their residency and banishes them from the city forever.

- Despite a shortage of 25,000 units, the Municipality grants only between 150 and 350 permits a year for

Arab housing and demolishes up to 152 homes a year (Margalit 2006a)—although in ICAHD's estimate Palestinians are forced to demolish two of their homes for every home demolished by the authorities, in order to avoid excessive fines. Some 22,000 Palestinian housing units, a third of all the housing in East Jerusalem, have been declared "illegal" and have had demolition orders issued against them. Because of the price of demolishing homes—dozens of police and Border Police have to be called out and commercial wrecking companies hired— the authorities cannot demolish the thousands of houses they would like to. They have therefore adopted a policy of "randomization." In order to diffuse the fear of demolition and deter Palestinians from building altogether, houses are demolished throughout East Jerusalem in a completely unpredictable way. Thus someone receiving a demolition order might have his or her home destroyed immediately, while a neighbor might live for a year, or five, or forever, in a home that received a demolition order long before. The authorities also use the courts as deterrence mechanisms. Palestinians who build "illegally" are fined up to $30,000 by the courts and, in a cruel twist, are often required to pay an additional $1,500 for the cost of demolishing their own homes. Paying the court fine has no bearing, however, on the threat of demolition.

• Permits, even in those few areas where it may be possible to acquire them, are nevertheless far too expensive for the average Palestinian resident. Israeli Jews do not bother with building permits since they do not own land and all construction in the Jewish sector is commercial, not private. Thus the government will release a certain amount of "state land" for a new neighborhood, and contractors bid on rights to build hundreds of apartment units. Costs involved in acquiring permits, often reaching $60,000 and more (fees, surveys, engineering plans, legal expenses, connection to infrastructure), are simply built into the price of the many units. And in places where the government wishes to encourage Jewish construction, as in the large settlements in East Jerusalem, fees are often waived entirely and building costs are subsidized. None of this exists in the Palestinian sector, where most building is done on privately-owned land for private family needs. Individual Palestinians must not only assume the astronomical costs of securing the permit and connecting to the infrastructure, but their costs are often higher than those of Jewish construction, since their residences are far from the Israeli infrastructure, making connection to sewage, electricity, water and telephone lines prohibitive.

- Even securing a building permit does not guarantee adequate housing, however. While Israeli contractors are allowed to build hundreds of percent the size of the property (that is, two to six or more stories), Palestinian building is confined to just 25 percent of their land. Jewish-Israelis, then, are able to acquire roomy apartments in medium- or high-rise buildings, or are able to purchase spacious "villas" (often marketed as desirable "Arab-style" housing), while Palestinians with large families are forced to make do in small single-story houses. Additional rooms added as the family grows—or because of the inability of married sons to obtain building permits for their own families—are often demolished. Palestinians thus suffer from overcrowded conditions: 2.2 persons per room on average for Arabs; 0.8 of a person per room in the Jewish sector.

- Although Palestinians are confined to 7 percent of the city's urban area in inadequate housing, Jewish-Israelis have access to spacious accommodation on both the eastern and western sides of the city. Between 1967 and 2006, some 90,000 housing units were built in East

Jerusalem for Jews, almost all with government subsidies. None were built for Palestinians with public financing. New settlements arise regularly on confiscated Palestinian land. In early May, 2007, the Jerusalem municipality announced its intention to construct 20,000 housing units for Jews in East Jerusalem (*Ha'aretz*, May 10, 2007).

- Discrimination against Palestinians exists also in the provision of municipal services. The Palestinian population comprises some 30 percent of the city's population but receives only 8–11 percent of the municipality's budget. Much of East Jerusalem is lacking such basic services as sewage systems, roads, parks, lighting, post offices, schools and community services.

- The "neighborhoods" built on "East" Jerusalem serve to isolate Palestinian populations in small and disconnected enclaves, and to prevent the development and expansion of the Palestinian side of the city. Together with a new system of Israeli "ring roads" and the creation of a "Greater" Jerusalem enveloped by a wall, Jerusalem is being transformed from a city into a region dominating the entire central portion of the West Bank.

Much of the same system exists for the West Bank, and for the same reasons: the confinement and induced emigration of the Palestinians and the expansion of Israel. Instead of the "open green spaces" of East Jerusalem, 70 percent of the West Bank is zoned as "agricultural land," which is why Salim was forbidden to build on his own property. In the early 1990s the Civil Administration further constricted Palestinian building by preparing "Master Plans" for about 400 West Bank villages which consisted of little more than merely drawing tight boundaries around the already built-up areas and prohibiting any further construction. In 1995 the Oslo II agreement carved the Occupied Territories into a complex mosaic of "areas": "A" drawn tightly around the major Palestinian population centers and, on paper, placed under Palestinian Authority (PA) control; "B" giving the PA civil control over additional concentrations of villages but leaving security under effective Israeli control; and "C," the 60 percent or so which contained the Israeli settlements, infrastructure and military facilities, under total Israeli control (see Map 2, p. xiii). The idea was that over a series of phased withdrawals "C" would become increasingly taken over by "B," "B" would steadily become "A," until, when final status negotiations began, the Palestinians would have all the territory except the settlements, infrastructure and military facilities, whose status would then be decided. The problem is that Israel hardly withdrew at all (except in Gaza, which is nevertheless subject to a total ground, sea and air blockade). Since 1995 the Palestinians have been locked into 70 tiny enclaves comprising only 42 percent of the West Bank. They are encircled by more than 500 checkpoints and other obstacles to movement, and isolated from one another by the settlements, Israeli-only highways and now the Separation Barrier (Halper 2005a, Amnesty International 1999a, 2004, B'tselem 2002).

Life for the 2.2 million Palestinians of Areas "A" and "B" is intolerable. They have been traditionally a farming society, and most own land outside of those enclaves where they not only farm, but where they have the only legacy they can pass on to their children: land. In Palestinian society a young man cannot marry until he can offer his bride a home. Land values in the congested areas where they are confined have risen to a point where they are unaffordable for families, 70 percent of whom live in poverty, on less than $2 a day. Their only option is to build on their own family land—but here, again, Israeli planning and house demolition policy prevents that since their lands fall into Area "C," the 58 percent of the West Bank under complete Israeli control. "There are no more construction permits for Palestinians [in the West Bank]," Colonel Shlomo Politus, legal advisor to the Civil Administration, flatly told the Israeli Parliament (Amnesty International 2004:4).

The only form of home demolition carried out for actual security reasons was "punitive," the destruction of family homes of individuals known or suspected of having participated in attacks on Israelis. Some 628 Palestinian homes have been demolished in this way during the second Intifada, the reasoning being that the knowledge that one's family would suffer if a family member engaged in a security offense would deter potential terrorists. On average twelve innocent people lost their home for every person "punished." Ultimately, however, this form of collective punishment was deemed counter-productive by the army itself, and was ended in 2004 (B'tselem 2004a:2).

Altogether Israel has demolished around 18,000 Palestinian homes in the Occupied Territories alone since 1967, only 5 percent having to do with security concerns (see Appendix 1). The demolitions constitute a war crime, being in direct violation of the Fourth Geneva Convention, in particular Article 53 which states: "Any destruction by the Occupying Power of real or personal property belonging individually or collectively to private persons...is prohibited." In May 2004, the UN Security Council adopted UN Resolution 1544 "Reiterating the obligation of Israel, the Occupying Power, to abide scrupulously by its legal obligations and responsibilities under the Fourth Geneva Convention...Expressing its grave concern at the continued deterioration of the situation on the ground in the territory occupied by Israel since 1967 [and expressing its grave concern over] the recent demolition of homes committed by Israel, the occupying Power, in the Rafah refugee camp" (where, during the second Intifada, Israel demolished 1,800 homes (B'tselem 2004b)).

THE MEANING OF A DEMOLISHED HOME

The human suffering entailed in the process of destroying a family's home is incalculable. Needless to say, one's home is not merely a physical structure. It is the center of your life, the site of your most intimate personal relations. In its furnishings and pictures it is the expression of you, your tastes, values, memories. It is a refuge. It is…"home," your sacred space. For Palestinians, homes carry additional meanings. Upon marriage, sons construct their homes close to that of their parents, thus maintaining not only a physical closeness but continuity on one's ancestral land—important in the world of farmers, especially so given the massive displacement the Palestinians have suffered over the past 60 years.

Having your home demolished is traumatic and shattering to everyone, particularly for a normal family, usually of modest means, generally traditional in orientation, unpolitical, not associated with security problems in any way, seeking nothing more than adequate shelter and personal security, fundamental human rights. But it is a very different experience for men, women and children. Men are probably the most humiliated, since loss of one's home means loss of one's connection to family and the land. The sense of powerlessness, the ultimate inability to provide a basic dwelling for your family, is emasculating. Men often cry at demolitions (and long after), but they are also angered and swear revenge, or plan to build again. Indeed, neighbors gathering immediately after a demolition sometimes rebuild a basic home for the family.

For women the loss of the home is the loss of one's life. Men at least go out to work; they have an outlet for their anger and frustrations. Most Palestinian women do not leave the house for employment; the domestic sphere defines them as persons, women, wives and mothers. When they lose that world they often become disoriented, as if the center of their lives has been taken away and they have no way to cope. Women who have suffered demolition tend to sink into mourning, their behavior—crying, wailing and then depression—resembles people who have lost loved ones. The demolished home can never be replaced, and many women, like Arabiya, undergo

THE MESSAGE OF THE BULLDOZERS

personality changes after demolitions, becoming more sullen or moody, often frightened by small sounds or unexpected events, prone to break into crying (Shalhoub-Kevorkian 2007, Amnesty International 2004:2–3).

For women, demolition represents a double tragedy. Not only do they lose their homes, but they are then forced to move into the homes of other women, their mothers-in-law or sisters-in-law. That is alright for a week or so, but bringing a family of four, six, eight children into the modest home of relatives must generate serious tensions over time. In particular a woman loses her authority over her own family responsibilities; she is subordinate to the woman whose house she is living in. She cannot conduct normal relationships with her husband and children, and since she is living in her husband's family's household, she is often isolated when conflicts do erupt. Her demands upon her husband for a home of their own frustrate and anger him. Even though he may own land—the land upon which he built the home that was demolished—he is limited by finances and the refusal of the Israelis to grant him a permit. Unable to provide shelter for his family, he may become sullen and withdrawn, or may stay away from home, alienated from his wife and kids whom he cannot face, or he may even become violent towards his wife. "Not only was our house lost," said Ina'am, "but our whole home too."

As for the children, the act of demolition—and the months and years of anxiety and tension leading up to it—unleashes the trauma suppressed all that time. To witness over your entire childhood the fear and powerlessness of your parents, to feel constantly afraid and insecure, to see loved ones (relatives and neighbors) being beaten and losing their homes, to experience the harassment of Civil Administration field supervisors speeding around your village in their dreaded white Toyota jeeps—and then to endure the noise and violence and displacement and destruction of your home, your world, your toys—these events mark children for life. Psychological services are missing in the Palestinian community despite many signs of trauma and stress among children: bed-wetting, nightmares, fear of leaving home lest one "abandon" parents and children to the army, dramatic drops in grades, school-leaving and exposure to domestic violence that occasionally follows impoverishment, displacement and humiliation.

I once went to the Palestinian Jerusalem neighborhood of Beit Hanina to visit the site of a demolished home and to comfort the family. Women often speak to me of their routine during the months or years of living with a demolition order. "When I woke up in the morning," said Huda, whose house was eventually demolished after eight years, "I would first go to the window to see if the home was surrounded by soldiers and police and bulldozers. When I saw that everything was OK, I would brush my teeth, dress and get the kids ready for school." In the case of the Beit Hanina family, the Jerusalem municipality came suddenly to demolish at about nine in the morning, after the kids had been packed off to school. As I sat in the mourning tent, I saw the children returning from school. All of a sudden, a six-year-old boy, coming over the hill, let out a scream and began going into convulsions. This is the stuff horror films are made of: you leave home one morning and return a few hours later—and it's gone. No home, no familiar landmarks, you don't see your parents. The child fell into hysterical convulsions. "Post-traumatic stress," the clinical term we give such experiences, lasts one's whole life and disfigures normal development. As Salim puts it, the demolition of a home is the demolition of a family.

Why, then, do Palestinians build "illegally" if they know their homes stand a good chance of being demolished? Well, many don't, like the 25,000 families who need decent shelter in Jerusalem yet are deterred from building through fear of demolition. But people cannot live without a home. And so many Palestinian families, barred by Israel from any possibility of obtaining decent, affordable and legal housing, do a simple, cold arithmetic: tens of thousands of demolition orders are outstanding, the various Israeli authorities destroy "only" 200–300 homes a year (military attacks and punitive demolitions aside), so if we build, the chances are that we might buy a year or two or three before the bulldozers arrive. As in a perverse reverse lottery, we might even "win" the jackpot and escape demolition altogether.

WHAT IN THE HELL IS GOING ON HERE?

Our "discovery" of the scope of the house demolitions policy in time, in space, in numbers and in human suffering was staggering; all the more so when it became clear it had nothing to do with security. Although we in ICAHD had backed into the house demolition issue, taking it as our focus yet considering it only one issue of the Occupation, we had unwittingly touched the very essence of the Israeli-Palestinian conflict: *nishul*, displacement. When one looks at Areas "A" and "B"—"cantons" as Sharon called them—they clearly form the contours of the emerging Palestinian bantustan, that non-viable, non-sovereign prison-state delineated so clearly by Prime Minister Olmert in his "Convergence Plan" presented before a joint session of the US Congress in May, 2006. Indeed, the policy of demolishing Palestinians homes in "East" Jerusalem and the Occupied Territories merely continues the campaign initiated by David Ben Gurion and his small band of ideologues and military personnel: a Jewish state extending over 85 percent of the Land of Israel, ideally free of Arabs but, failing that, containing them in truncated enclaves that do not threaten Israel control of the entire country from the Mediterranean to the Jordan River.

For the house demolition policy, as we've seen, did not begin in 1967; nor are demolitions limited to the Occupied Territories. The campaign of creating a Jewish ethnocracy continues apace on both sides of the Green Line. The security

of Arab citizens of Israel in their homes is only marginally
better than that of Salim and Arabiya, and "Israeli Arabs" face
almost exactly the same restrictions. I knew that Palestinian
citizens of Israel, fully 20 percent of the population, are confined
by law and zoning to a mere 3.5 percent of the country, but
I was astounded to hear the government announce, in mid
2004, the establishment of a "Demolition Administration"
within the Ministry of Interior, charged with overseeing the
demolition of between 20,000 and 40,000 homes *of Israeli
[Arab] citizens*! Targeted are the homes—if you can call them
that—of more than 150,000 "internal refugees" from 1948 and
their descendants, Palestinians who left their homes in the heat
of battle and hid out in nearby valleys or hillsides, but who,
despite Israeli army orders to leave the country, managed to
remain. Well, sort of. They managed to stay in the country and
were eventually given Israeli citizenship. But their homes were
lost, either turned over to Jews (Shosh's parents were given
an Arab house in the village of Tira, renamed Tirat Yehuda,
when they immigrated in 1949) or demolished to prevent any
refugees from returning. Now, after 60 years, these citizens
of Israel still live where they found night refuge, in more than
100 "unrecognized villages" denied by the authorities housing
permits, sewage, electricity, roads or schools, and they face
once again the demolition of their shanty-homes. According to
the Interior Ministry, 868 Palestinian homes were demolished
inside Israel in 2006. In the spring of 2007, four entire Bedouin
villages were flattened.

Since neither Palestinians in Israel nor refugees like Salim
and Arabiya can return to their ancestral homes inside Israel or,
because of the demolition policy, can find refuge in new homes
in the Occupied Territories, the Message of the Bulldozers is
clear: "Get out. You do not belong here. Just as we uprooted
you from your homes in 1948 and prevented your return, we
will uproot you from the entire Land of Israel."

Why? What reason would the state of Israel have for wanting the Shawamreh family out of the country, for demolishing its home, indeed, for not letting them return to Amishagav? The answer obviously goes beyond the granting of a permit. Nor can it have anything to do with security, since Salim and Arabiya's home, like almost all the other Palestinian homes demolished in the past 60 years on both sides of the Green Lines, was not destroyed for security reasons. Was the demolition somehow crucial to maintaining the Occupation? But, again, Salim and Arabiya are refugees from Israel; occupation policies don't explain the destruction of their ancestral village. No, something else is going on here, something big. Salim and Arabiya's lost home was only the tip, a miniscule tip, of something much greater, much more fundamental to Israel's concept of itself, its rights and aims, and its relationship to the other people claiming a national home in "our" country: the Palestinians.

Part II

The Sources of Oppression

3
The Impossible Dream: Constructing a Jewish Ethnocracy in Palestine

The terms "democracy" or "democratic" are totally absent from the Declaration of Independence. This is not an accident. The intention of Zionism was not to bring democracy, needless to say. It was solely motivated by the creation in Eretz-Israel of a Jewish state belonging to all the Jewish people and to the Jewish people alone. That is why any Jew of the Diaspora has the right to immigrate to Israel and to become a citizen of Israel.

—Ariel Sharon, "Democracy & the Jewish State,"
Yedioth Ahronoth, 28 May 1993

Mark Twain once said that the Jews are like everyone else, but more so. If one goes by Zionist ideology, Israeli government policy, the aggressiveness of the military, the success of the militant settlers and the willingness of the public to elect governments that only deepen the Occupation and foreclose any possibility of peace and security, it appears as if Israeli Jews indeed prefer land to normalcy, exclusivity to coexistence, going it alone in a kind of "Fortress Israel" rather than joining the wider world. This is not the case. Casting Israeli Jews as a passive collective defined by blind adherence to a particular nationalist doctrine eliminates the wide range of opinion that exists in the country (twelve parties are represented in the current Knesset), as well as its ethnic, religious and class

pluralism. It only creates a simplistic, unhelpful caricature.
If anything, polls reflect great public confusion, uncertainty
and radical swings of opinion when it comes to issues such as
Zionism, Israel as a Jewish state, security, democracy, adherence
to the Greater Land of Israel ideology and the prospects of
peace with the Arab world. The late Tanya Reinhart, an Israeli
professor of linguistics and a keen observer of the Israeli scene,
offered a more nuanced and most useful formula:

> About one third [of the Israeli population] is firmly against the
> occupation and the settlements on moral and ideological grounds;
> another third believes in Israel's right over the whole land and
> supports the settlements; the middle third is people with no fixed
> ideological view on that matter—people whose sole concern is
> the ability to lead a normal life.
>
> In 1993, at the time of Oslo, the middle third joined the end-
> the-occupation camp....[T]wo-thirds of Israelis supported Oslo in
> all polls, though it was conceived as leading to Israeli withdrawal
> and evacuation of the settlements. This majority has remained
> stable....Thus it is not the Israeli people who hinder progress,
> but the Israeli political system, which has been working, in fact,
> against the will of the majority. To numb this majority, it has been
> necessary to keep alive the illusion that the occupation is about
> to end, and at the same time to convince the majority that this
> cannot possibly happen overnight. (Reinhart 2002:226)

I'll go a step further. I would argue that the two-thirds Israeli
public Reinhart identifies as being anti-occupation and
somewhere in the middle has little interest in maintaining
the Occupation or in the right-wing and religious scheme of
settlements securing a Greater Land of Israel. It would be
difficult to describe them as ideological at all; even the term
"Zionist" has the air of irrelevancy, of an outmoded quaintness,
to most Israeli Jews, especially the secular population and the
younger generations, for whom "Israeliness" precedes Jewish
identity (Magid 2007). I would argue that the vast majority
of Israelis simply want to get on with their lives. "Peace and
quiet" best describes Israeli aspirations; "peace" in a political

sense is considered by most Israeli Jews as unattainable. They may have various views about it, but the Israeli public has largely disconnected itself from the political process. Even those who support peace with the Palestinians have accepted Barak's contention that we have "no partner for peace." Barak's message fell on fertile ground, since Israeli Jews have been conditioned to believe that there is no political solution to the conflict with the Arabs. As early as 1919 Ben Gurion had put his finger on this fundamental "reality":

> Everybody sees the problem in relations between the Jews and the Arabs. But not everybody sees that there is no solution to it. There is no solution!...The conflict between the interests of the Jews and the interests of the Arabs in Palestine cannot be resolved by sophisms. I don't know of any Arabs who would agree to Palestine being ours—even if we learn Arabic....and I have no need to learn the Arabic language. Woe to us if we have to conduct our lives in Arabic. On the other hand, I don't see why "Mustafa" should learn Hebrew....There's a national question here. We want the country to be ours. The Arabs want the country to be theirs. (quoted in Segev 1999:116)

If that is the case, Israeli Jews reason, if there is no political solution or any possibility of normalcy in this region, all that's left is to hunker down, get on with our lives and trust that the army, if not the government, will keep us safe. The entire conflict with the Palestinians has been thus reduced to one consideration: personal security. The complete reversal between the vote for Barak in 1999, a massive rejection of Netanyahu's confrontational approach and a clear mandate to make peace with the Palestinians, and the ever more massive rejection of Barak in early 2001 in favor of the militaristic Sharon, cannot be explained by ideology. Two intervening factors came into play. First, Barak's charge that the Palestinians did not want peace, and second, the outbreak of the second Intifada in late September, 2000. That seemingly irrational about-face is easy to explain: Israeli Jews prefer peace and compromise, but

only if they are convinced that their prime preoccupation—
security—has been credibly addressed.

The leap from Barak to Sharon exposed another element
of Israeli life that frustrates the attempts of us in the critical
Israeli peace movement to engage with the wider public. That
is, Israelis live in a bubble, in a self-contained world where
perceptions and opinions are formed, and political decisions
made, on the basis of ideological internal arguments rather
than upon a comprehensive grasp of political realities. In
other words, Israelis do not know a thing about either the
realities on the ground in the Occupied Territories or what
Palestinians think and want (and don't really care). They
seldom venture into the Occupied Territories, including East
Jerusalem, and if they do they do so either as soldiers—not
exactly the way to understand the other side—or as settlers
travelling Israeli-only highways. So when we come to them
with our presentations on house demolitions or our analysis
on how to end the conflict in a win–win manner, or if we
offer them tours of the Occupied Territories so they can see
for themselves, there are few takers. Israeli Jews live within an
ideological membrane which filters out anything not having
to do with them. Arab citizens of Israel have been rendered as
invisible as the Palestinians of the territories. The "villages"
they inhabit (everywhere Arabs live is considered a "village")
have been reduced to a quaint background. Almost autistic in
their preoccupation with themselves and unwilling to listen
to other voices, including ours, Israeli Jews have neither the
information necessary to make informed political decisions
nor the willingness to entertain ideas that fall outside of the
accepted parameters of discussion.

But how can this be in an open society like Israel's? By
almost every standard—economic or educational, in the
numbers of personal computers or cell phones, having a
critical press unhampered by government interference, in the
time devoted to political discussion and news in the popular

media, in the numbers of libraries and cultural offerings in all their diversity—Israel compares favorably with Western European countries. Politicians and "experts," especially from the military, dominate much of the public discussion, but this is true elsewhere as well. On the surface there is no reason why Israelis shouldn't understand what is going on in the nearby Palestinian territories or even in the Arab world around. Why the disconnect? Why do they persist in electing leaders who only deepen their involvement in the occupation, when what they desire is separation? Why, with all the information available, can they not break out of The Box?

I suggest three major elements at play that keep the Israelis "domesticated" and prevent them from taking an active role in achieving a just peace with their neighbors. A national ideology and the political system emerging out of it—an ethnocracy; a closed-circuit security framing; and small group decision-making.

CAUGHT IN A TRIBAL PARADIGM

The Zionist movement created a national narrative while still in Europe. It had little to do with the actual country of Palestine, and certainly did not include Arabs. It was a completely Jewish story, compelling and self-contained, of national birth in the biblical Land of Israel, exile and triumphant return two millennia later. In it the Jewish nation had the natural and straightforward right to repossess their homeland, which was anyway portrayed as "empty," desolate and waiting for their return. But it also contained the seeds of future defensiveness, anxiety and even fear among its adherents, since the reality they found in Palestine could not be reconciled with the ideology; Zionism required a suppression, violence and dispossession, a situation that could never be relaxed or normalized.

It took me many years to appreciate how central exclusivity was to the way Israeli Jews saw and reacted to things. No

satisfying explanation of why Salim's home had been
demolished was apparent to me. Nor could I understand why
the demolition of Palestinian homes, like everything else having
to do with "Arabs," is such a non-issue in Israeli society. Only
after months of reflection following the traumatic experience
at Salim's did I finally detect that unspoken yet critical element
in the Zionist paradigm: exclusivity and its handmaiden,
privilege. With that element in place I could finally grasp the
implications of Zionism, including its political dynamics *vis-
à-vis* the Palestinians.

The Zionist narrative of national birth and rebirth in
the Land of Israel is well-known and straightforward. Its
most official framing comes from Israel's Declaration of
Independence in 1948:

> The Land of Israel [*Eretz-Israel*] was the birthplace of the Jewish
> people. Here their spiritual, religious and political identity was
> shaped. Here they first attained to statehood, created cultural
> values of national and universal significance and gave to the world
> the eternal Book of Books. After being forcibly exiled from their
> land, the people remained faithful to it throughout their Dispersion
> and never ceased to pray and hope for their return to it and for
> the restoration in it of their political freedom. Impelled by this
> historic and traditional attachment, Jews strove in every successive
> generation to re-establish themselves in their ancient homeland.
> In recent decades they returned in their masses. Pioneers, defiant
> returnees and defenders, they made deserts bloom, revived the
> Hebrew language, built villages and towns, and created a thriving
> community controlling its own economy and culture, loving
> peace but knowing how to defend itself, bringing the blessings
> of progress to all the country's inhabitants, and aspiring towards
> independent nationhood.
>
> In the year 5657 (1897), at the summons of the spiritual father
> of the Jewish State, Theodore Herzl, the First Zionist Congress
> convened and proclaimed the right of the Jewish people to national
> rebirth in its own country. This right was recognized in the Balfour
> Declaration of the 2nd November, 1917, and re-affirmed in the
> Mandate of the League of Nations which, in particular, gave
> international sanction to the historic connection between the

Jewish people and *Eretz-Israel* and to the right of the Jewish people to rebuild its National Home.

The catastrophe which recently befell the Jewish people—the massacre of millions of Jews in Europe—was another clear demonstration of the urgency of solving the problem of its homelessness by re-establishing in *Eretz-Israel* the Jewish State, which would open the gates of the homeland wide to every Jew and confer upon the Jewish people the status of a fully privileged member of the comity of nations. Survivors of the Nazi holocaust in Europe, as well as Jews from other parts of the world, continued to migrate to *Eretz-Israel*, undaunted by difficulties, restrictions and dangers, and never ceased to assert their right to a life of dignity, freedom and honest toil in their national homeland.

In the Second World War, the Jewish community of this country contributed its full share to the struggle of the freedom- and peace-loving nations against the forces of Nazi wickedness and, by the blood of its soldiers and its war effort, gained the right to be reckoned among the peoples who founded the United Nations.

On the 29th November, 1947, the United Nations General Assembly passed a resolution calling for the establishment of a Jewish State in *Eretz-Israel*; the General Assembly required the inhabitants of *Eretz-Israel* to take such steps as were necessary on their part for the implementation of that resolution. This recognition by the United Nations of the right of the Jewish people to establish their State is irrevocable. This right is the natural right of the Jewish people to be masters of their own fate, like all other nations, in their own sovereign State.

The Declaration of Independence also touched on the apparent contradiction between Israel as a Jewish state and Israel as a democratic state of all its citizens, though only in a declarative fashion. Following the claim "of the Jewish people to be masters of their own fate, like all other nations, in their own sovereign State," the text goes on to say:

[T]he Jewish State, to be called "Israel,"…will be open for Jewish immigration and for the Ingathering of the Exiles; it will foster the development of the country for the benefit of all its inhabitants; it will be based on freedom, justice and peace as envisaged by the prophets of Israel; it will ensure complete equality of social and political rights to all its inhabitants irrespective of religion, race or sex; it will guarantee freedom of religion, conscience, language, education and culture; it will safeguard the Holy Places of all religions; and it will be faithful to the principles of the Charter of the United Nations....We appeal—in the very midst of the onslaught launched against us now for months—to the Arab inhabitants of the State of Israel to preserve peace and participate in the upbuilding of the State on the basis of full and equal citizenship and due representation in all its provisional and permanent institutions.

It's true that the Arab citizens of Israel technically received equal rights. They are citizens, they do enjoy freedom of religion, conscience, language and culture and they have the vote. Their situation, however, is far less than that of "complete equality." By the time the Declaration of Independence was declared, 200 Palestinian villages in the area partitioned for the Jewish state had already been demolished by Jewish paramilitary forces. By January 1949, 85 percent of the Arabs who were to be citizens of Israel were gone, their villages destroyed and their lands expropriated (Badil, quoted in Pappe 2006:179). But the issue of exclusivity, which is cast in positive terms in the Zionist framing, must clash with Arab rights and claims simply because the Jews were (and still are) attempting to create an ethnically pure space in a country where the vast majority of the inhabitants are not Jewish. Concerns of exclusivity and Jewish claims, then, are often cast in terms of demography. In December 1947, six months before Israel would be declared a state, Ben Gurion laid this out in a speech to members of his party. "There are 40% non-Jews in the areas allocated to the Jewish state," he told them.

> This composition is not a solid basis for a Jewish state. And we have to face this new reality with all its severity and distinctiveness. Such a demographic balance questions our ability to maintain Jewish sovereignty....Only a state with at least 80% Jews is a viable and stable state. (quoted in Pappe 2006:48)

The crime of ethnic cleansing that Israel carried out from December 1947 to April 1949, well within memory and well documented, shares an essential feature with its current policies in the Occupied Territories: it is both denied and justified by educated people with full access to the facts—including many liberal Diaspora Jews. How could this be? How could such blatant acts of injustice be committed in the light of day, fundamental violations of human rights (not to mention the killing), and yet be ignored, minimized and rationalized by good and enlightened people? And to go back to an earlier question, how could all this be done—an ongoing campaign of ethnic cleansing now entering its 60th year—without arousing more dissent and soul-searching within the Israeli public?

Part of the answer lies in the compelling Zionist narrative and the integral, organic, tribal nationalism it engendered. In fact, exclusive Jewish claims come from two sources: the Bible and nineteenth-century nationalism. The Bible is basic to Zionist claims to the Land of Israel. For religious Jews, the claim is absolute and irrefutable, beginning in Genesis 12:7 where God says to Abraham: "Unto thy seed will I give this land." Yet for the secular as well—and Zionism was primarily a secular, even anti-religious movement—the Covenant was folded into the national narrative. Israel's Declaration of Independence provides its *Eretz-Israel* nationalist spin: is "the birthplace of the Jewish people [where] their spiritual, religious and political identity was shaped [and where] they first attained statehood." Although the ancient Israelites and Judeans had sovereignty over the country for only 1,300 of its 10,000 years of recorded history (and a third of which was under Babylonian, Greek or Roman suzerainty), in Zionist thought our claims trump any others, including the 1,300 years of Muslim rule.

The Jews, however, were a nation in the political sense during the centuries preceding the Roman Exile, whether or not they were actually sovereign. In the Diaspora—or the Exile in Zionist terms—they maintained an ethno-nationalism within the framework of religion. This was especially true during their 1,000 years in Europe, where the Jews lived as a "people apart" from their Christian neighbors. With the rise of political nationalism in Europe during the nineteenth century, that national core came to the fore, especially in Eastern and Central Europe. There the overwhelming masses of Jews lived in poverty and absolute segregation, mostly within the Russian Pale of Settlement, a rural area which they needed permits to leave. Unlike in Western Europe and America, where a civil form of nationalism emerged in the wake of the French and American Revolutions and where the Jews enthusiastically embraced citizenship, retaining only a loose ethnicity if not choosing total assimilation, the nationalism that emerged in Eastern and Central Europe was "organic," tribal as opposed to the civil nationalism of the West. In Russia, Poland, Bulgaria, Hungary, Serbia and elsewhere in Eastern Europe where pan-Slavism ruled, and in the pan-Germanic parts of Central Europe, a country did not belong to its citizens but rather to a particular national group.

It was within the context of tribal nationalism, in the countries where the vast majority of Jews lived, that Zionism emerged. Zionist nationalism reflected the sentiments of the other organic nationalisms surrounding it: that every nation has its own distinct homeland (Sternhell 1998). And since the homeland of the Jews is indisputably the Land of Israel, expanding that form of tribal nationalism to Palestine was simple and unproblematic. "Palestine" was a "land without a people for a people without a land" not only because its Arab population was seen as sparse and lacking any features of a national entity, but because it could belong to only *one* people, its rightful historic owners, the Jews, who had been exiled against their will. Arabs may live there as the Declaration of Independence affirms (again, after a thorough campaign of ethnic cleansing), but only that. They lack any legitimate historic or national claims to the country that the Jews have, and even as citizens they must accept the fact that the state of Israel "belongs" exclusively to the Jews.

One cannot understand Israel's policies in the Occupied Territories—although, in light of what we've said, Israel denies any occupation, since one cannot occupy one's own country—without reference to its exclusive claims. Yet, while the claims are stated clearly, proudly and even assertively, the element of exclusivity is muted, mainly because it would contradict Israel's image as a Western democracy. It is, therefore, an unstated but absolutely essential part of the Zionist/Israeli narrative. It affirms that:

> The Land of Israel [from the Mediterranean to the Jordan River] belongs exclusively to the Jewish people. There is no other people with valid national rights over or claims to the country. Although Arabs live in the Land of Israel, they do not constitute a collectivity that in any way challenges Jewish exclusivity. Since the Land belongs to the Jews, only they have the prerogative to decide its fate. Any political solution to the current conflict, even one in which a Palestinian state may emerge, will be decided solely by Israeli Jews. Arabs might be consulted, but genuine negotiations based upon the notion that the Palestinians have a right of self-determination in the Land of Israel are out of the question.

The claim of exclusivity renders Zionism an either–or equation: either the country is made "ours" or we lose it to "them." This explains the Israeli bubble, and why crossing the membrane is so frightening. It explains the ideologically-motivated myopia that renders Israeli Jews unable to see anyone but ourselves or admit to any shortcomings, in particular anything to do with Palestinians. And it explains the inability of the critical peace movement to conduct any meaningful political discussion with the very Israeli Jewish public of which we are a part. Yet without crossing that membrane separating Salim and Arabiya's home from ours, there is no way to step out of the tribal paradigm to critically comprehend "the situation."

AN UNEASY ETHNOCRACY

The political upshot of all this is a Jewish ethnocracy (Yiftachel 1999a). Israel presents itself as a Western democracy (the "only democracy in the Middle East") and, on the surface, it resembles one. In fact, it is something quite different, an ethnocracy based on an Eastern European tribal nationalism.

An ethnocracy is the opposite of a democracy, although it might incorporate some elements of democracy such as universal citizenship and elections. It arises when one particular group—the Jews in Israel, the Russians in Russia (and, more evidently, in the former Soviet Union), the Protestants in pre-1972 Northern Ireland, the whites in apartheid South Africa, the Shi'ite Muslims of Iran, the Malay in Malaysia and, if they had their way, the white Christian fundamentalists in the US—seizes control of the government and armed forces in order to enforce a regime of exclusive privilege over other groups in what is in fact a multi-ethnic or multi-religious society. Ethnocracy, or ethno-nationalism, privileges *ethnos* over *demos*, whereby one's ethnic affiliation, be it defined by race, descent, religion, language or national origin, takes precedence over citizenship in determining to whom a country actually "belongs." Israel is referred to explicitly by its political leaders as a "Jewish democracy."

It's not easy for Israel's own Jewish citizens, or for Jews abroad, to discern the difference between ethnocracy and democracy. If the dominant group constitutes as large a majority as do the Jews of Israel (between 70 percent and 75 percent), there is little need for repressive measures to enforce ethnic domination, so a democratic façade can be maintained. Hence the formal rights of citizenship bestowed upon the "Israeli Arabs;" hence the Israeli sociologists Smooha and Hanf's (1992) preference for the term "ethnic democracy" over ethnocracy. But in every aspect of Israeli life, the *ethnos* takes precedent over the state or civil society. Most obvious are the symbols that represent the state. The very name of the country denotes its belonging to the Jews, as do the exclusively Jewish motifs on our flag and the exclusively Jewish content of our national anthem: "As long as deep in the heart / The soul of a Jew yearns / And the eye looks east toward Zion / Our hope is not lost / Our hope of two thousand years / To be a free nation in our land / In the land of Zion and Jerusalem." The "story" of Israel is that of the official Zionist narrative, with no other viewpoints permitted or legitimized. Israel's national holidays either arise out of the Jewish religion (the Sabbath and major Jewish holidays for which the public life of the entire country halts) or out of the Israeli/Jewish experience (Independence Day, Holocaust Day, Remembrance Day for fallen Israeli soldiers and victims of terror attacks, Jerusalem Day in which we "celebrate" the "liberation" of Jerusalem in 1967, and others). Israel has no official holiday which is inclusive, to which all "Israelis" can identify. Ramadan or Christmas is marked solely by the Muslim or Christian communities; Jews go about their daily routine largely unaware of them. And who could ever even imagine a joint Independence/Naqba Day which would commemorate both the *Naqba*, or "catastrophe," suffered by the Palestinians in 1948 together with "our" independence? The only "Arab" event noted, if not commemorated except by the Palestinian community itself, is Land Day, when Palestinian citizens of Israel mark the killing in 1976 of six demonstrators shot by the Israeli police as they were protesting the massive and ongoing expropriation of their lands.

More serious, however, are the structural inequalities inherent in any ethnocracy. Arabs may sit in the Parliament, but no government decision is considered legitimate unless it enjoys a "Jewish majority"—that is, the support of the majority of Jews in the Parliament rather than a parliamentary majority that requires Arab votes. This is the basis of the charges that Rabin's government, which refused to take the Arab parties into the coalition but relied on them for its parliamentary majority, had no "mandate" to conduct negotiations in Oslo. How, it was argued, could Arabs, by definition anti-Zionist, be the deciding factor in a decision to relinquish Judea and Samaria or the Golan Heights or the Temple Mount? Structural discrimination goes even deeper. The Law of Return that determines who can immigrate to Israel applies only to Jews. I immigrated from Minnesota and received citizenship automatically; a Palestinian who was born here but lived for an extensive time outside is denied citizenship and the right to return. And then there is the land issue, discrimination in housing and education which are strictly segregated, house demolitions solely targeting Arabs—even the construction of walls between Jewish and Arab neighborhoods in the "mixed cities" of Ramle and Lod. There is not even a civil mechanism by which Jewish, Christian and Muslims citizens of Israel can marry each other, since personal status—citizenship, marriage, death, inheritance—is regulated by religious and not civil law. Non-Jews cannot even be buried in Jewish cemeteries, even immigrant soldiers killed in battle whose Judaism is in doubt.

Today the liberal façade of democracy is falling away. After 1948, when the Jews had achieved a demographic majority in Israel of 89 percent due to the expulsion of most of the Arab population and the massive waves of immigration in the late 1940s and early 1950s (Israeli Ministry of Foreign Affairs 1998), it was possible and desirable from a PR angle to grant the remnants of the Palestinians citizenship. At that time they were a shattered population of only 150,000 souls (down from a little over 1 million before 1947), property-less, impoverished, traumatized, intimidated and concentrated in urban and rural locales, living under a strict military regime until 1966—hardly a threat to the Jewish ethnocracy which could afford to appear liberal. Today the situation has changed and ethnocracy, always present but concealed, is beginning to assert itself. Palestinian citizens of Israel now account for a full 20 percent of the population and are beginning to demand equal civil rights, even recognition as a "national minority," since the Israeli system is based, in the end, on national identity (a "Jewish state" that by definition excludes non-Jews from full membership and identification) rather than on citizenship. Ahmed Tibi, a member of the Knesset, states the case clearly:

> We maintain that the Jewish character of the State of Israel must be abolished. We do not accept the fact of exclusive Jewish hegemony in the state, completely disregarding 20 percent [of the population] who are not Jewish. We are not subletting here, and the definition of who we are has to be anchored in the definition of the state; therefore we absolutely support the idea of a "state of all its citizens"....It is impossible to talk about a Jewish state and a democratic state in the same breath. It is either a democratic state or a Jewish state. It would be enough for me if it were a democratic state. (quoted in Schueftan 2003:77)

The Israeli ethnocracy is responding accordingly. In 2002 the then Interior Minister Eli Yishai threatened to revoke the citizenship of Arab Israelis who are involved in attacks on Israeli targets, a move praised by Prime Minister Sharon. The very next year Yishai's successor, Avraham Poraz of the liberal Shinui party, initiated the Citizenship and Entry into Israel Law which prohibits spouses of Arab citizens of Israel who come from the West Bank, Gaza or any Arab country from entering Israel or receiving residency rights or citizenship—including the children of such marriages. He went so far as to explain that Palestinians already married to Palestinian citizens of Israel "will have to go back to the West Bank regardless of how long they have been living in Israel." And, indeed, on January 24, 2006, Border Police troops invaded the Arab Israeli town of Jaljulya, arrested 36 wives and mothers of Israeli citizens, and deported eight of them to the West Bank. This law, described as a "defense measure," has successfully withstood a challenge before the Supreme Court (Pappe 2006:249). In 2006 Prime

Minister Olmert appointed Avigdor Lieberman, the head of the extreme right-wing "Israel is Our Home" party that calls openly for the transfer of Arabs out of the Land of Israel— including Arab citizens of Israel—Minister of Strategic Affairs and *Deputy Prime Minister.* Citing the "demographic threat" posed by the Arab population, he proclaimed that 90 percent of Israel's 1.2 million Palestinian citizens would "have to find a new Arab entity" in which to live beyond Israel's borders. "They have no place here. They can take their bundles and get lost" (quoted in the Wikipedia entry on Lieberman). In a recent poll, 68 percent of Israeli Jews expressed their wish to see them "transferred" (*Ha'aretz*, May 9, 2006).

The struggle between ethnocracy and democracy in Israel has its own place. What concerns me here is how it impacts on the chances of reaching a just accommodation with the Palestinians. For Zionist peace groups, whether more mainstream ones like Peace Now or more critical ones like Gush Shalom, as well as for the political parties like Labor and Meretz and think-tanks such as the Peres Center for Peace, the two-state solution is an absolute and unassailable one; they cannot even contemplate another one, and in particular anything smacking of a bi-national state. This is because they are Zionists, and for them a Jewish ethnocracy—or a "Jewish democracy" as they prefer to say—is sacrosanct. The only way to leave the Israeli ethnocracy intact is to insist that the conflict began in 1967, for if the problem is only to end to the Occupation, then Israel as a Jewish state is off the hook. We at ICAHD took part in a wide coalition of peace organizations marking the 40th anniversary of the Occupation. When we then suggested similar activities marking the 60th anniversary of 1948, almost all the peace groups backed away.

This brings up an interesting convergence of right-wing Zionist, Hamas and our critical non/post/anti-Zionist position that Israel should be a truly democratic country. Lieberman and I—and we could include Ben Gurion in our company—

agree that the conflict originates with the start of Zionism. From the Lieberman/Ben Gurion point of view, the conflict is not territorial, but ideological: the Arabs simply do not accept the presence of a Jewish state in Palestine. The only solution, then, is transfer, getting the Arabs out of "our" state and, to paraphrase Jabotinsky, thoroughly transforming Palestine into the Land of Israel. Hamas, too, sees the problem as inherent in Zionism: the only way to prevent Palestine from being transformed into the Land of Israel is by liberating it altogether. Unlike my fellow peaceniks who support the two-state solution, I agree that the conflict cannot be limited to the territories occupied in 1967, that its roots go back to 1948 and beyond. Needless to say, however, I don't share the view that transfer—be it of either Palestinians or Jews out of the country—is the answer. Ideally, a genuine two-state solution would be a first step towards ending the political conflict with the Palestinians. That would address their claims to national self-determination. Most Palestinians and the leaders of the Palestine Liberation Organization (PLO) have indicated that this would be enough to end the conflict and to even achieve a meaningful degree of reconciliation, on condition that the refugee issue be resolved in a *mutually agreed-upon* way. The Palestinians, gatekeepers of the process of reconciliation between Israel and the Arab world, would be prepared to signal that their national aspirations have been satisfied and the time has come to normalize relations with Israel. The second step in the process of reconciliation and normalization would then be an internal one: Israel transforming itself from an ethnocracy into a democracy, the only way Palestinian Israelis can fully achieve their own civil rights.

So if pressed then, yes, I too accept a two-state solution—if it's a genuine two-state solution that leads to a viable and fully sovereign Palestinian state. But here is where the problem of Zionist exclusivity enters in. There is no place in that tribal ideology for recognizing the legitimate claims of another people to the Land of Israel; indeed, the very existence of that "other people" is denied. The two-state solution has been on the table since 1988, when the PLO officially adopted it as its political program. It is the preferred solution of the international community, the basis of every international plan for peace from UN Resolution 242 in 1967 to the current Road Map. It has been adopted by the Arab League in the "Saudi Initiative" of 2002 and, again, polls indicate that most Israeli Jews would accept it as well (although they waffle over the extent of territorial concessions). So what is the problem? Why wasn't it implemented 20 years ago? Because, I would contend, Zionism's exclusive claim to the *entire* Land of Israel prevents it. The idea that Palestinians should be allowed to establish a state on all the Occupied Territories—only 22 percent of the country—has never been seriously entertained by *any* major Israel political leader or party (Gorenberg 2006). From the Allon Plan of 1967 through Oslo and until Olmert's "Convergence Plan" of today, it's simply not on the cards. On the contrary, the physical expression of exclusivity, Israel's official and explicit policy of "Judaization" (*yihud* in Hebrew), goes on apace as Israel's Matrix of Control over "Judea and Samaria," including the consolidation of seven major "settlement blocs," becomes all-encompassing and permanent.

The problem, then, is that the only political solution that would leave Israel's ethnocracy intact has been rejected. Instead, Israeli leaders of all the major parties persist in pursuing the Zionist agenda of more than a century: creating an ethnically pure Jewish space over a "Greater" Land of Israel. To be sure, Israel seeks "separation" from the Palestinians, lest it open the door to Palestinian demands for equal civil rights in a bi-national state created by Israel itself—the Israeli nightmare. So some kind of Palestinian state will be finessed, but at a risk. Even if Israel proves strong and clever enough to engineer the emergence of a Palestinian state which nevertheless leaves Israel in control of the country's borders and resources, that state will by definition be little more than a bantustan, an artificially supported prison-state. This form of a two-state "solution" represents nothing less than apartheid, the only possible outcome acceptable to exclusive Zionist claims, besides transfer and ethnic cleansing.

ISRAEL'S SECURITY FRAMING

A compelling, self-contained national ideology that has given rise to a powerful ethnocracy whose right to exist as such has been rendered unquestionable and eminently moral and just by both Israeli Jews and much of the international community goes a long way towards explaining why the Israeli Jewish public cannot see beyond The Box and continues to support political parties that only deepen its entanglement in a conflict it desperately wants to escape. But there's a potential flaw in this which Israel's ideologues and decision-makers must address: What if the public begins to believe that the conflict can be resolved and, in its desperation for normalcy, begins to question whether or not the ethnocracy must be as maximalist in its territorial demands as it is? What if Zionism has "weakened" to a point where Israelis begin to see themselves as normal people desiring to live in a normal country that does not need to control the Greater Land of Israel to survive—a process that seems to be happening? According to *Ha'aretz* (January 18, 2005),

> Some 63 percent of the Palestinians support the proposal that after the establishment of the state of Palestine and a solution to all the outstanding issues—including the refugees and Jerusalem—a declaration will be issued recognizing the state of Israel as the state of the Jewish people and the Palestinian state as the state of the Palestinian people....On the Israeli side, 70 percent supported the proposal for mutual recognition.

How, then, do we keep the public on our side—"our side" being that of the political leaders and their military collaborators, Labor and Likud alike, who jointly share an overriding fixation on the need to preserve a maximalist ethnocracy? Enter the next piece of the equation: security. "The battle against Palestinian terrorism" is the lynchpin of Israel's security framing, together with a general distrust of the wider Arab and Muslim worlds, often slipping into outright enmity and conflict. The framing presents the Israel-Palestinian/Arab conflict not as a *political* one that can be resolved, but as a preordained "situation," de-politicized, mystified, a win–lose proposition: either we "win" or "they" do. A localized clash of civilizations. The purpose of the framing is to convince Israeli Jews that there is no political solution. Former Prime Minister Yitzhak Shamir put it graphically: "The Arabs are the same Arabs, the Jews are the same Jews and the sea [into which the former seek to throw the latter] is the same sea." By casting the conflict as irresolvable, the powers-that-be, the Framers, ensure broad support for the notion that Israel must control the entire country for its own survival. All other options are eliminated, the public is completely disempowered.

This is the power of framing. It is a crucial intervening variable between facts and reaching particular conclusions. In any debate, the party that succeeds in framing the issue, in determining the parameters of the discussion and the terms used, control the flow of the discussion and usually wins. Conclusions follow naturally from the framer's presentation. The other side (called "the negative" in college debates) can only rebut. It lacks the space to present a coherent and persuasive framing of its own; it comes across as defensive, inarticulate and unconvincing. And if a framing like Israel's is lavishly funded by state agencies, painstakingly constructed by PR agencies and communicated by professional spokespeople enjoying unlimited access to the media, it must be effective. How effective is indicated in the following report:

> According to the poll, which was conducted during the third week of December 2005 by the Geocartography Institute for the

Center Against Racism, half of Israel's Jews feels uncomfortable and fearful when they hear people speaking Arabic, and 18 percent feel hate. The survey revealed that 68 percent of the Jewish public would not agree to live in the same apartment building with Arabs, while 26 percent would agree. Forty-six percent of Jews said they would refuse to allow an Arab to visit their home....Forty-one percent of Jews support the segregation of Jews and Arabs in places of recreation....63 percent agreed with the statement that "Arabs are a security and demographic threat to the state".... Forty percent agreed that "the state should encourage Arab citizens to emigrate"....Thirty-four percent agreed that "Arab culture is inferior to Israeli culture." (*Ha'aretz*, March 23, 2006)

Israel's security framing has been characterized by the Israeli sociologist Baruch Kimmerling as "civilian militarism." "Conflict and war," says Kimmerling (2001:109), became "a self-evident and routine part of everyday life."

Civilian militarism is systematically internalized by most statesmen, politicians and the general public as a self-evident reality whose imperatives transcend partisan or social allegiances. The gist of civilian militarism is that military considerations, as well as matters that are defined as national security issues, almost always receive higher priority than political, economic or ideological problems. Thus, dialectically, making peace is also a military matter.

The security framing that underlies civilian militarism— which both justifies and promotes tribal nationalism and ethnocracy—has been pushed on the Israeli and international publics by all Israeli governments, Labor, Likud and Kadima alike. Its main elements are these:

- Israel is fighting for its existence, the victim of implacable hatred on the part of Arabs who don't want peace. Since they (and the Palestinians in particular) are our permanent enemies, the conflict is a win–lose proposition: either we "win" or "they" do.

- The core of the conflict problem is Palestinian terrorism. As a peace-loving democracy and the victim of aggression Israel bears no responsibility for creating or perpetuating the conflict. Because the threat to Israel is existential and Israel's policies are based solely on concerns for security, it is exempt from accountability for its actions under conventions of human rights, international law or UN resolutions.

- There is no Occupation.

- Since no political solution is possible, any future arrangement must leave Israel in control of the entire country, including control over the Palestinians. Still, in order to remain a Jewish state, Israel must establish a Palestinian state to "relieve" itself demographically of that population. That state, however, must for security purposes be truncated, encircled by Israel, non-viable and only semi-sovereign.

This framing represents a logical extension of pre-state Zionist and Israeli government, an extremely centralized form of government, actually a kind of civilian-army coalition, in which military considerations trump all others (Eldar and Zartal 2004, Peri 2006). The *bitkhonistim* as we call those security-minded people (*bitakhon* means "security" in Hebrew) who dominate the major parties and determine foreign and defense policies, convey to government decision-makers, the media and the general public the notion that we are in a permanent state of conflict with the Arabs in which political accommodation is impossible. This view has a long history; it was been dominant among the pre-state *Yishuv* leadership from the time of the very first Palestinian Intifada in 1936, which in de-politicized Zionist terms are called "riots." Ben Gurion made the army the primarily vehicle of nation-building (Maoz 2006). With a few very brief exceptions—the terms of Prime Ministers Moshe Sharett (1954–55), Levi Eshkol (1963–69) and, perhaps, Rabin

in his Oslo phase (1992–95)—the *bitkhonist* position has held
the upper hand.

In 1957, Sharett described in detail the assumptions of the
military "activists" with whom he struggled (unsuccessfully in
the end) and who until this day dominant Israeli government
policy and decision-making:

> The activists believe that the Arabs understand only the language
> of force....The State of Israel must, from time to time, prove
> clearly that is it strong, and able and willing to use force, in a
> devastating and highly effective way. If it does not prove this, it
> will be swallowed up, and perhaps wiped off the face of the earth.
> As to peace—this approach states—it is in any case doubtful;
> in any case very remote. If peace comes, it will come only if
> [the Arabs] are convinced that this country cannot be beaten....
> If [retaliatory] operations...rekindle the fires of hatred, that is no
> cause for fear for the fires will be fueled in any event. (quoted in
> Morris 1999:280)

Adds Yoram Peri, a well-known Israeli journalist, professor of
political sociology at the Hebrew University and the author of
Generals in the Cabinet Room (2006):

> The centrality of the army depends on the centrality of war....But
> the moment the political leadership opted to create a "mobilized,"
> disciplined and inequitable society by turning the army into the
> "nation builder" and making war a constant, the politicians
> became dependent on the army. It was not just dependence on the
> army as an organization, but on military thinking. The military
> view of political reality has become the main anchor of Israeli
> statesmanship, from the victory of Ben Gurion and his allies over
> Moshe Sharett's more conciliatory policies in the 1950s, through
> the occupation as a fact of life from the 1960s, to the current
> preference for another war in Lebanon over the political option.
> (*Ha'aretz*, August 25, 2006)

Taken together, the three parts of the Israeli framing—the
paradigm of tribal nationalism, ethnocracy and security—form
a complete, self-contained, compelling and rational worldview
and political structure. The upshot of all this is a country—or

rather a mentality—we call "Fortress Israel." It is testimony to the power of paradigms. Even as I write these words (August 10, 2007), the headline in big black letters in Israeli's largest daily newspaper, *Yedioth Ahronoth*, carries an unequivocal message: "Barak: There is No Possibility of an Agreement with the Palestinians." The sub-headline continues: "He says about the efforts to renew the political process: 'Fantasy'. There is no difference between Hamas and Fatah. I will not remove any roadblocks in the West Bank." If this firm pronouncement comes from the former army Chief of Staff, the most decorated soldier in Israel's history, a former Prime Minister during the Oslo peace process, the current Minister of Defense and the head of the *Labor Party*, not the Likud, then who am I, says the average citizen, to doubt his words?

The security framing does not only provide Israeli Jews with a coherent and compelling rationalization for their government's policies, thus keeping them in line, but it also relieves them of any responsibility. A catch-all "first cause" element asserts that the entire conflict derives from Arab rejection of Zionism and that the Arabs keep it going with their intransigence. The corollary insists that we are the victims who have only sought peace. Thus all our conflicts with the Arabs, from wars with Arab countries to the construction of the Separation Barrier through Palestinian neighborhoods and farms are characterized by the same Hebrew term: *ain brera*, "no choice." If *we* are the victims, as the security framing claims, then by definition *they* are the perpetrators. All our actions are defensive; we play no role in perpetuating the conflict. As Golda Meir put it most bluntly: Israel had no responsibility for the wars because it had nothing to do with starting them (McGreal 2003). As recently as the second Lebanon war in 2006, Amir Peretz, the Israeli Defense Minister and veteran "peacenik," invoked the *ain brera* rational.

The security framing also simplifies. You don't have to formulate sophisticated political arguments, you merely have to memorize the main slogans (our interns have collected 51 over the years and put them together in a booklet entitled "Reframing the Israel-Palestine Conflict"). And if confronted by incontrovertible facts that contradict the framing, you can always minimize their significance. If all Israel's policies are defensive and security-related, you may ask, then why did it build 250 settlements in the Occupied Territories? Most Israelis cannot answer that question—it doesn't fit the framing—and so we revert to the ultimate trump card, exclusivity. "Because Jews should be able to live anywhere in the Land of Israel." OK, you may answer, but what if the settlements present an obstacle to peace? That's when minimization kicks in: "Well, they [or the Wall or any of the other elements of the Occupation] can always be dismantled." Minimization is the mechanism whereby we are able to dismiss facts that contradict the logic of the framing. And if we don't want to get into these issues, the framing also acts as a filter: what "fits" gets in, what doesn't is filtered out as "anti-Israeli," "anti-Zionist," "anti-Semitic" or "leftist," and is rebuffed as essentially hostile.

The worst feature of the security, however, is that it forecloses any possibility of peace, genuine security and reconciliation. Paradigms are compelling because they possess an internal logic; they lead effortlessly to certain conclusions, they "make sense," and thus they eliminate other conclusions from consideration. If it is true, as Israel's framing asserts, that the Land of Israel belongs exclusively to the Jews, that Palestinians have no legitimate claim to the country, that the cause of the conflict is an irrational and everlasting refusal to accept the state of Israel, that Israel has done all in its power to achieve peace with its neighbors and that everything it does in Judea, Samaria, Jerusalem and Gaza is purely for self-defense, then a two-state solution in which our intractable enemies receive a state in the very belly of our tiny country (and in its most sacred part to boot) makes no sense whatsoever. The ball is entirely in the Arabs' court; we are blameless and have no responsibility.

Ze'ev Maoz (2006), in an article entitled "Israel's Nonstrategy of Peace," sums it up well:

> Israel has a well-developed security doctrine [but] does not have a peace policy....Israel's history of peacemaking has been largely reactive, demonstrating a pattern of hesitancy, risk-avoidance, and gradualism that stands in stark contrast to its proactive, audacious, and trigger-happy strategic doctrine. The military... is essentially the only government organization that offers policy options—typically military plans—at times of crisis. Israel's foreign ministry and diplomatic community are reduced to public relations functions, explaining why Israel is using force instead of diplomacy to deal with crisis situations.

A compelling framing that lets Israel off the hook is a powerful weapon in the war for public opinion. Yet in the long run, if Israel aspires in any way to regional peace and security, if not actual integration and reconciliation, a framing which eliminates those possibilities can boomerang; it can foster a myopic view of political realities that prevents people from accurately evaluating their situation—a perilous posture in a world of shifting geopolitics. That became evident at the start of the Oslo peace process. Without being prepared in any way, Israelis turned on their TVs one day in September, 1993, and saw their Prime Minister shaking hands with the person whom they had been told for a generation was the arch-terrorist, the ultimate foe of Israel, the incarnation of the biblical Satan Amalek. Suddenly their whole world was turned upside down. If Arafat is now a good guy and our partner for peace, the official framing doesn't work anymore. That handshake sent the Israeli Jewish public into a paradigm panic. Bumper-stickers appeared on cars reading: "This is a nightmare peace." A sudden lack of orientation, not knowing who is friend or foe, is the very stuff of nightmares and horror movies; it became a living nightmare for those in The Box who had always been prevented from considering other options. Yigal Amir, Rabin's assassin, acted as much the alter ego of many mainstream Israeli Jews as he did the representative of a particular community of religious or ideological opposition to the Oslo peace process. He killed not a Prime Minister or legendary Israeli war hero but rather the greatest threat to Israel's existence that had ever emerged, the slayer of the exclusivist security framing from which Israelis drew their very moral universe. Within five months the Israeli public voted in Rabin's antithesis, the very personification of the security framing, Benjamin Netanyahu.

Still, a paradigm shift had occurred in the first two years of Oslo. Netanyahu, whose election was certainly aided by a spate of Hamas suicide bombings, was soundly defeated by Ehud Barak, who at that time presented himself as Rabin's successor and who was given a mandate to negotiate a peace settlement. When, however, Barak failed to impose his dictates on Arafat, he himself quickly reverted to the security framing. Barak's proclamation that Israel has "no partner for peace" has probably done more to convince Israeli Jews to support a hard line against the Palestinians than anything else. In 2007 he was elected again to head the Labor Party. The second subheading in a recent *Yedioth* was: "Barak moves to the right of Netanyahu."

TAKING RESPONSIBILITY

It is only fair to note, as even peace-oriented Israeli liberals insist, that there is some substance to the security paradigm. Israel, they point out, has been embroiled for the past 120 years in a conflict with the Arabs and, to this day, there are Palestinian, Arab and Muslim voices calling for Israel's destruction. The security framing is not all smoke-and-mirrors.

The problem with the security framing is not that it holds the Arabs responsible for their actions—there has certainly been much to criticize on their part over the years—but that it removes from Israel any responsibility. "I argue," says Alan

Dershowitz (2003:7), Israel's most vociferous and well-known advocate, "that it is impossible to understand the conflict in the Middle East without accepting the reality that from the very beginning the strategy of the Arab leadership has been to eliminate the existence of any Jewish state, and indeed any substantial Jewish population, in what is now Israel....The goal has always been the same: eliminating the Jewish state and transferring most of the Jews out of the area."

This may be an effective position in a debate or PR campaign, but it can hardly serve the cause of resolving the conflict, which is the only way Israel can ultimately achieve peace, security and normalization. For the security framing ignores Israel's responsibility for the conflict. It ignores the fact that since the end of the First World War the Zionist *Yishuv* and subsequently the state of Israel have been the strong party. It ignores the Jews' exclusive claim to the entire country, their denial of Palestinian national rights, ethnocracy and occupation. It also demonizes the Arabs and ignores opportunities that have arisen to end the conflict, and Arab gestures in that direction. "The files of the Israeli Foreign Ministry," writes the Israeli-British historian Avi Shlaim (2001:49), "burst at the seams with evidence of Arab peace feelers and Arab readiness to negotiate with Israel from September 1948 on." To take just a few examples of opportunities deliberately spurned:

- In the spring and summer of 1949, Israel and the Arab states met under the auspices of the UN's Palestine Conciliation Committee (PCC) in Lausanne, Switzerland. Israel did not want to make any territorial concessions or take back 100,000 of the 700,000 refugees demanded by the Arabs. As much as anything else, however, was Ben Gurion's observation in a cabinet meeting that the Israeli public was "drunk with victory" and in no mood for concessions. No concessions "maximal or minimal," according to Israeli negotiator Elias Sasson.

- In 1949, Syria's leader Husni Zaim openly declared his readiness to be the first Arab leader to conclude a peace treaty with Israel—as well as to resettle half the Palestinian refugees in Syria. He repeatedly offered to meet with Ben Gurion, who steadfastly refused. In the end only an armistice agreement was signed (Morris 1999:264–265).

- King Abdullah of Jordan engaged in two years of negotiations with Israel but was never able to make a meaningful breakthrough on any major matter before his assassination. His offer to meet with Ben Gurion was also refused. Foreign Minister Moshe Sharett commented tellingly: "Transjordan said—we are ready for peace immediately. We said—of course, we too want peace, but we cannot run, we have to walk." Three weeks before his assassination, King Abdullah said: "I could justify a peace by pointing to concessions made by the Jews. But without any concessions from them, I am defeated before I even start" (Morris 1999:262).

- In 1952–53 extensive negotiations were held with the Syrian government of Adib Shishakli, a pro-American leader who was eager for accommodation with Israel. Those talks failed because Israel insisted on exclusive control of the Sea of Galilee, Lake Huleh and the Jordan River.

- Gamal Abdel Nasser made repeated offers to Ben Gurion beginning soon after the Revolution in 1952 to talk peace, with no success. That effort was finally ended by the refusal of Ben Gurion's successor, Moshe Sharett, to continue the contacts, and by a devastating Israeli attack (led by Ariel Sharon) on an Egyptian military base in Gaza (Morris 1999:265–268).

- In general, Israel's post-1948 war inflexibility was due to its success in negotiating the armistice agreements, which left it in a politically, territorially and militarily superior position. "The renewed threat of war had been pushed back," writes the Israeli historian Benny Morris in his book *Righteous Victims*. "So why strain to make a peace involving major territorial concessions? In a cable to Sharett, Ben Gurion stated flatly what would become Israel's long-term policy, essentially valid until today: 'Israel will not discuss a peace involving the concession of any piece of territory. The neighboring states do not deserve an inch of Israel's land....We are ready for peace in exchange for peace'" (Morris 1999:265). In July, 1949, he told a visiting American journalist: "I am not in a hurry and I can wait ten years. We are under no pressure whatsoever." Nonetheless, this period saw the emergence of the image of the Arab leaders as intractable enemies, curried so carefully by Israel and representing such a powerful part of the Israeli framing. Morris (1999:268) summarizes it succinctly and bluntly:

> For decades Ben-Gurion, and successive administrations after his, lied to the Israeli public about the post-1948 peace overtures and about Arab interest in a deal. The Arab leaders (with the possible exception of Abdullah) were presented, one and all, as a recalcitrant collection of warmongers, hell-bent on Israel's destruction. The recent opening of the Israeli archives offers a far more complex picture.

- In late 1965 the head of the Mossad, Meir Amit, was invited by Abdel Hakim Amer, the vice-president and deputy commander of the Egyptian armed forces, to come to Cairo. The visit was vetoed after stiff opposition from Isser Harel, Eshkol's intelligence advisor (Morris 1999:305). Could the 1967 war have been avoided? We'll never know.
- Immediately after the 1967 war Israel sent out feelers for an accommodation with both the Palestinians of the West

Bank and with Jordan. The Palestinians were willing to enter into discussions over peace, but only if that meant an independent Palestinian state, an option Israel never even entertained. The Jordanians were also ready, but only if they received full control again of the West Bank and, in particular, East Jerusalem and its holy places. King Hussein even held meetings with Israeli officials, but Israel's refusal to contemplate a full return of the territories scuttled the process. Israel's annexation of a "greater" Jerusalem area and an almost immediate program of settlement construction foreclosed any option for a full peace, then and until today (Gorenberg 2006:175–176; Shlaim 2000:264).

- In 1971 Sadat sent a letter to the UN Jarring Commission expressing Egypt's willingness to enter into a peace agreement with Israel (Morris 1999:388–389). Israeli acceptance could have prevented the 1973 war. After the war Golda Meir summary dismissed Sadat's renewed overtures of peace talks.

- Feelers put out by Arafat and other Palestinian leaders in the early 1970s expressed a readiness to discuss peace with Israel; Arafat's offer to discuss peace was flatly shut down by Secretary of State Kissinger, who refused all contact (Aburish 1998:134).

- In 1978 Sadat attempted to expand the Israel-Egypt peace process to resolve the Palestine issue; he was rebuffed by Begin who refused to consider anything beyond Palestinian "autonomy" (Morris 1999:469).

- In 1988 in Algiers, as part of its declaration of the Palestinian independence, the PLO publicly recognized Israel within the Green Line in 1988 and expressed a willingness to enter into discussions (Morris 1999:605–610).

- In 1993, as the very start of the Oslo peace process, Arafat and the PLO reiterated in writing their recognition of Israel within the 1967 borders (that is, on 78 percent of historic Palestine). Although they recognized Israel as a "legitimate" state in the Middle East, Israel did not reciprocate. The Rabin government did not recognize the Palestinian's national right of self-determination, but was only willing to recognize the Palestinians as a negotiating partner. Neither in Oslo nor subsequently has Israel ever agreed to relinquish the territory it conquered in 1948 in favor of a Palestinian state, although this is the position of the UN (in its Resolution 242) and the international community (including, until Bush, the Americans), and has been accepted by the Palestinians since 1988 (Savir 1998:53).

- Perhaps the greatest missed opportunity of all, the undermining by successive Labor and Likud governments of any viable Palestinian state by doubling Israel's settler population during the seven years of the Oslo "peace process" (1993–2000), thus effectively eliminating the two-state solution and destroying Oslo's potential for bringing an agreed-upon peace.
- In late 1995, Yossi Beilin, a key member of the Oslo negotiating team, presented Rabin with the "Stockholm Document" for resolving the conflict, which had been negotiated with Abu Mazen's team. So promising was this agreement that Abu Mazen had tears in his eyes when he signed off on it. Rabin was assassinated a few days later, and his successor, Shimon Peres, turned it down flat (Shlaim 2000:555).
- Sharon completely disregarded the Arab League's 2002 offer of recognition, peace and regional integration in return for relinquishing the Occupation, an offer reiterated and made the basis of the Arab and Muslim world's peace initiative ongoing as of 2007.
- Because Arafat would not play the role of quisling and agree to a Palestinian bantustan, Sharon eliminated him

as a negotiating partner (in whatever way you want to interpret that term), although he was by far the most congenial and cooperative partner Israel ever had and the last Palestinian leader who could "deliver." He subsequently boycotted his successor, Mahmoud Abbas (Abu Mazen).

- In mid 2006 Sharon's successor Olmert declared "irrelevant" the Prisoners' Document in which all Palestinian factions, including Hamas, agreed on a political program of seeking a two-state solution. Instead, he has continued in his attempts to destroy the democratically-elected government of Hamas by force, by economic boycott and by outright starvation, and through his "Convergence Plan" to finesse a Palestinian Bantustan.

- Beginning in the fall of 2006 and continuing as this book is being written, Bashar Assad of Syria again made repeated overtures for peace with Israel, declaring in public: "I am ready for an immediate peace with Israel, with whom we want to live in peace." On the day of Assad's first statement to that regard, Prime Minister Olmert declared "we will never leave the Golan Heights," accused Syria of "harboring terrorists" and, together with the entire Israeli leadership of all the major parties, announced that "conditions are not ripe for peace with Syria" (*Ha'aretz*, August 22, 2006).

- As the Palestinians push for peace within the framework of the Road Map and the Arab League initiative, the Israeli government in mid 2007 announced the building of two new cities in the West Bank, Givat Yael and Meskiot, as well as the construction of 20,000 new housing units in East Jerusalem and the surrounding West Bank areas. The policy of economic "closure" of the Occupied Territories and the construction of the "Separation Barrier" continues apace.

In the end, as we have said, the security framing, based on the exclusive claims of tribal nationalism, locks the Israeli public into a paradigm of conflict in which there is no way out. For Israel cannot "complete 1948" and transfer the Palestinians out of the country altogether; nor can it allow a viable Palestinian state to emerge in the Occupied Territories because of its exclusive claims to the Land, backed up by ever-expanding settlement blocs; nor can it offer the Palestinians of the territories citizenship since Israel would then cease to exist as a Jewish state. The only possible outcome can be apartheid, a regime of separation (*hafrada*, Israel's own term for its policies *vis-à-vis* the Palestinians) in which one population permanently and institutionally dominates another. The thrust of our work in the Israeli peace movement is thus to prod and push Israel into taking responsibility for its actions while prodding the international community to hold Israel accountable for its actions under human rights covenants, international law and UN resolutions. We realize, however, that genuine peace will require Israel to rethink Zionism and to reconceptualize itself as a country. We need to help it reframe. In the meantime, we must also specify what steps must be taken for truly resolving the conflict.

4
Dispossession (Nishul): Ethnocracy's Handmaiden

It must be clear that there is no room for both people [Jews and Palestinian Arabs] in this country....If the Arabs leave the country, it will be broad and wide-open for us. And if the Arabs stay, the country will remain narrow and miserable...and there is no way besides transferring the Arabs from here to the neighboring countries—to transfer them all. Except maybe for Bethlehem, Nazareth and Old Jerusalem, we must not leave a single village, not a single tribe. And the transfer must be directed to Iraq, to Syria and even to Trans-Jordan.

> —Joseph Weitz, Director of the Jewish National Fund,
> *My Diary and Letters To My Children* (1965)

These operations can be carried out in the following manner: either by destroying villages (by setting fire to them, by blowing them up, and by planting mines in their rubble), and especially those population centres that are difficult to control permanently; or by mounting combing and control operations according to the following guidelines: encirclement of villages, conducting a search inside them. In case of resistance, the armed forces must be wiped out and the population expelled outside the borders of the state.

> —Plan D (*Dalet*) of the Hagana, drafted December 1947

Some 46 percent of Israel's Jewish citizens favor transferring Palestinians out of the territories, while 31 percent favor transferring Israeli Arabs out of the country, according to the Jaffee Center for Strategic Studies' annual national security public opinion poll. When the question of transfer was posed in a more roundabout way, 60 percent of respondents said that they were in favor of encouraging Israeli Arabs to leave the country.

> —Amnon Barzilai, *Ha'aretz*, March 12, 2002

I felt I was making progress in answering the question I had posed for myself, a question which touched on all the major issues of the Israeli-Palestinian conflict: Why in the hell did the Israeli authorities demolish the home of Arabiya and Salim Shawamreh? Moving back and forth between the Occupied Territories and my own life in Israel, trying to reconcile what I was witnessing on the ground with what I was being told by my political leaders, I was constantly trying to put the micro (the Shawamreh house, the positioning of a particular checkpoint or settlement, the behavior of the soldiers) into the context of the macro (Zionism, ethnocracy, occupation, global geopolitics) and vice versa.

Understanding Zionist aspirations and the goals of Israeli ethnocracy provided much of the background I needed, but I was still caught in the 1948/1967 conundrum: If the Occupation began unintentionally in 1967, if it was the product of the Six Day War and stands on its own as a political issue and therefore the Israeli-Palestinian conflict can be resolved merely by ending the Occupation, then why doesn't Israel let it go? "Security" didn't provide a satisfactory explanation. Although it is invoked as a "selling point" to an insecure population by the political and military establishment, few of the major elements of the Occupation actually seemed to have anything to do with security. Israel did not establish some 250 settlements because of security—indeed, some military people see them as a liability since they eliminate the strategic depth provided by the West Bank; from the start they were proactive assertions of Jewish claims to the entire Land of Israel. The economic closure suddenly imposed upon the Palestinians *at the start of the Oslo "peace process,"* the severe restriction on their movement *within the West Bank*, the demolition of 18,000 homes, the uprooting of a *million* olive and fruit trees, the devastation of Palestinian agriculture, industry and infrastructure, the crazy route of the Separation Barrier intruding far into

Palestinian areas—*none* of these measures could be explained by security. No, something else was going on.

Was the Occupation really an isolated event forced upon Israel and having nothing to do with Israel itself? What of Occupation-like policies inside Israel? The demolishing of entire villages that goes on in the Negev until today, or of house demolitions in Arab areas throughout Israel proper? What of the expropriation of 93 percent of the lands of Israel, the vast majority of them Palestinian-owned, and the confinement of that population to tiny enclaves? And what of the Koenig Document, a confidential memorandum circulated in 1976 by Israel Koenig, the then Interior Ministry Commissioner in the Galilee, which recommended policies designed to counter the growing Arab "demographic problem" within Israel? In that policy paper he laid out a number of draconian measures, many of which have since been carried out. The territorial contiguity of Arab towns and villages should be broken up, he suggested, by strategically establishing Jewish communities around them. Dozens of Jewish-only *mitzpim* (outposts) and "community settlements" in the Galilee, and expansive Jewish-only "farms" in the Negev, accomplish this purpose. Opportunities for a better life through education, adequate housing and appropriate employment should be denied Israel's Arab citizens, said Koenig, so that their middle class, from where the community's leaders come, would be weakened. Intensifying tax collection, limiting the number of Arabs employed in major economic enterprises and obstructing the marketing of Arab-produced goods would convince the more ambitious Arabs to pursue their lives elsewhere. He proposed a "reward and punishment" system in which "cooperative" Arab mayors would be granted somewhat larger budgets and "recalcitrant" ones denied. He even suggested founding an Arab party of "collaborators"—personalities "of high intellectual standard" identified and groomed by government officials—to coopt the less cooperative ones. Arab students should be encouraged to study abroad, and then not allowed to return (Lustick 1980:256, Sa'di 2003). And on and on up to the latest Citizenship and Entry into Israel Law. No, the Occupation does appear to be an isolated phenomenon removed from the core ideology, policies and practices of Israel itself. It does seem to harken back to 1948, if not well before. This is far more than philosophical speculation. 1948 and 1967 are intimately linked. I would contend that the end of occupation will come only when Israel is able to conceive of itself as a normal country with borders, rather than as a tribal ethnocracy whose national and territorial demands can be assuaged only when the entire Land of Israel is "redeemed" exclusively for Jews. Alternatively, only if we in the Israeli peace movement succeed in prying the Occupied Territories from Israeli control—with a lot of help from our friends abroad—will Israel be able to normalize and transform its ethnocracy into a democratic state of all its citizens.

In search of the 1948/1967 connection, I began to search for the thread connecting the demolition of Salim and Arabiya's home to the Israeli ideology and policies that caused it. I began casting around for the overarching concept, and came up with *nishul*, dispossession, the operative part of exclusive national claims and the natural extension of ethnocracy.

NISHUL

"The idea of transfer," says the Israeli historian Benny Morris (Shavit 2004a), "is as old as modern Zionism and has accompanied its evolution and praxis during the past century. And driving it was an iron logic: There could be no viable Jewish state in all or part of Palestine unless there was a mass displacement of Arab inhabitants."

Nishul has assumed many forms over the years, all of them by necessity violent since the population being displaced can never agree to it or ever be reconciled with it. It has a double face, as we've seen: "de-Arabization" and "Judaization" are by necessity part and parcel of the same process. *Nishul* is not a term we use in Israel; "transfer" is much more common. Still, *nishul* is not seen negatively by Israeli Jews. For most it was merely a consequence of the 1948 war, and without examining it much the vast majority of Jewish Israelis accept as fact the notion that the Arabs fled or were told to leave by the Arab countries. Again, we bear no responsibility for the exodus of 711,000 Palestinians (according to the UN), and we certainly will not allow them or their descendants to return. Whatever happened in 1948 left us with precisely the Jewish space we had craved, and any resolution of the conflict will have to omit the Right of Return. Besides, the rise of a Jewish state represents nothing more than restitution for a history of persecution and isolation, an affirmation of Jewish national rights. The restoration of the Jews to their historic homeland is a morally justified act recognized as such by the international community in the UN vote which created the state. Israel normalizes Jewish life after centuries in which we suffered displacement, dispossession, *nishul*.

In Israel, then, we prefer more positive terms which focus exclusively on our rights and needs; our "return" to our historic homeland, for example, or the process of "redeeming the Land" (*ge'ulat ha'aretz*) by settling and developing it. Since the Palestinians play no role in our national narrative, they are outside of our sphere of concern—except when, in their assigned roles as "terrorists" or "gangs," they seek to foil our justified reclaiming of our country. "Zionism's point of departure," notes the Israeli historian Kolatt (1983), "was not in the actual realities of Palestine, but rather in the problem of the Jews and the Jewish people and in the notion of Jewish rights to and bonds with the Land of Israel."

Despite the power of framing, however, we must look squarely and honestly at the process of displacement that lies at the very root of Zionism's attempt to wrest the Land of Israel

from its Palestinian inhabitants. Surveying the past century and
more until this day, we may discern seven stages of *nishul*:

1. Localized displacement (1904–14)
2. Systematic national Zionist expansion and the articulation
   of the idea of *nishul* (1918–47)
3. Active *nishul* (1948)
4. The consolidation of *nishul* (1948–66)
5. Occupation, colonization and the construction of a
   permanent Matrix of Control (1967–present)
6. The first attempt to complete the process of *nishul*: the
   Oslo process (1993–2000)
7. Taking a new approach to completing the process of *nishul*:
   unilateral "separation" (2001–present).

Let's look briefly in this chapter at the first four historical
stages. In the following chapters we'll examine in greater
detail the three later phases, since they define the present
political moment.

1. Localized Displacement (1904–14)

The problem began with the first settlement wave of proto-
Zionist "pioneers" in 1882, but had already reached significant
proportions in the very first years of Zionist settlement. Read
what Yitzhak Epstein, a Russian-born teacher who settled
in the Upper Galilee in 1886, said in a speech called "The
Hidden Question" delivered before a Jewish group in Basel,
Switzerland, in 1905:

> Faithful Zionists have not dealt with the question of what our
> attitude to the Arabs should be when we come to buy property in
> the Land of Israel, to found villages, and in general to settle the
> land. The Zionists certainly did not intentionally ignore one of the
> main conditions of settlement; they did not recognize its reality
> because they did not know the country and its inhabitants—and
> even more, they lacked human and political sensitivity....We pay
> close attention to all the affairs of our land, we discuss and debate

everything, we praise and curse everything, but we forget one small detail: that there is in our beloved land an entire people that has been attached to it for hundreds of years and had never considered leaving it. (quoted in Shatz 2004:36)

Epstein's words were echoed by other strong voices, *critical* voices; some of the Sephardi Jews like Albert Antebi (Halper 1991:210–211) and Eliahu Eliashar (1997) whose roots were in the Arab world, others part of a non-colonial Jewish national movement in Palestine known as "Cultural Zionism." One of its leading voices was the essayist Ahad Ha'am (a pen name meaning "One of the People"), whose writing can be found in the Israeli school curriculum. In 1891, upon his return to Russia from Palestine, four years before Epstein's seminal speech and six years before Herzl convened the first Zionist Congress, he wrote "Truth From the Land of Israel" (not one of the essays Israeli students read). There he writes:

> From abroad we are accustomed to believe that the Land of Israel is presently almost totally desolate, an uncultivated desert, and that anyone wishing to buy land there can come and buy all he wants. But in truth it is not so. In the entire land, it is hard to find tillable land that is not already tilled....
>
> From abroad we are accustomed to believing that the Arabs are all desert savages, like donkeys, who neither see nor understand what goes on around them. But this is a big mistake....
>
> There is certainly one thing we could have learned from our *past and present* history: how careful we must be not to arouse the anger of other people against ourselves by reprehensible conduct. How much more, then, should we be careful, in our conduct toward a foreign people among whom we live once again, to walk together in love and respect, and needless to say in justice and righteousness. And what do our brethren in the Land of Israel do? Quite the opposite! They were slaves in the land of exile, and they suddenly find themselves with unlimited freedom, the kind of wild freedom to be found only in a country like Turkey [the Ottoman Empire]. This sudden change has engendered in them an impulse to despotism, as always happens when "a slave becomes a king," and behold they walk with the Arabs in hostility and cruelty, unjustly encroaching on them, shamefully beating them for no

good reason, and even bragging about what they do, and there is no one to stand in the breach and call a halt to this dangerous and despicable impulse. (quoted in Shatz 2004:32–33)

From the writings of Epstein, Ahad Ha'am and others, both Jewish and Arab, *nishul* appear to be a major element of Zionism from the very beginning. While Zionists saw themselves as "returning natives," they often employed such terms as "conquest" and "colonization" to describe the process of "reclaiming" the Land. One of the most important Zionist organizations to acquire land and settle immigrant Jews was the Jewish Colonization Association (ICA).

Physical displacement began in an organized way in 1904 with the establishment of the Palestine Office of the World Zionist Organization. It was then that the systematic purchase of lands began, mainly from absentee Arab landowners, many residing in Beirut. Purchases of large tracts of lands necessitated the removal of the Palestinian peasantry. The first tangible expression of physical displacement took place in the years before the First World War, when *Ha-Shomer* ("The Guard"), a heavily armed paramilitary group of Jews mounted on horses and grotesquely attired as Arabs to emphasize their "authenticity" as "natives of the East," forcibly evicted Palestinians from lands they had cultivated for generations (Khalidi 1997:105–111). The Zionists adopted progressive-sounding "socialist" language to conceptualize and justify the nascent process of *nishul*. Arabs were not being displaced from their lands and economy, Jews were merely engaged in the "conquest of labor." Yet as early as 1911 we encounter the term "transfer." Arthur Ruppin, the Director of the Zionist Organization's Palestine Office, publicly proposed that dispossessed Arab peasants be transferred to Syria. Israel Zangwell, the Zionist figure who coined the expression "A land without people for a people without a land," lobbied for an "Arab Trek" à la trek of the Boers into Transvaal—though in the direction of other Arab lands (Flapan 1979:259).

Palestinians—or simply "Arabs," as we still call them—
played only one role in the Jewish national narrative, as foils.
Resistance to displacement began already in the 1880s in
reaction to absentee land purchases on the part of "First Aliya"
settlers, who then forced the peasants out. In fact, resistance to
Zionism preceded the rise of Palestinian nationalism, which only
came into being after the Young Turk Revolt of 1908 and after
Palestine was severed from Syria in the wake of the First World
War. In 1899 Yusuf Diya' al-Din Pasha al-Khalidi, a former
mayor of Jerusalem who had corresponded with European
Jewish and later Zionist leaders since the 1870s and even knew
some Hebrew, sent a letter to Theodor Herzl acknowledging
that Zionism was "in theory a completely natural and just
idea," but pointing out that Palestine was heavily populated by
non-Jewish inhabitants who had claims of their own. "By what
right do the Jews demand it for themselves?" Warning Herzl
that the Palestinians would resist the aspirations of Political
Zionism, which could only be achieved at their expense, he
concluded: "For the sake of God, leave Palestine in peace"
(Khalidi 1997:24, 75).

None of this apparently impressed Herzl who, in the words
of the Israeli historian Benny Morris (1999:21), sang a tune of
displacement and transfer of Arabs. In 1895 he wrote in his
diary: "We must expropriate gently....We shall try to spirit the
penniless [Arab] population across the border by procuring
employment for it in the transit countries, while denying it
employment in our country." He then added: "Both the process
of expropriation and the removal of the poor must be carried
out discreetly and circumspectly" (Morris 1999:21–22).
Resistance to displacement, instead of being seen by Zionists
as warning signs of future conflict, were dismissed—as they
are today—as merely the criminal behavior of Arab "gangs"
inherently hostile to the innocent Jews' claims to "their" ancient
homeland. But while resistance may have been de-legitimized
and dismissed as futile acts of irrelevant "natives," the image

of the irrational, violent, anti-Jewish, Arab fanatic served the colonial project well, as it has many other colonial projects employing similar images. It was nurtured and disseminated not because the Zionist leaders thought it was true, but because it legitimized whatever measures they wished to take to further their national aims. Mystifying the conflict, making it into the classic colonial struggle between civilized (white) people of the West versus (dark) barbarians of the East, intentionally obfuscate the other side of the issue, the Palestinians' right to self-determination in their historic homeland.

Nishul did not get very far in these early years of Zionism. Dispossession was still an incipient idea. By the end of the First World War the Jews comprised only 10 percent of the country's population, the vast majority being non- or anti-Zionist Sephardi and ultra-orthodox Jews of the "Old Yishuv." And the Ottoman/Turkish rulers were firmly against outward expressions of Zionism or any other manifestation of nationalism among their constituent peoples. Still, the chief elements dispossession—the ideology, framing and organization—were already taking form.

2. Systematic National Zionist Expansion and the Articulation of the Idea of Nishul (1918–47)

The Zionist movement began in earnest in 1917. That is the year the British conquered Palestine and the year the Balfour Declaration was issued. Although promising the Arabs independence if they would enter the war against the Turks (which they duly did, led by Lawrence of Arabia), the British government declared in the Balfour Declaration that "His Majesty's Government view with favour the establishment in Palestine of a national home for the Jewish people, and will use their best endeavours to facilitate the achievement of this object." In one fell swoop the British betrayed that commitment to the Arabs and gave the Zionist movement the international credibility and support it sorely needed. The idea of the Declaration was initiated by Herbert Samuel, a Jewish member of the British Cabinet who would soon after be appointed the first High Commissioner for Palestine under the British Mandate. Haim Weizmann, the Zionist representative in London and later the first President of Israel, lobbied effectively for it. Lord Balfour, the Foreign Secretary whose own declaration "I am a Zionist!" derived partly from a desire to see the Jews leave England, issued it. And it was approved by Lloyd George, the British Prime Minister, who had once been legal counsel to the Zionist Federation (Segev 1999:38). While the Balfour Declaration diplomatically hedged its support for Zionism by adding "it being clearly understood that nothing shall be done which may prejudice the civil and religious rights of existing non-Jewish communities in Palestine," the effect, as the writer Arthur Koestler put it, was that "one nation solemnly promised to a second nation the country of a third."

Emboldened by the Balfour Declaration and the assumption of British rule over Palestine, the years 1918–20 witnessed the emergence of "Maximalist Zionism," the attempt to establish a Jewish state with an overwhelming Jewish majority that would arise on both sides of the Jordan River (Kolatt 1983). This development, it is important to note, had nothing to do with any conflict with the Palestinians; in fact, this radicalization of Zionism took place at a time of quiet in Jewish-Palestinian relations. Later, following an outbreak of Arab "riots" and a subsequent British White Paper which seemed to retreat from the promises of the Balfour Declaration, Maximal Zionism received its clearest ideological expression when, in 1923, Vladimir Ze'ev Jabotinsky, the founder of Revisionist Zionist and the ideological source of today's Likud party, formulated his "Iron Wall" doctrine. "Every indigenous people will resist alien settlers as long as they see any hope of ridding themselves of the danger of foreign settlement," wrote Jabotinsky, using colonial terminology Zionists would never use today.

This is how the Arabs will behave and go on behaving so long as
they possess a gleam of hope that they can prevent "Palestine"
from becoming the Land of Israel. [The sole way to an agreement,
then,] is through the iron wall, that is to say, the establishment
in Palestine of a force that will in no way be influenced by Arab
pressure....A voluntary agreement is unattainable....We must
either suspend our settlement efforts or continue them without
paying attention to the mood of the natives. Settlement can thus
develop under the protection of a force that is not dependent
on the local population, behind an iron wall which they will be
powerless to break down. (Jabotinsky 1923 (1937))

This seminal doctrine represents one of the first times *nishul*
was explicitly articulated. For this Jabotinsky deserves some
credit; his doctrine was one of the rare Zionist formulations
that actually brought the "natives" into the picture. Lustick
(1996) and Shlaim (2000:19) argue that the Iron Wall doctrine
was fully adopted by Ben Gurion and became a central tenet
of Zionist policy, operational until this very day. While
Ben Gurion entertained notions that the Jewish state could
"expand to the whole of Palestine" through the good offices
of Transjordan's Emir Abdullah, in the end the Iron Wall
approach, if taking "natives" into account, also rendered them
irrelevant to Zionism's goals. Indeed, it sought to bypass them
completely by reaching separate political arrangements with
Arab leaders. We had to be wary of the Palestinians, but in
terms of actual rights and claims to "our" country there was
simply no "other side."

By 1932, when, according to the British census, the Jews
constituted only 17 percent of the population of Palestine, the
vision, indeed the program of ethnocracy, was clearly articulated
by Haim Arlosoroff, a leading Labor Zionist figure and Director
of the Political Department in the Jewish Agency Executive. In
a letter to Weizmann, Arlosoroff discusses the strategic options
facing the Zionist movement, and concludes:

Zionism cannot be realised without a transition period during
which the Jewish minority would exercise organised revolutionary

rule...during which the state apparatus, the administration, and the military establishment would be in the hands of the minority, in order to eliminate the danger of domination by the non-Jewish majority and suppress rebellion against us....During this period a systematic policy of immigration, colonisation, and development would be practised. (quoted in Khalidi 1971:253)

How, it might be asked, did a small minority justify the displacement of an overwhelming native majority? Kolatt (1983) makes a perceptive observation. Palestine, in the eyes of the Zionists, "belonged" to two unequal peoples: the entire Jewish people of 14 million, the country's "true" natives who were returning to claim their historic patrimony, and a static population of only 600,000 Arabs, generally cast as recent immigrants from other Arab countries and therefore "intruders" with no legitimate counter-claims to the land. The rapid rise of Jewish immigration from Europe during the 1930s—the "Fourth Aliya" brought about 60–70,000 immigrants, mainly from Poland, between the years 1924 and 1929, while the "Fifth Aliya," comprised mainly of middle-class German Jews, brought 200–250,000 immigrants to the country between 1932 and 1939, doubling the *Yishuv*'s population (Sachar 1981:189)—only bolstered this perception.

Although characterized as mere "riots," the organized Arab Revolt of 1936–39 finally convinced the Zionists that, like it or not, they were facing a growing nationalist movement— although they would never publicly dignify it in such terms. It is at this juncture that notions of a "voluntary transfer" or "resettlement" of displaced Arab peasants give way to explicit Zionist consideration of "compulsory transfer." In June 1938, Ben Gurion reported to the Jewish Agency: "I am for compulsory transfer; I don't see anything immoral in it....We have to state the principle of compulsory transfer without insisting on its immediate implementation" (Morris 1999:144).

The "riots," accompanied by the 1937 Peel Commission report which for the first time proposed the partition of the country, galvanized the *Yishuv* leadership. From this point on, Jewish sovereignty over the entire country became a priority over any attempts to reconcile the conflict with the Palestinians. It might be best to characterize the *Yishuv*'s approach to the Palestinian as pragmatic rather than ideological. It was not directed against Arabs, if only because Arabs did not matter in any way except demographically. It was hoped the Arabs would leave voluntarily, but all the extensive discussion of transfer in the 1930s, as today, was a purely intra-Jewish discussion; the opinions of the Arabs were neither solicited nor considered necessary. Most of the major Zionist figures repeated what Menachem Ussishkin said succinctly to the Jewish National Fund in 1930: "We must take over the land. We have a greater and nobler ideal than preserving several hundred thousand of Arab peasants" (Morris 1999:141). The issue was purely technical, as it is today. Sooner or later, the Iron Wall and Jewish immigration would lead the Arabs to accept the Zionist presence and, if not, that they would have both the power and moral right to enact a wholesale transfer (Morris 1999:138–144).

This is why Ben Gurion and other Zionist leaders said such contradictory things, at times denying any wish to expel the Arabs, at other times stating flatly that transfer is inevitable; occasionally expressing an understanding of Arab national feelings, their attachment to the land and the reasons for their resistance, more often condemning Arab resistance as the work of a bloodthirsty fringe of primitive Arabs who do appreciate the benefits Jewish colonization. If it is impossible to define a precise "Zionist position" on the Arabs, it is because they simply don't figure in. One thing is clear: very early in the Zionist program the idea of bi-nationalism, of two nations claiming the same country and thus necessitating some kind of accommodation, was rejected. Ben Gurion set this position out very clearly to the Peel Commission. The Jews, he said, had emerged as the only national group in Palestine. Aside from the Jews, who had full historic rights to Palestine, "there is no other nation—I do not say population, I do not say sections of a people—there is no other race or nation as a whole which regards this country as their only homeland" (Lustick 1980:34). When in 1942 the Zionist movement formally adopted the Biltmore Program, it asserted "that Palestine be constituted as a Jewish Commonwealth," the Palestinians were not even mentioned.

3. Active Nishul (1948)

By the end of the Second World War, faced with what it considered an anti-Zionist turn in British policy, the *Yishuv* leaders agreed to reevaluate the idea of partition. In the wake of the Holocaust, the need to establish a Jewish state as soon as possible was considered paramount; so, too, was the need to exploit the political "opening" that emerged in the wake of the war. In November, 1949, the UN approved the partition of Palestine. The Jews, then only about a third of the population, would receive 56 percent of the country, the Arab majority 42 percent. (The other 2 percent, Jerusalem and Bethlehem, were to be under internationalized trusteeship.)

The partition plan, however, created the necessity of displacement. If the area designated for the Jewish state was to be truly Jewish, a solution had to found for the fact that 397,000 of the people living there, a full 43 percent, were Arabs. Nor could a Jewish state be limited to that area, since another 10,000 Jews lived in what was to become the Arab state, an area essential for territorial contiguity. If the map presented to the Paris Peace Conference by the World Zionist Organization in 1919 showed a Jewish state incorporating all of Israel, the Occupied Territories of today and large adjacent strips of Sinai, Transjordan, the Golan Heights and southern

Lebanon including the cities of Tyre and Sidon, the minimum the Zionist movement under Ben Gurion would settle for was 80 percent of Palestine—roughly the area taken by Israel in 1948 (Pappe 2006:48).

This is not the place to go into the details of the ethnic cleansing campaign begun in December, 1947 and ending, at least in its warfare mode, in January 1949. In my view, both the case for an ethnic cleansing campaign and the demographic reasons behind it have been convincingly presented by Ilan Pappe (2006), Walid Khalidi (1992), Nur Masalha (1992) and others. Since I have argued that the policy of *nishul* extends over a century, the most pertinent point here is that plans for the dispossession of the Palestinian population were prepared even before war. "Prior to March 1948," writes Pappe (2006:41),

> the activities of the Zionist leadership carried out to implement their vision could still be portrayed as retaliation for hostile Palestinian or Arab actions. However, after March this was no longer the case: the Zionist leadership openly declared—two months before the end of the Mandate—it would seek to take over the land and expel the indigenous population by force: Plan Dalet.

Israeli Jews, including a sizable chunk of my own critical crowd, could never come to terms with what happened in 1948. Pappe (2006:xiii) calls it a "crime [which] has been erased almost totally from the global public memory." Few Israeli Jews could bring themselves to use the terms "crime" or "ethnic cleansing." They simply do not jibe with their view, critical as it may be, of what Ben Gurion and the *Yishuv*-cum-Israeli leadership were capable of. So deeply have the progressive ideals and fundamental humanism of the mainstream Labor Zionist movement etched themselves into the Jewish public's image of itself, that the cabal of eleven and the evil deeds ascribed to them by Pappe are absolutely ungraspable. They simply could not be. The liberal wing of the Labor Zionist movement, Mapam, spoke of "coexistence" before, during and after the war even though it was aware of an Israeli military intelligence report from July 1948 stating authoritatively that 70 percent of the Palestinians who fled from areas which had been allocated by the UN to the Jewish state, plus another 150,000 from Jerusalem and the areas allocated to the Arab state, did so due to "direct, hostile Jewish operations against Arab settlements" (Beinin 2004:41). 1948 has never registered with Israeli Jews of any political persuasion. That their leaders had planned and carried out a deliberate and cold-blooded campaign of ethnic cleansing including, by Pappe's (2006) count, 36 massacres and the destruction of 517 entire villages, towns and cities, is too much to absorb. It could never be squared with the Zionist narrative as voiced powerfully by Leon Uris in *Exodus* (1958):

> There was never a question of the Jews' willingness to die for Israel. In the end they stood alone and with blood and guts won for themselves what had legally been given them by the conscience of the world....If the Arabs of Palestine loved their land, they could not have been forced from it—much less run from it without real cause. The Arabs had little to live for, much less to fight for. This is not a reaction of a man who loves his land.

Meron Benvenisti is a supremely critical and unflinching Israeli historian who has written on, among other things, the process of Judaizing Palestine. Yet even he hedges when it comes to describing what happened. The second half of the 1948 war, he says (2000:145), "came dangerously close to fitting the definition of 'ethnic cleansing.'"

> Although not as severe as in the case of Bosnia [when the term "ethnic cleansing" was coined to characterize Serbian policies and actions towards the Bosnian Muslims during the war of 1992–95], atrocities that could be defined as war crimes did occur....[S]ome of the Arabs were expelled not on military grounds but with the objective of taking over their homes and land expressly for the settlement of Jews. Even if the pretext for the expulsions was related to military security (and there undoubtedly were legitimate reasons for them), those responsible knew that Israel's leaders

had laid down two principles that transformed the abandonment of the Arab settlements into a matter whose implications went beyond the fulfillment of the short-term requirements of the military-security situation. They had determined, first, that the Arabs would not ever be allowed to return to their homes and, second, that the abandoned areas were designated for the settlement of Jews....

Benny Morris, too, in a *Ha'aretz* interview (January 9, 2004), skirts the issue: "There is no explicit order of [transfer] in writing, there is no orderly comprehensive policy, but there is an atmosphere of [population] transfer. The transfer idea is in the air. The entire leadership understands that this is the idea. The officer corps understands what is required of them. Under Ben Gurion, a consensus of transfer is created."

A deliberate campaign to expunge or conceal the facts of 1948—physical, documented and oral—has also helped, as Pappe says, to totally erase the events from public memory. After reading *The Ethnic Cleansing of Palestine*, I asked Pappe why it took 58 years for that book to be written. It did not depend, after all, upon the opening of new archival material; on the contrary, a good deal of the source material comes from Ben Gurion's diaries and other contemporary sources published years ago. Why, then? He replied that Israeli Jewish scholars simply did not want to confront the events, did not want to "go there." The only exception, he said, was Simcha Flapan, a prolific Israeli journalist and critical, though non-university-affiliated, historian.

Besides his position, still rejected by mainstream Zionist historians and, of course, by Israel's PR machine, that a planned and deliberate campaign of transfer was carried out in 1948, Morris added a caveat in his *Ha'aretz* interview which shocked even the interviewer (Shavit 2004a). "[I]n certain conditions," he opined, "expulsion is not a war crime. I don't think that the expulsions of 1948 were war crimes. You can't make an omelet without breaking eggs....There are circumstances in history that justify ethnic cleansing." That bald statement was shocking not because of what it said—most Israelis would probably agree with it—but because, like the idea of "transfer in the air" itself, such thoughts are seldom expressed outright.

Morris is singular in his forthright description and support of ethnic cleansing—until, that is, when one travels to the far right of Lieberman and the settlers where outrageous statements are taken for granted and thus dismissed (even if they do, in fact, express a significant view within the Israeli public). Here, too, a kind of coy vagueness enables Israelis to gloss over the massive campaign of dispossession out of which Israel was born. Since the government never took an actual decision to expel the Arabs, Ben Gurion could later claim disingenuously that "Israel did not expel a single Arab" (Morris 1999:258).The significance of this act of deception should not be lost on us; it underpins the success Israel has had over the years in both deflecting criticism of its policies in the Occupied Territories and maintaining Israel's democratic, defensive façade. "Doing and not talking about it," as Sharon would later put it, enables Israel to mobilize support for policies most people, in Israel and abroad, could not support if they were laid out honestly, as Morris does in promoting ethnic cleansing. As we shall see, Israeli decision-makers decided from the start of the Occupation that Israel would never relinquish military and economic control of the West Bank. Their success in keeping the "two-state solution" alive, in convincing the world (and its own people) that Israel is committed to peace and in blaming the Palestinians for the continued conflict, shows how efficacious that approach can be.

4. The Consolidation of Nishul (1948–66)

Benvenisti (2000:151) quotes from the diary of Joseph Weitz, the head of the Jewish National Fund, who had lobbied vigorously for the expulsion of the Arabs and would soon spearhead the efforts to destroy the "abandoned" villages, written as he toured the country toward the end of 1948:

> And the road continues eastward between mountains and over mountains, and the Galilee is revealed in its splendor, its hidden places and folds, its crimson smile and its green softness and its desolation. I have never seen it like this. It was always bustling with man and beast. And the latter predominated. Herds and more herds used to descend from the heights to the valleys of the streambeds, their bells ringing with a sort of discontinuous sound, which vanished in the ravines and hid among the crevices, as if they would go on chiming forever. And the shepherds striding after them like figures from ancient times, whistling merrily and driving the goats towards the trees and the bushes—to gnaw at them hungrily; and now the picture has disappeared and is no more. A strange stillness lies over all the mountains and is drawn by hidden threads from within the empty village. An empty village; what a terrible thing! Fossilized lives! Lives turned to fossilized whispers in extinguished ovens; a shattered mirror; moldy blocks of dried figs and a scrawny dog, thin-tailed and floppy-eared and dark-eyed. At the same time—at the very same moment—a different feeling throbs and rises from the primordial depths, a feeling of victory, of taking control, of revenge, and of casting off suffering. And suddenly the whispers vanish and you see empty houses, good for the settlement of our Jewish brethren who have wandered for generation upon generation, refugees of your people, steeped in suffering and sorrow, as they, at least, find a roof over their heads. And you knew: War! This was our war.
> But has it ended?...

During the 1948 war Israel expanded to 78 percent of Mandatory Palestine—the 56 percent allocated to the Jews by the UN plus an additional 22 percent, more than half the land that was to become an Palestinian Arab state, which was conquered and annexed. The problem was now not the Arab population itself—75–80 percent of the Arabs in the expanded territory of Israel had left or been driven out—but how to keep them out. If the refugees were allowed to return—or more precisely, if Israel was forced by the international community to accept their return—the enormous Jewish space created by the Palestinian exodus would be reoccupied by Arabs and the "miraculous" success of the transfer campaign would be reversed. The refugees' Right of Return is, after all, an inalienable right embodied in international law. As early as April, 1948, even before the state of Israel came into being, the US and Britain tried to impress this fact upon the Zionist leaders (Morris 1999:258). As a condition for its creation as a state, the *Yishuv* leadership had solemnly promised that Israel would respect UN resolutions. How could it refuse to honor General Assembly Resolution 194, passed in December, 1948, calling upon it to respect the wishes of the refugees to return home? Refugee rights were also embodied in Geneva Conventions of 1949, the foundations of modern human rights and international humanitarian law. Seeking to protect civilian populations living under hostile conditions, including occupation, they drew their inspiration and immediacy from the Jewish experience in the Holocaust. Indeed, Jewish organizations abroad, possessing considerable clout as the horrors of the Holocaust emerged, had labored hard for their adoption (Korey 1998). It is supremely ironic that the first country called upon to honor the Geneva Conventions—unsuccessfully—was Israel.

Israel's strategy, which would later be applied to the Occupied Territories, was to create "facts on the ground" that effectively foreclose the refugee's return. On June 16, 1948, the Cabinet took a political decision to bar their return. It was from this time that various Israeli actors—the army, the Jewish National Fund and even the refugees' former neighbors, the Jews of the *kibbutzim* (collective farming settlements) and *moshavim* (cooperative farming settlements)—began razing their villages, taking over their lands and, mainly in the urban areas, occupying their homes (Morris 1999:256–257). Presaging the use it would later make of law, administration and planning as mechanisms of territorial expansion after 1967, Israeli leaders prepared Kafkaesque legal means by which Palestinian property could be "legally" appropriated, thus ensuring that the refugees would have nowhere to return while retroactively legalizing the destruction or stealing of their properties. Kimmerling (1976) and Jiryis (1976:75–134) describe four stages whereby Israel alienated Palestinian land within Israel from its Palestinian owners—and continues to do so both within Israel and in the Occupied Territories:

Stage 1. *Israel claims sovereignty.* The "Abandoned Areas Ordinance" Section 1(A) defines "abandoned territory" as "any area captured by the armed forces or surrendered to them or land abandoned by all or some of its inhabitants." This definition allows land to be declared "abandoned" whether or not its residents have left it.

Stage 2. *Freezing the "lack of ownership."* The Provisional Council of the State (1948) created a "Custodian" for the "abandoned areas." The "Absentees' Property Law—1950" defines an "absentee" as an owner of a property in 1947–48 who was: (a) national or a citizen of Lebanon, Syria, Transjordan, Iraq, Egypt, Saudi Arabia or Yemen; (b) who was in any of these places or in parts of Palestine outside of Israel (West Bank/Gaza and East Jerusalem) during 1947–48; or (c) was a Palestinian citizen who left his ordinary place of residence in Palestine for somewhere else before September, 1948, or for "a place in Palestine held at the time by forces which sought to prevent the establishment of the State of Israel or which fought against it after its establishment." This definition includes almost all Palestinians, including Israeli citizens, who left their homes, as most did, even to go to a neighboring village. Thus were created the "internal refugees" or, in a truly Orwellian term, the "present absentees," especially residents of the "Triangle" area of the eastern Galilee.

Palestinians were also removed from their land by other means. The "Emergency Defense Regulations (1945)" empower military commanders to declare certain areas as "closed areas," prohibiting both entrance or exit. Thirteen Palestinian villages and their lands were declared "closed areas," and this policy of restricting Palestinians from their own lands was reinforced by the Curfew of 1948–66.

Actual evacuation of populations was made possible by several military orders such as "Regulation 8(A) of the Emergency Regulations, Security Areas, 1949," which reads: "An authorized source may command a permanent resident of a security area to leave the area." Most of the upper and eastern Galilee, as well as a ten-kilometer strip along the border with Jordan, were declared "security areas," as were sections of the Negev. This allowed the expulsion of the residents of Ikrit and Baram, for example, as well as Bedouin groups from the Negev, like the Jahalin tribe. This was reinforced by the "Law of Land Acquisition in Time of Emergency," which empowered the authorities to issue a "Land Acquisition Order" in cases deemed "necessary for the defense of the state and public security."

Extra-legal means of expulsion were also employed between 1949 and 1959. Whole communities were expelled—Mag'dal, now Ashkelon, to Gaza in 1950, for example, or the Jahalin Bedouin from the Negev to Lod and subsequently to Jordan— as well as thousands of individuals. This was presented as a "voluntary" evacuation.

Stage 3. "Israelification:" from "lack of ownership" to Israeli ownership. A number of legal means were instituted in the early years of the state to expropriate Palestinian lands and hand them over to Israeli owners. The "Emergency Regulations for the Cultivation of Fallow Lands, 1948" empowered the Ministry of Agriculture to seize lands not (or "under-") cultivated to "ensure" their cultivation. When used together with the "Security Areas Regulations" and the "Regulations on Closed Areas," both of which prevented Palestinians from reaching their fields, these regulations proved an effective means of confiscation.

In 1950 a "Development Authority" was created with the goal of acquiring "abandoned" Arab territories and lands and "developing" them. This was in line with the policy of not accepting back Palestinian refugees or "present absentees"; the Development Authority developed into the Israel Lands Authority. Although compensation was offered for lands (at 1950 rates, well below later market prices), most Palestinian owners refused it because taking compensation would validate the loss of their lands and signal their relinquishing them. Many owners also had no authority to "sell" what were collectively-owned lands, or could not agree to do so with other family members. Regulations issued in 1953 allowed the state to expropriate the lands of 250 "abandoned" Arab villages and individual parcels of land belonging to "absentees," equaling 586 square miles.

Stage 4. De-Arabization. In general, Palestinian ownership of land or even their territorial presence was perceived as a threat to Israeli sovereignty and the "Jewish character" of the state. The land had to be "nationalized."Israel emerged after the 1948 war consisting of 7,812 square miles, or 72 percent of Palestine. But the Jewish National Fund owned only about 390 square miles, while Palestinians owned 2,000 square miles, or 25 percent of the land in Israel, mainly in the Galilee. The Law of Absentee Property (1950) allowed it to acquire millions of acres more, so that by 1962, 92.6 percent of the land belonged to either the state (6,000 square miles) or to the Jewish National Fund (1,400 square miles). Palestinian ownership was down to 7.3 percent (580 square miles). By the time the process of physical displacement was largely completed within Israel proper, the Jews had sovereignty over the entire country and actual control of almost 93 percent of the land (Abu Hussein and McKay 2003).

Some 75 percent of the Palestinians were now refugees beyond Israel's borders, and of those that remained, about half (75,000 out of 150,000) were classified as "internally displaced"—or, in a classic Orwellian term, "present absentees"—and forbidden to return to their homes and lands. Instead nearly 200,000 Jewish immigrants, including my in-laws, were settled in "abandoned" Arab villages, both because of the availability of housing and in order to prevent the refugees' return (Lustick 1980:57–58).

Yet Israeli governments still felt their hold over the country to be tenuous, and the process of *nishul* continued by other means. One of the key elements of consolidation was the use of settlements to "constitute a human wall against the dangers of invasion," as Ben Gurion stated plainly. "Our territorial conquests and redemptions will not be assured," he went on,

> if we do not succeed in erecting a great and closely linked chain of settlements, especially settlements of soldiers, on the borders, in the Negev, on the coast, in the Jerusalem corridor, around Safed, and in all other areas of strategic importance. (quoted in Lustick 1980:41)

Between 1948 and 1953, 370 new Jewish settlements were established, 350 of them on "abandoned" lands expropriated from the Arabs. And not necessarily Arabs who had fled or been expelled from the country. Sixty thousand acres of land taken for the new Jewish settlements belonged to Arabs who still lived in the country, often adjacent to their fields that now became Jewish agricultural settlements or towns (Lustick 1980:51). In the Galilee, where by the early 1960s only 8 percent of the population were Jews (10,000 of 120,000 people), a vigorous policy of Judaization was adopted. Thousands of acres of Palestinian-owned land were expropriated for the building of Carmiel, Upper Nazareth and other Jewish "development towns." When the Jewish population in the Galilee still did not reach a critical mass, dozens of "outposts" (or "community settlements") were established on hilltops to ensure territorial control. Identical policies of *nishul* and Judaization were carried out in the center of the country and in the Negev. By 1954 more than a third of Israel's Jewish population lived either in "abandoned" Arab neighborhoods, towns or villages, or on expropriated Arab lands (Lustick 1980:58). The model for what would occur later in the Occupied Territories was clearly emerging.

At the same time, legislation was strengthened (such as the "Basic Law: Israel Lands –1960") to prevent lands or houses built on either State Lands or lands controlled by the Jewish National Institutions (the World Zionist Organization (WZO), the Jewish Agency (JA) and the Jewish National Fund (JNF)) from being sold, leased or rented to Palestinian citizens of Israel. This ploy of sub-contracting state authority over land to non-state yet "national institutions" allows Israel to formally maintain its promise to "ensure social and political rights to all its inhabitants" while institutionalizing discrimination unofficially. In the critical areas of immigration, settlement and land development, writes Uri Davis in his exhaustively detailed book *Apartheid Israel* (2003),

> the Israeli sovereign, the Knesset, which is formally accountable to all its citizens, Jews and non-Jews alike, has formulated and passed legislation ceding state sovereignty (including taxation) and entered into Covenants vesting its responsibilities with organizations such as the WZO, the JA and the JNF, which are constitutionally committed to serving and promoting the interests of Jews and Jews only. It is through this procedure of legal duplicity...that legal apartheid is regulated in Israel. And it is through this mechanism of legal duplicity that the State of Israel has successfully veiled the reality of Zionist apartheid in the guise of legal democracy since the establishment of the State of Israel to date. (Davis 2003:48)

As a result, Palestinian ownership (formal or customary) has been reduced from 93 percent in pre-war 1948, to 25 percent immediately after the war, to just 4 percent in 2007.

In the years immediately following the 1948 war, *nishul* faced a new problem: "infiltration," the attempt of Palestinian refugees to return to the homes and properties. No orderly evacuation had been decided upon or organized, and the

711,000 Palestinian refugees who now found themselves outside of Israel also found themselves in a kind of dazed limbo. They were stateless, yet in many cases no more than an hour or two away from their homes, fields and relatives from whom they had been suddenly torn. There had been no mental preparation for their flight or expulsion, no time to plan or get ready, not even a chance to say goodbye to family, to collect some precious personal items or even a modest nest egg, a cow, maybe, or a professional tool. They had neither sold nor given up their properties in any way. Foreshadowing the latter use of the term "terrorism," "infiltration" was presented as a threat to Israeli security, a blurring of the expanded borders Israel had created. Most seriously, infiltration, as a kind of refugee "return," threatened to upset the extremely favorable demographic domination the Jews had achieved. Thus framed, it was appropriate to employ military force against these hapless people. A "free fire" policy was instituted in which soldiers were ordered—or at least allowed—to shoot at any Arab attempting to cross the ceasefire lines (Morris 1999:260, 269–281).

Yet, then as now, the Israel authorities knew the infiltrators were not terrorists. True, massive infiltration along the borders with the West Bank and Gaza began even as the war was being fought, during the first truce in mid 1948. Some 10–15,000 "incidents" occurred annually until 1954, when they started to drop off (Morris 1999:269). "During 1948–49," writes Morris (1999:269), "most of the infiltrators crossed the borders to harvest crops left behind, to plant new crops in their abandoned lands, or to retrieve goods. Many others came to resettle in their old villages or elsewhere inside Israel, or to visit relatives, or simply to get a glimpse of their abandoned homes and fields." As time went on and the refugees began to grasp the finality of their separation from their former lives, impelled by both poverty and the need for revenge, "the vast majority came to steal crops, irrigation pipes, farm animals or other property belonging to the [Israeli] settlers, or to graze their flocks. " Most of the infiltrators, Morris (1999:270) writes,

> were unarmed individuals, though it appears that the proportion who came armed and in groups increased after 1950, largely in reaction to the IDF's violent measures. Many of the Israeli victims of infiltration were incidental casualties of raids whose aim was theft or smuggling....
> Only a very small proportion, certainly far less than 10 percent, of the infiltrators came with the express purpose of attacking people or sabotaging Israeli targets....Until 1955 the Arab states officially opposed infiltration and generally attempted to curb it.

At partition, when the UN passed Resolution 181 (November 29, 1947), the Jews, just a third of the population and owning but 6 percent of the land, were allocated 56 percent of historic Palestine. By the time the 1948 war had concluded, Israel controlled 78 percent of the country and the Palestinians had nothing—Jordan, which had taken the West Bank by agreement with Israel (Shlaim 1988), annexed it in 1950, while Gaza came under Egyptian rule.

The dual process of de-Arabization and Judaization described by Kimmerling and Jiryis formalized an apartheid system in which one ethnic/national/religious community both separates itself from the others and imposes upon them a permanent regime of domination in which it has exclusive privilege. From 1948 to 1966, Israel imposed a strict military administration on its Arab citizens. While the rationale given was, as usual, "security"—"Israeli Arabs" were considered a potential fifth column, as they are until today—the military regime also broke any cohesiveness that the decimated Arab society might have retained. But it also had an important economic role in the days when Israel's fledgling economy, burdened by the costs of war and massive immigration, was struggling. Although given unwillingly and by force, the land, labor and agricultural produce appropriated by Israel played a major role in its nation-building (Lustik 1980). While the military government ended in 1966, the very next year Israel's occupation of the West Bank and Gaza began, with many of the same issues and problems Israel had confronted since 1948. The fact that Israel had a military administration already in place, complete with policies, laws, institutions and trained personnel, allowed it to move quickly from military occupation to a mixed regime, similar to Israel, of martial law for Arabs and an ever-expanding space exclusively for Jewish citizens under Israeli law.

After the ethnic cleansing which accompanied the establishment of an expanded Israel, *nishul* took the form of removing Palestinians from vast tracts of the country and concentrating them in small, disconnected and densely-packed enclaves or cantons. To be sure, policies to induce emigration remained in place, targeting in particular the Palestinian middle classes, but the thrust of dispossession and de-Arabization shifted from expulsion to confinement. This is what happened in Israel after 1948, and it continues to characterize policies of *nishul* in the Occupied Territories, where the goal is to complete the expansion of Israel over the entire country between the Mediterranean and the Jordan River while finessing, under the guise of a "two-state solution," a Palestinian bantustan that leaves intact Israeli control.

5
The Narrative of Exodus

There was never a question of the Jews' willingness to die for Israel. In the end they stood alone and with blood and guts won for themselves what had legally been given them by the conscience of the world....If the Arabs of Palestine loved their land, they could not have been forced from it—much less run from it without real cause. The Arabs had little to live for, much less to fight for. This is not a reaction of a man who loves his land.

—Leo Uris, *Exodus* (1958)

What you've read so far is not the story as we have always heard it. More familiar is the rendition made popular by Leon Uris in his 1958 saga, *Exodus*, read and internalized my millions of people worldwide:

The Arabs, mainly the Egyptians in the Gaza Strip, organized *fedayeen* ["infiltrators" in Hebrew, "men of sacrifice" in Arabic; the former meaning is being used here] gangs for the purpose of murdering Israelis. These gangs crossed the border nightly to kill, to burn fields, to cut water-pipes, to destroy. Tormented Palestinian refugees were used in these gangs, goaded by hate-spewing leaders.

Israel, with all of her other burdens, had to adopt an axiom of reality: "When Hitler said he was going to exterminate the Jews, the world did not believe him. When the Arabs say it, we in Israel believe them."

This is the story—the Israeli critic Rachel Weissbrod (1999) calls it a melodrama—we all grew up with, heroic little Israel standing bravely against hoards of bad Arabs bent only on our destruction, is eerily similar to a lot of other stories we in Europe and North America often hear: the brave American pioneers struggling against the dark Indian savages; the handsome British colonial officer overwhelmed by the dark Indians (of India); Tarzan and Jane amongst the African "natives." Are the stories really the same, or should their similarity caution us that they may be constructed to justify if not glorify the taking of territory, as Jabotinsky says, "without paying attention to the mood of the natives."

It is in this period of Israeli history that the familiar colonial narrative emerges full-blown, and no narrative in history has ever approached *Exodus*, the template which emblazoned an idealized image of Israel upon an entire generation and until today defines "pro-Israel" *hasbara* (PR). What 17-year-old in the entire Western world did not read the compelling story of Ari Ben Canaan, ironically introduced in the book as "a Palestinian in charge of the escape of German Jews" (the Palestinians themselves are called simply "Arabs"); Dafna, Ari's girlfriend horribly raped and murdered by Arabs; Karen, the beautiful Holocaust survivor killed by "a gang of *fedayeen* from Gaza"; Kitty, Ari's American lover, and a whole host of idealistic yet determined youngsters—Dov, Barak, Sarah, Jordana, David, and Mussa, the "loyal Druze" member of the Hagana—as they battled "crafty" Bedouin, Nazis, British and bloodthirsty, Nazi-infested Arab "henchmen" for only a small Jewish state which "held out its hand in friendship to its Arab neighbors"? No sympathetic Arab figures here, only the hate-filled Haj Amin, "the brigand Kawukji", and cynical, despotic and fanatical Arab leaders. "The avowed intention of murdering the Jewish people and completely destroying the State of Israel," says Barak Ben Canaan, Ari's diplomat-father, "was the Arab answer to law and friendship."

In *Exodus*, the Zionist enterprise received its classic formulation. The Jews were cast as victims—"righteous victims," as Morris entitles his survey of the Zionist-Arab conflict. We were the survivors of centuries of persecution, a people broken by the Holocaust. We sought only our simple, normal right, to return to our ancient homeland, our tiny sliver of an ancient homeland, and resume our existence as a nation among the nations. And that right had been recognized by the international community in its decision to create a Jewish state on just over half of "our" country. We had gone along with that decision, but were then attacked by five Arab armies determined to wipe us out. We have been fighting for our survival ever since. The War of Independence, for example, constituted, according to the British-Israeli historian Avi Shlaim (2001:79–80),

> a glorious contrast to the centuries of powerlessness, persecution, and humiliation. Yet the traditional Zionist narrative of the events surrounding the birth of the state of Israel was still constructed around the notion of the Jews as the victims. This narrative presents the 1948 war as a simple, bipolar no-holds-barred struggle between a monolithic and malevolent Arab adversary and a tiny peace-loving Jewish community. The biblical image of David and Goliath is frequently evoked in this narrative. Little Israel is portrayed as fighting with its back to the wall against a huge, well-armed and overbearing Arab adversary. Israel's victory in the war is treated as verging on the miraculous, and as resulting from the determination and heroism of the Jewish fighters rather than the from the disunity and disarray on the Arab side. This heroic version of the War of Independence has proved so enduring and resistant to revision....It is also the version of history that Israeli children are taught at school.

The main problem with this formulation is "agency," academic jargon for taking your fate in your own hands, for accepting responsibility. "Agency" is completely missing in this version of events; we are, again, history's ultimate victims. "The traditional Zionist version of the Arab-Israeli conflict," writes Shlaim (2001:79),

> places the responsibility on the Arab side. Israel is portrayed as the innocent victim of unremitting Arab hostility and Arab aggression. In this respect, traditional Zionist accounts of the emergence of

Israel form a natural sequel to the history of the Jewish people, with its emphasis on the weakness, vulnerability, and numerical inferiority of the Jews in relation to their adversaries. The American Jewish historian Salo Baron once referred to this as the lachrymose view of Jewish history.

It was a framing that proved extremely effective, especially when applied in later years to the Occupation. For if we can cast ourselves as victims, we are off the hook. Victims are victims; they cannot be held responsible or accountable for their actions, which are by definition defensive in nature. "Agency" is gone. Also gone from view is the fundamental fact that the pre-state *Yishuv* was never the weaker party. It enjoyed tremendous political support from Europe, and especially Britain, thanks to powerful lobbying on the part of the Zionist movement. It also received massive financial support from the Zionist movement that made immigration and settlement possible, as well as the development of strong industrial and agricultural sectors. And Israel was able to marshal equipment and resources that, together with European models of military organization, allowed it to vanquish the Arab armies and forces arrayed against it in the 1948 war. Shlaim (2001:80) argues

> that the Arab coalition facing Israel in 1947–49 was far from monolithic; that within this coalition there was no agreement on war aims; that the inability of the Arabs to coordinate their diplomatic and military moves was partly responsible for their defeat; that throughout the conflict Israel had the military edge over its Arab adversaries; and, finally, and most importantly, that Israel's leaders were aware of the divisions inside the Arab coalition and that they exploited these divisions to the full in waging the war and in extending the borders of the state.

Until this day, Israel, the world's fourth largest nuclear power, a strategic ally of the world's only superpower and the power occupying Palestinian territories these 40 years, still casts itself as the victim.

The reversal is complete. In the eyes of the world, the Arabs are the aggressors and we are merely agency-less victims preoccupied with self-defense. Golda Meir made an art-form out of self-righteous, self-serving and outrageous reversals. Two of her most famous are: "We will have peace with the Arabs when they love their children more than they hate us," and "When peace comes, we will perhaps in time be able to forgive the Arabs for killing our sons. But it will be harder for us to forgive them for having forced us to kill *their* sons." Through this mechanism Israel effectively deflects attention from the actual products of its agency: the imposition of a Jewish ethnocracy over an Arab majority then reduced to subordinate status through a process of *nishul*. Capturing the role of victim relieves us of all responsibility while turning the tables on the Palestinians; our victims could now be cast as the wicked enemy of the righteous survivors, the perpetrators of the conflict, the strong against the weak. We are justified in doing anything we want to them.

This is a trickier proposition than meets the eye. For Zionism is based on agency, on the notion that the Jewish people has to take its fate in its own hands. The perceived passivity of Diaspora Jewry, the disgrace, shame and cowardice displayed by the Jews of the Diaspora as they were "taken to the slaughter like sheep," invoked derision from Zionist nationalists, the new, strong, atavistic "Hebrew Men" (Elon 1971:272–273). So at the same time we must take pride in our prowess on the battlefield, the foundation of our usefulness to our American "ally" and the fount of our hegemony over the Arabs, we must deliberately understate our political, economic and military power lest we be held responsible for our actions. The delicate, calculated acrobatics of such a manipulative dance are revealed in the following anecdote:

> In 1965, Ezer Weizman, the commander of the air force, was sent to Washington with a long shopping list, which included a good number of Skyhawks as well as forty-five A-6 Intruders.

Weizman went to see the minister of defense [Levi Eshkol, who was also the Prime Minister] to ask for help with a small problem. On the one hand he had to exhibit a certain degree of weakness, to persuade the Americans to sell the planes. On the other hand he had great confidence in the ability of his pilots and did not want the Americans to get the idea that they were dealing with a feeble little air force. Eshkol did not hesitate for a moment before proffering his famous advice: "Present yourself as *Shimshon der nebichdicker!*"—a poor little Samson, or a pitiful Samson [in Yiddish]. (Shlaim 2000:219)

The point of reversal, of course, is to shift responsibility and culpability for the conflict and its atrocities onto "the Arabs" while relieving us of any blame. In the *Exodus* framing, physical *nishul* was now complemented by a conceptual *nishul*. Not only had they no right to resist the good and just Zionist cause, they had no legitimate national claim to the country in the first place. And not only did they lose their land, they *deserved* to lose it. Uris discovers the startling truth: the Arabs really don't care about the Land at all. "Some of the Arabs and their armies fought with valor," he generously concedes:

Most of them did not. They had been promised easy victories, loot, and rape. They had bolstered each other with a false illusion of Arab unity. Obviously, the "cause" was not so great it was worth bleeding for.

There was never a question of the Jews' willingness to die for Israel. In the end they stood alone and with blood and guts won for themselves what had legally been given them by the conscience of the world....

If the Arabs of Palestine loved their land, they could not have been forced from it—much less run from it without real cause. The Arabs had little to live for, much less to fight for. This is not a reaction of a man who loves his land.

So finally, after thousands of years of abuse, the Land of Israel would be restored to the loving hands of its true owners, the only ones who ever cared for it, the Jews. Dov, the traumatized Holocaust survivor now transformed into a brave soldier, "a handsome young man with sensitive features"

who "worshipped" the doomed Karen, is sent by the Army
to "study specialized courses for the ambitious water projects
being planned for the redemption of the Negev." (Needless to
say, he "proved a brilliant scholar.")

Even in this early phase of nation-building one discerns
disturbing realities, policies, attitudes and behaviors that were
to emerge more clearly during the course of the Occupation.
Extreme disproportionality, for instance. "The army of
Israel swore to kill ten [*fedayeen*] for one [Israeli victim],"
writes Uris, who then articulates yet another principle of the
Israeli framing: "Unfortunately, reprisal seemed to be the
only language that the Arabs understood." During the eight
years of "infiltration" (1948–56), between 3,000 and 5,000
mostly unarmed refugees were killed, and 10,000 "suspected
infiltrators," including a number of Bedouin tribes living in
the Negev, were expelled (Morris 1999:270, 274–279). True,
Israel had every right to protect its citizens during this period;
after all, 200 of its people and scores of soldiers were killed
by infiltrators. But as Morris points out, most were casualties
of clashes the Palestinians did not seek; they were victims
of Israel's exclusively military response just as much as the
refugee infiltrators were. A genuine attempt to deal with the
problem on a human basis—compensating the refugees for
their lands and property, for example, or allowing them to
collect their belongings and farm animals, or providing for
some form of family reunion, whatever—would likely have
reduced the need for the refugees to "infiltrate" altogether.
But as in the case of the Occupation, a genuine solution was
not the aim; *nishul* was.

A cold, calculated ruthlessness also becomes evident at this
time. Listen to Moshe Dayan, then head of the Israeli Defense
Force's (IDF's) Southern Command, as he responded to Sharett's
criticism of the excesses of the policy of killing, brutalizing and
expelling infiltrators and "suspected" infiltrators:

Using the moral yardstick mentioned by [Sharett], I must ask: Are [we justified] in opening fire on the Arabs who cross [the border] to reap the crops they planted in our territory; they, their women, and their children? Will this stand up to moral scrutiny...? We shoot at those from among the 200,000 hungry Arabs who cross the line [to graze their flocks]—will this stand up to moral review? Arabs cross to collect the grain that they left in the abandoned villages and we set mines for them and they go back without an arm or a leg....[It may be that this] cannot pass review, but I know of no other method of guarding the borders. If the Arab shepherds and harvesters are allowed to cross the borders, the tomorrow the State of Israel will have no borders. (quoted in Morris 1999:275)

This coldness, the unfeeling hardness that I encounter daily among Israeli soldiers at checkpoints or at home demolitions in the Occupied Territories, among clerks of the Civil Administration as they turn down a request for dialysis treatment in an Israeli hospital, among settlers in Hebron who proudly watch as their kids kick or torment Palestinian children or the elderly, as well as among our politicians who pursue the most hateful policies towards our own Arab citizens (such as the law forbidding Palestinian citizens of Israel from either bringing their spouses into Israel from the Occupied Territories or joining them)—where does this disturbing element of Israeli culture and policy come from? I am continually asked: How can Jews do these things after what they have been through? It does not come from Jewish culture, although it must have been part of our national culture in biblical times if we obeyed the biblical command to kill every Canaanite man, woman and child. That latent manifestation of power, violence, exclusivity and cruelty, suppressed over the 2,000 years of diaspora, seems to have surfaced again, if we listen to the testimony of Epstein, with the rise of modern Jewish settlement in Palestine. The very act of carving an ethnocracy out of someone else's country must require a calculated cold-heartedness, transformed into a virtue when "heroically" confronting "cruel" Arab mayhem—which is how we have always characterized their resistance, another example of narrative reversal. The evolution from tender Jew to tough Hebrew takes place in five pages of Uris's book, as the idealistic Jossi goes from being a "friend of the Arabs" opposed to using arms against them, to joining The Guardsmen (after being accused of being a "ghetto Jew" by refusing to fight for "your own property"), to meting out a brutal whipping to the Bedouin sheikh Suleiman, "an old renegade and smuggler."

> "Suleiman, you gave me your hand in a bargain and you lied. If you or your kinsmen ever again set foot in our fields I will cut your body apart with this whip and feed the pieces to the jackals."
> Jossi turned and his eyes pierced the astonish Bedouins. They were all too stunned to move. Never had they seen a man so powerful and fearless and angry. Showing utter disdain for their rifles, Jossi turned his back on them, walked to his horse, mounted, and rode off.
> Suleiman never touched a Jewish field again.

Amos Elon, in his insightful book *Israelis: Founders and Sons* (1971), ascribes what I call an unfeeling coldness to Arabs to a kind of fatalism described in Hebrew as *ain brera*, "no choice." "For almost its entire existence Israel has been in a state of war or semi-war," writes Elon:

> Early Zionism was predicated upon faith in peaceful change. The discovery that this was nearly impossible has profoundly affected the Israeli temper. As in other liberation movements, whether social or national, the Zionist mystique of redemption has become powerfully intertwined with a mystique of violence....
> Israelis are fond of saying that in this prolonged entanglement with forces that have often been superior, their main weapon has been an awareness of *ain brera*, there is no choice. *Ain brera* deserves to be inscribed on the currently motto-less national coat of arms....It implies a fatalistic, daily shrugging of the shoulders; it excuses much and explains even more....Israelis often say, "Yes, we live dangerously. *Ain brera!* There is no choice. But we are free!"...
> The first thing to note is a spreading cult of toughness....A spartan rigidity has developed over the years and now marks

large segments of the younger adult population. It often spills over from the military life, where it was acquired, to the civilian sphere....Frequent and prolonged periods of service in the army breeds a stark, intensely introverted, icy matter-of-factness in the young that contrasts sharply with the externalized, rather verbose emotionalism of their elders. (Elon 1971:222–224, 236–237)

As Elon says, *ain brera* excuses much; it was most recently invoked by Amir Peretz, the current leader of the Labor Party and Minister of Defense, a self-proclaimed "person of peace," to justify the Israeli invasion of Lebanon. It is not the solely the result of long-term conflict, in my opinion, but of conflict from which there is no way out, no possible "victory." In the case of Israel, I would argue that this special kind of conflict and the *ain brera* mind-set it induces arises out of the unavoidable and irresolvable collision of interests inherent in imposing an exclusivist ethnocracy in a country with a competing national entity. The exclusive claim of my people to the entire Land of Israel and the negation, both implied and asserted, of Palestinian national claims, rights and even existence cannot, in fact, be resolved as long as the ethnocracy exists in that form. If that is true, then *ain brera* reflects an objective situation—and then closes any option of supplanting the ethnocracy with a more inclusive political system because, ipso facto, *ain brera*, "they" hate us so much that we simply cannot live together. Cutting the Arabs some slack, being lenient towards them, showing them any compassion or understanding is interpreted in Israel as showing "weakness." As long as Israel exists as an ethnically-defined state the conflict is, in truth, absolute and permanent; its very existence requires a cold-heartedness towards its eternal enemies.

A hard-hearted approach to the natives is intrinsic to colonialism and ethnocracy. The land must be taken and a relationship of domination established. Everything truly human, let alone personal, must be eliminated lest the native "raise his head" (Judges 8:28). In *The Flame Trees of Thika*, her classic book about growing up in colonial Kenya, Elspeth Huxley describes how the membrane (or, in her analogy, "a fragile spider's web") preserved power differentials even in situations of close personal contact:

> "No more words," Tilly said snappily. Juma [the family's African "houseboy"] had a patronizing air that she resented, and she doubted if he was showing enough respect....Indeed respect was the only protection available to Europeans who lived singly, or in scattered families, among thousands of Africans accustomed to constant warfare and armed with spears and poisoned arrows, but had themselves no barricades, and went about unarmed. The respect preserved them like an invisible coat of mail, or a form of magic, and seldom failed; but it had to be very carefully guarded. The least rent or puncture might, if not immediately checked and repaired, split the whole garment asunder and expose its wearer in all his human vulnerability. Kept intact, it was a thousand times stronger than all the guns and locks and metal in the world; challenged, it could be brushed aside like a spider's web. So Tilly was a little sensitive about respect, and Juma was silenced. (Huxley 1959:15)

While I've said I don't equate Jewish settlers in Palestine with British farmers in Kenya, we cannot escape strong colonial elements in Zionism. Unlike the case of other ethnocracies—the Serbs or the Russians, for example—but as in Kenya, Jewish settlers arrived from abroad. And as in Kenya they had to pacify the natives by force, since the latter could never accept dispossession voluntarily. De-humanization was necessary and inevitable. My cause, whether "bringing civilization to the benighted" or "reclaim our ancient homeland," must, as Jabotinsky astutely noted, stand on its own merits, for if the claims and rights of the indigenous are seriously entertained, our whole colonial enterprise will be called morally into question. In order to preserve my humanity while carrying out objectively immoral acts, then, I must make my victims unworthy of a human response; indeed, I must justify my actions as mere responses, forced upon me by the savage natives. "Had the Arab leaders obeyed the decision of the highest international tribunal and adhered to the law, there would have been Arab refugee problem," declares Uris's character Barak Ben Canaan. Having carved a Jewish ethnocracy out of Arab Palestine, a skein of membranes then insulates us from "the Arabs" living in the nooks and crannies of our country. Within our protective bubble our humanity and goodness is preserved, and "unpleasant" but necessary behaviors and situations are kept safely on other side of the membrane, filtered out of our reality.

Thus were the Palestinians—the "Arabs"—doubly removed from their land. Physically, of course, but also existentially. In what was to become Israel, their very claim to peoplehood, to having any legitimate collective existence whatsoever, would be negated. The process of de-Arabizing Palestine, a component of *nishul*, steadily and thoroughly became the mirror process of "Judaizing" the landscape and creating the Land of Israel.

Part III

The Structure of Oppression

6

Expanding Dispossession: The Occupation and the Matrix of Control

Seven years ago, I felt I had to write something about the occupation. I could not understand how an entire nation like mine, an enlightened nation by all accounts, is able to train itself to live as a conqueror without making its own life wretched. What happened to us?

Years passed [and] I also became an artist of sublimation. I found myself developing the same voluntary suspension of questions about ethics and occupation. I did not visit the territories; I did not even go to Old Jerusalem....Like so many others, I began to think of that kidney-shaped expanse of land, the West Bank, as an organ transplanted into my body against my wishes, and about which soon, when I had time, I would come to some sort of conclusion and decision.

—David Grossman, *The Yellow Wind* (1988:212–213)

For many of the founders of Israel still prominent in the Labor Party at the time the West Bank, "East" Jerusalem and Gaza were taken in 1967, 1948 represented a "job undone." Yigal Allon, a minister in the government in 1967 and the commander in 1947 of the military operations responsible for the expulsion of the greatest number of Arab refugees, wrote just before the outbreak of the Six Days War: "In case of a new war, we must avoid the historic mistake of the War of Independence and,...must not cease fighting until we achieve total victory, the territorial fulfillment of the Land of Israel" (Morris 1999:314). Yitzhak Rabin, the then Chief of Staff,

141

exhorted his troops on the Jordanian front to "complete what we were unable to finish" in 1948 (Oren 2002:191).

The conquest of the West Bank may have not been intended when the Six Day War began, but almost immediately the claim to the entire Land of Israel came to the fore, as much among secular "left-wing" politicians and military figures as Allon, Dayan and the poet Nathan Alterman as among Begin's Revisionists and the modern orthodox who would soon form the avant-garde of the settlement movement. From the start it was clear that Israel would retain control over the territories. Massive settlement construction commenced immediately in Jerusalem and within weeks the Allon Plan was presented—bearing a canny resemblance to Sharon's later scheme of "cantonization" and Olmert's plan of "convergence"—in which a third of the West Bank is annexed, including the Jordan Valley, what later became known as "Greater" Jerusalem and all the Judean Desert between Hebron and the Dead Sea. The West Bank would be truncated into two chunks, connected to Jordan by an Israeli-controlled "road link" and a corridor. Within less than a year Jewish settlement was approved in Hebron (Gorenberg 2006). The fifth stage of the process of *nishul* had begun, and continues to this day.

If Israel would retain control of the territories, the central question was, as it is today, how to find an Arab partner who would agree, especially after Israel unilaterally annexed East Jerusalem, including the Old City with its Muslim and Christian holy sites. Prime Minister Levi Eshkol preferred the "Palestinian option," to offer the Palestinians autonomy under Israeli control. When that didn't work out he tried a "Jordanian option," giving to Jordan the populated Palestinian areas but keeping a third of the West Bank for security reasons. That was not acceptable either (Shlaim 2000:264).

The issue at first was not territory but security. Eshkol and the others feared the consequences of territorial annexation; it would mean incorporating 1 million Palestinians into an Israel which itself had less than 2.5 million Jews. Hence the Allon Plan, which became the unofficial policy of the government until the rise of Begin's Likud government in 1977: a third of the West Bank along the border with Jordan would be retained for security; the rest, including those parts heavily populated by Palestinians, "given back" to Jordan. The rise of Labor's "hawks" in the government of Golda Meir which took power in early 1969—Defense Minister Moshe Dayan, who later became Begin's Foreign Minister; senior Cabinet minister Yisrael Galili; Yigal Allon; and Shimon Peres, who had just bolted to the expansionist Rafi party of Ben Gurion—gave rise to a policy they knew was unacceptable to the Arab world at that time: no return to the pre-war borders without direct negotiations and peace treaties with the Arab states (Shlaim 2000:285). And no Palestinian state. "There is no Palestinian people," Meir declared; "there are Palestinian refugees....How can we return the Occupied Territories? There is nobody to return them to."

Despite the lack of clear political goals, the double-barreled agenda of "security" and "redeeming the Land" soon put into motion an unofficial, unspoken but effective policy of *nishul*, just as it had in 1948. The Occupation began, predictably, with physical displacement. During the 1967 war itself, 350,000 Palestinians, most of them refugees from the 1948 war, once again left their homes and refugee camps, most fleeing to Jordan. After the fighting subsided 120,000 of these Palestinian refugees applied to the Israeli authorities to return to their homes, their absolute right under international law. Only 14,000 were allowed to do so (Morris 1999:329).

Indeed, the very first act of the Occupation, carried out even before the fighting had ended, was a wanton act of home demolition for the express purpose of Judaization. On June 11, having no jurisdictional authority over the occupied eastern part of Jerusalem but with the active cooperation of the army, West Jerusalem mayor Teddy Kollek ordered the destruction of the Arab Mughrabi Quarter of the Old City, situated at the entrance to the Wailing Wall. The army provided the bulldozers, although the operation had nothing whatsoever to do with either the hostilities or security. In the middle of the night, Lieutenant Colonel Yaakov Salman ordered the 135 families of the neighborhood roused from their beds. They were given just a few minutes to evacuate their homes, and when they refused, Salman ordered the Engineering Corps to begin the demolition anyway. The first house hit by a bulldozer collapsed on top of its inhabitants, killing an elderly woman, Hajji Rasmia Tabaki (Gorenberg 2006:42–43). She was perhaps the first victim of the Occupation.

The Jewish Quarter was then declared off-limits to Arabs and the Palestinian families living there were forcibly removed by court order, even while hundreds of Jewish families and institutions began moving into the Muslim, Armenian and Christian Quarters. Seeking revenge for having lost the Latrun area near the foothills of the Jerusalem Mountains to the Jordanians in 1948, and wishing to cleanse the approach to Jerusalem of Arabs, Israel summarily expelled 5,000 residents from the villages of 'Imwas, Yalu and Beit Nuba and razed them to the ground. (The ruins were subsequently "Judaized," covered over by a recreational forest planted by the Jewish National Fund and called "Canada Park.") In the West Bank, the entire city of Qalqilya was slated for demolition; a third was actually destroyed before the government relented. Just as it had done to the Arab population of Israel from 1948 to 1966, Israel placed the entire population of the West Bank and Gaza under military rule (Morris 1999:328).

UNILATERAL ANNEXATION

Israeli governments until the election of Begin's Likud in 1977 may not have had a clear conception of where they were going in terms of the territories conquered in 1967, but they did have a strong inclination to hold onto the newly conquered parts of the Land of Israel and a ready-made template of control, the military administration ruling over the Palestinians within Israel 1948 to 1966. It didn't take long to extend that system to the Occupied Territories and begin constructing, piece by piece, a comprehensive Matrix of Control intended to perpetuate Israeli control forever. Within days and weeks of the war the government moved to create permanent "facts on the ground." Here, however, it encountered a problem it had not faced inside Israel. International law prohibits the acquisition of territory by force (as well as the alienation of sovereignty by force). The only acceptable way of resolving the status of an occupied territory is through negotiations. So as not to prejudice those negotiations, an Occupying Power is therefore prohibited from taking any measures that might render its occupation permanent. It cannot transfer its civilian population into an occupied area or build settlements or any other permanent infrastructure, except for an immediate and legitimate military purpose. An Occupying Power cannot deport or harm the local population in any way, or exploit the resources of an occupied territory (such as using its water). It cannot impose its own laws and regulations or, of course, unilaterally annex territory. Overall, an Occupying Power is not allowed to alter the status quo except in the strict sphere of military defense, and then only until negotiations are concluded (Benvenisti 2004, Pacheco 1989, Kretzmer 2002).

Had international law been respected, Israel would not have been able to create those "facts on the ground" that today make the Occupation impossible to uproot. How, then, did it reconcile its self-image as a progressive Western democracy and its desire for territory? Meir Shamgar, a former member of Begin's pre-state terrorist militia, the Irgun, a former army general, Israel's Attorney-General at the time of the 1967 war and later President of the Supreme Court, came up with the solution. If there was no occupation, he reasoned, then international law, and in particular the Fourth Geneva Convention governing the rights of civilian in occupied territories, did not apply. And so, creating his own legal definition of "occupation" that had absolutely no standing in international law, Shamgar put forth an original argument: "occupation" occurs only when the territory on one sovereign state is conquered by another sovereign state. Since Jordan itself had conquered the West Bank and East Jerusalem in 1948, it had no legitimate claim, and the same applied to Egypt in Gaza. Declaring the principle of "a missing sovereign" over the territories, Shamgar argued that no country had an undisputed claim to the Occupied Territories, and that Israel's claim was as good as anyone else's.

But what about the Palestinians, the indigenous population that had been promised self-determination by the UN in 1947? Under Shamgar's interpretation they had no standing whatsoever since they had never enjoyed sovereignty at all. In one fell stroke they were rendered irrelevant and the lands upon which they lived—the last remnants of their country from 1948—were ruled neither occupied nor theirs: "disputed territories." Israel, Shamgar ruled, was free to annex whatever it pleased and to "administer" the rest as it saw fit for as long as it wants (Benvenisti 1989, Kretzmer 2002). And as an extra benefit: neither does the Fourth Geneva Convention apply.

This decision has absolutely no basis or legitimacy in international law, says Eyal Benvenisti, an Israeli human rights expert who has written extensively on this issue. Indeed, one of the oldest principles of international law stipulates that sovereignty rests with the people, not with any particular royalty, government or regime. The latest affirmation of this principle, Benvenisti points out, is Security Council Resolution 1483 of May 22, 2003, having to do with "regime change" in Iraq. Since sovereignty inheres in the people, regime collapse does not extinguish sovereignty. Resolution 1483 grants a mandate to the inhabitants of occupied Iraq "freely to determine their own political future and control their own natural resources…to form a representative government based on the rule of law that affords equal rights and justice to all Iraqi citizens without regard to ethnicity, religion, or gender." Hence, concludes Benvenisti (2004:3), the law of occupation connotes respect to popular sovereignty, not to the demised regime. Besides, he points out (2004:110), the concern of the Fourth Geneva Convention for the rights and well-being of *individuals* under Occupation stands alone, without any connection to conflicting claims of sovereignty. This was expressed unequivocally in opinion of the International Court of Justice (ICJ), which ruled that the Wall (as the ICJ called it) was illegal both because it violated the Fourth Geneva Convention, Israel's own rejection of it notwithstanding, as well as the principle of proportionality. So disproportionate was the negative impact of the Wall on Palestinian life it overrode Israel's political and security concerns.

Shamgar's ruling, although flying in the face of international law, has nevertheless formed the basis of Israeli Supreme Court rulings ever since. It is the reason that Israeli governments are careful never to refer to the territories as "occupied," but only as "administered" or "disputed." But how does Israel get away with it? It is explained best and mostly candidly by an Israeli expert in international law who, understandably but tellingly, chose to remain anonymous:

> International law is the language of the world and it's more or less the yardstick by which we measure ourselves today….So you have to play the game if you want to be a member of the world community. And the game works like this. As long as you claim you are working within international law and you come up with a reasonable argument as to why what you are doing is within the context of international law, you're fine. That's how it goes. This is a very cynical view of how the world works. So, even if you're being inventive, or even if you're being a bit radical, as long as you can explain it in that context, most countries will not

say you're a war criminal. (*Jerusalem Post, Up Front* magazine, April 15, 2005, p. 34)

Just to show how absurd Israel's interpretation of international law goes, yet how it succeeds in providing an effective legalistic smokescreen over such illegal practices in the Occupied Territories as settlement, here is what Dr. Alan Baker, the Foreign Ministry's advisor on international law has stated: "The legal claim today and the arguments [for the legality of the settlements]," he explains, "rest on the Oslo accords. It was resolved—and the Palestinians agreed—that the settlements' fate would be determined in a future peace agreement. After we signed those accords, which are still legally in force, we are no longer an occupying power, but we are instead *present in the territories with their consent* and subject to the outcome of negotiations" (Gorali 2003; italics added). Wow! We are in the West Bank and East Jerusalem, which are "no longer" occupied (interesting, since we always denied we were an Occupying Power in the first place), with the consent of the Palestinians! Legally, at least, Israel has achieved what it always desired: occupation-by-consent. The Palestinians must be the first people in history to actually agree to have their lands, their farms, their homes expropriated by another people for that people's own exclusive benefit. And to think we were the only "generous" party!

So cynical and untenable are these legal gymnastics that even Shamgar had to issue a ruling undercutting his own previous position. In 1988 he ruled that the laws of occupation do apply to the Gaza Strip since occupation is defined as the "effective control of territory" (Benvenisti 2004:111). Israel gets away with its legalistic maneuvering, of course, only because of steadfast and uncritical American support. Since 1967 the US has vetoed 84 UN resolutions condemning Israeli policies or actions in the occupied lands. Still, play the game we must. Towards that end, and in order to bypass the prohibition on extending Israeli law to the territories, Israel has developed a sophisticated approach: consolidating some 2,000 military orders, a selective mix of Ottoman and Jordanian law, plus once-hated British "Emergency Regulations," all of which do not require judicial review as do laws and procedures affecting citizens. At the same time Israel has a large population of its own citizens—almost half a million as of this writing—over whom (and over whose settlements) it must extend Israeli law. It also desires to have Israeli rule accepted as normally and routinely as it is in Israel, by the Israel public and the international community, if not by the Palestinian themselves. Thus, in response to a Supreme Court ruling calling for the government to harmonize its "occupier's law" with the legal system of Israel, it established in 1981 a "Civil Administration." Intended to lower the Occupation's military profile and bring Israeli administration within the sphere of its own civil law (without, of course, actually integrating the two systems), the "Civil" Administration is actually run by the Ministry of Defense. Its head is a colonel and its staff mainly soldiers— or settlers like Micha, the building inspector who issued the demolition orders on Salim and Arabiya's home and carried it out.

Over the years, then, the distinction between Labor and Likud governments has blurred almost entirely in terms of both settlement activity throughout the Occupied Territories or the de facto annexing of the West Bank. Already by 1972, over 9,300 square miles of Palestinian land had been confiscated, a full 28 percent of the West Bank. Much of that land, expropriated for "military purposes" as international law demands, sooner or later found its way into the hands of the settlers. By the time the Labor Party lost power to the Likud in 1977, about 10,000 homes had been demolished (by our count), hundreds of Palestinians had been deported or not allowed to return home and nearly 80 settlements had been established, home to more than 70,000 settlers (Gorenberg 2006:358).

THE MATRIX OF CONTROL

Labor's policy of "creeping annexation" ended abruptly when, in 1977, Menachem Begin was elected Prime Minister. Begin's government was openly annexationist. "There is not a shadow of doubt regarding our intention to remain in Judea and Samaria," stated the 1978 "Drobless Plan" of the World Zionist Organization. "A dense chain of settlements on the mountain ridge running southward from Nablus to Hebron will...minimize the danger of the establishment of another Arab state in the region" (Benvenisti and Khayat 1988). Begin needed little time to formulate and implement a plan of separation, annexation, control and *nishul*; he had a ready-made model developed *vis-à-vis* Israel's own Arab population since 1948 and refined over ten years of Labor "administration" of the territories.

Immediately following the 1967 war the Labor government had already annexed Palestinian "East" Jerusalem, an artificial entity that absorbed the lands of 28 West Bank villages (Cheshin et al. 1999, Gorenberg 2006:58–59). Now Begin formally declared his government's intention of integrating Judea, Samaria and Gaza to Israel. His first public act as Prime Minister was to inaugurate a synagogue in the Kaddum settlement. He also issued a ban on the terms "occupation," "occupied territories" or "West Bank" in the state-owned media, and since that time they are seldom used. Anxious to begin the rapid and systematic incorporation of the territories into Israel, he turned to his Minister of Agriculture, Ariel Sharon, nicknamed "the bulldozer," appointing him to head a Ministerial Committee on Settlements. Sharon was charged with two tasks: first, to create "facts on the ground" so massive that Israel's domination and control would be irreversible; and second, to foreclose forever the establishment of a Palestinian state—or, as Sharon would later amend it, a *viable and truly sovereign* Palestinian state. These directives conformed to

Begin's conception of what Israel was prepared to offer the Palestinians: autonomy. Sharon was charged with formalizing and systematizing the Matrix of Control that had been so tentatively emerging under Labor (Benvenisti and Khayat 1988, Kimmerling 2003:63–64, 76–78).

He proved the ideal person for the job, and he had a ready-made strategy. A few years before, as chief of army's Southern Command, Sharon had taken great exception to the static row of fortified bunkers being built along the Suez Canal, called the Bar-Lev Line. So much exception, if fact, that Haim Bar-Lev, the army Chief of Staff, fired him. When, however, the fortifications were quickly breached by the Egyptians at the start of the 1973 war, Sharon leapt into the fray, carrying out with startling effectiveness his alternative strategy—a dynamic matrix composed of a series of strong points (ta'ozim). The IDF would take strategic points rather than try to hold a static line; that way, it could advance to more forward points or retreat from others without giving up either its offensive or defensive positions, without having to hold an all-or-nothing line. It worked beautifully, and soon the Israel forces, led by a swashbuckling Sharon, his head dramatically wrapped in a bandage, had out-flanked the Egyptians. The IDF took the Egyptian side of the Canal, thereby entrapping the Egyptian army on the other side.

Four years later, now heading the Ministerial Committee on Settlements, Sharon applied this innovative conception and strategy to ensuring permanent Israeli control over the Occupied Territories. It is an approach the Israeli architect Eyal Weizman (2003) calls "the geometry of occupation" and describes as follows:

> As chief of southern command of the Israel Defense Forces before the Yom Kippur war in 1973, where he rejected the effectiveness of linear fortification along the edges of the Suez Canal and conceived a defense system based on of a matrix of elevated strong-points spread throughout the depth of the Sinai desert; as a minister with

various portfolios in a number of Likud-led governments where his "location strategy" for the West Bank was implemented by the seeding of the depth of the territory with civilian mountain-top settlements and outposts; as a politician who rode to power as prime minister following the collapse of the Oslo peace process, who now draws the meandering and splintered path of the barriers—Ariel Sharon, more than anyone else, is the man who has shaped the spatial and physical environment in which the Israeli-Palestinian conflict takes place.

Sharon's strategy was strikingly similar in concept to the East Asian game of "Go." Unlike chess, where two opponents try to "defeat" each other by eliminating one another's pieces, the aim of "Go" is not to actually defeat but rather to immobilize your opponent by taking control of key points on the game board which is, indeed, a matrix. It was a strategy used effectively in Vietnam, where small forces of Viet Cong were able to pin down and virtually paralyze half a million American soldiers possessing overwhelming firepower. Israel's Matrix of Control accomplishes the same with the Palestinians. Unlike the concept of a "forward line" (that can be breached, as happened with the Bar-Lev Line),

> defense based on a "network of points in depth" relies on a matrix of interlocking strong points connected by physical and electromagnetic links: roads and electronic communications. Each point can connect and communicate with any other, and each point overlooks, and, whenever necessary, covers the other with firepower. This creates an interlocking, fortified surface. When the defensive matrix is attacked it can become flexible and adapt to the fall of any number of points by forming new connections across the matrix.
>
> The geography of nodes in a matrix cannot be conventionally measured in distance. [More important is] the speed and reliability of the connection—that is, how fast and how secure can one travel between given points. The network defense is a spatial trap that allows the defenders a high level of mobility while acting to paralyze any possibility for enemy movement. (Weizman 2004:174–175)

Employing innocuous planning policies and procedures to create a matrix of *ta'ozim*, Sharon succeeded in constructing an almost invisible system of control that, repressive as it got, conceal its actions behind a façade of "proper administration," thus protecting Israel's image as a peace-seeking democratic country. The conception was also brilliant.

> In 1982, a few months before the Israeli invasion of Lebanon, Sharon, then minister of defense, published his *Masterplan for Jewish Settlements in the West Bank Through the Year 2010*— later known as the Sharon Plan. In it he outlined the location of more than a hundred settlement points, placed on strategic summits. He also marked the paths for a new network of high-volume, interconnected traffic arteries, connecting the settlements with the Israeli heartland. In the formation of continuous Jewish habitation, Sharon's plan saw a way towards the wholesale annexation of the areas vital for Israel's security. These areas he marked onto the map attached to his plan in the shape of the letter H. The "H-Plan" contained two parallel north–south strips of land: one along the Green Line containing the West Bank from the west, and another along the Jordan Valley, accepting the presence of the Allon Plan to contain the territory from the east.
>
> These two strips separated the Palestinian cities, which are organized along the central spine of the West Bank's mountain ridge, from both Israel proper and from the Kingdom of Jordan. Between these north–south strips Sharon marked a few east–west traffic arteries—the main one connecting through Jerusalem, thus closing a (very) approximate H. The rest—some 40 percent of the West Bank, separate enclaves around Palestinian cities and towns—were to revert to some yet undefined form of Palestinian self-management.
>
> The small red-roofed single-family home replaced the tank as the smallest fighting unit. District regional and municipal plans replaced the strategic sand table. Homes, like armored divisions, were used in formation across a dynamic theatre of operations to occupy strategic hills, to encircle an enemy, or to cut communication lines. (Weizman 2004:176–177, 181)

The brilliance of Sharon's Matrix of Control was not only in its strategic use of geography and settlements, but in the way it interlocks four strategic modes of control: administrative, economic, physical ("facts on the ground") and military. Unless we grasp these critical details, we cannot possible "get it."

1. Administration, Bureaucracy, Planning and Law as Tools of Occupation and Control

One of the foundations of the Matrix is the Kafkaesque skein of rules, restrictions, procedures and sanctions Israel has imposed over the Occupied Territories. Military orders regulate every detail of Palestinian life. Order 59 (1967), for example, grants the Israeli Custodian of Abandoned Properties the authority to declare uncultivated, unregistered land as Israeli "state land." Since Israel refuses to recognize Ottoman- or British-era deeds and Order 291 (1968) stopped the process of land registration, Israel was thus able to classify a full 72 percent of the West Bank as "state lands," making expropriation from their Palestinian owners an easy administrative matter. Order 270 (1968) designated a further 400 square miles of West Bank land as closed "military zones," which could then be handed over to settlements or used for Israeli infrastructure. Order 363 (1969) imposes severe restrictions on construction and land use in yet other areas zoned as "nature reserves." Order 393 (1970) grants any military commander in Judea and Samaria the authority to prohibit Palestinian construction if he believes it necessary for the security of the Israeli army or to ensure "public order." Order 977 (1982) authorizes the Israeli army or its agencies (such as the Civil Administration) to proceed with excavation and construction without a permit, providing an avenue for settlement construction that bypassed legal and planning systems. Hundreds of other military orders prohibit Palestinian building around army bases and installations, around settlements and whole settlement areas, or within 200 meters on each side of main roads. They effectively curb the development of Arab communities and alienate tens of thousands of acres of land from their Palestinian owners.

With the necessary legal and bureaucratic mechanisms in place, Sharon proceeded rapidly to expand the settlements. Because of international opposition to new settlements, each settlement, upon its founding, was allocated an expansive master plan. When, then, additional settlements were established nearby, the government could argue that it was merely "thickening" existing ones in response to "natural" population growth. During the five years of Sharon's own government, yet another planning innovation was introduced. The "hill-top youth," as the second generation of settlers is called, taking its nickname from Sharon's 1998 call on the settlers to "grab every hill top," have hastily erected more than 100 "outposts" in the West Bank. Though unplanned, they easily receive retroactive approval by the Civil Administration because they invariably fall within the existing master plans.

Government control utilizes every possible bureaucratic tool. A little-noted provision of British planning law, for instance, gave the District Commission (now the Civil Administration) the "power to grant a relaxation of any restriction imposed by this scheme." Employing this obscure regulation from a bygone period enables the Israeli authorities to construct hundreds of thousands of housing units for Jews on lands zoned for agriculture, while strictly enforcing the Regional Schemes in the case of the Palestinians. Administrative restrictions penetrate into even the most intimate areas of their personal life. Due to Israeli fears that any kind of Palestinian self-sufficiency would help the population withstand its policies of expansion and *nishul*, it requires Palestinians to acquire permits for planting and marketing their crops, including the right to grow vegetable gardens next to their houses! The opening of banks and businesses is severely curtailed, and even seemingly routine practices such as licensing and inspection of Palestinian

businesses are exploited as a way to harass businesspeople and
stunt the local economy.

International humanitarian law, particularly the Fourth
Geneva Convention, accords a great deal of importance to
the protection and well-being of people under occupation.
Israel attempts to bypass this responsibility in many ways,
including rejecting the very fact of occupation. With the
outbreak of the second Intifada, it found novel ways to avoid
constraints on its military. Israel declared the Intifada "a
conflict short of war," invoking a concept of "almost war"
unknown in international law. Oppressed peoples have a right
to resist under international law, even in an armed fashion,
although not involving attacks on civilians. The "conflict short
of war" notion casts all forms of resistance as "terrorism,"
even as sheer criminal activity, thereby effectively nullifying
Palestinian human rights to self-determination. This construct
also relieves Israel of all responsibility for state terrorism,
for attacks on civilian populations equally prohibited under
international law. Being "inventive" bestows on Israel the
privilege of unconstrained military license under the guise of
an "almost war" without any of the restrictions or responsibilities. Palestinian political leaders and those engaged in
legitimate resistance can be "legally" assassinated, while the
killing of civilians is justified as "collateral damage." By the
same token, thousands of Palestinians can be arrested and
held indefinitely in prison without being granted the status
and rights of prisoners of war. Unfortunately the international
system has not progressed to a point where its laws can be
enforced, so besides bringing shame on Israel for its human
rights violations, there is little we can do to end it abuses.

2. Economic Warfare

In the Matrix of Control, policy, administration, physical
control and economic subordination are interwoven and

mutually supportive. For the first two and half decades of the Occupation, from 1967 through the first Intifada and until the economic closure following the Gulf War, Israel's economic policy towards the Occupied Territories was one of controlled development—"asymmetric containment" (UNCTAD 2006). On the one hand, Israel wanted to incorporate the territories' economy into Israel. The Palestinian population thus became one of Israel's major agricultural export markets, the Old City of Jerusalem became its most important tourist venue, and Palestinians themselves provided cheap produce and labor. On the other hand, however, the economy of the territories had to be kept under strict control lest their cheap products and labor undermine or compete with Israel's own market—and lest a feeling of economic strength and independence create demands for political independence as well.

As time went by, economic development in the Occupied Territories fell under ever greater limitations. Palestinians were not to allowed to open a bank of their own; tariffs, subsidies of Israeli produce and import controls prevented the Palestinian economy from seriously competing with the Israeli one; and economic ties between the Palestinians and Arab countries were severely curtailed (Hever 2007b). At the same time, Israel actively de-developed the Palestinian economy. It invested almost nothing in infrastructure, housing or services, which were (and are) supported completely by taxes on the poor Palestinian population channeled, after 1981, through the Civil Administration. In the agricultural sector, a pillar of the Palestinian economy, farm land continued to be expropriated at a rapid pace. The closure policy prevented Palestinian produce from reaching Israeli markets, and a steadily tightening internal closure closed access even to Palestinian markets within the Occupied Territories. Any benefits the Palestinians may have derived from Israeli Occupation—new roads, for example, that passed by their communities on their way to settlements, or employment opportunities in construction—were merely by-products of the development of Judea, Samaria, the Jerusalem area and Gaza for Jews.

A certain economic liberalization took place during the Oslo years when Palestinians could finally open banks of their own, though severe restrictions remain on the development of financial and credit institutions. But just as the Oslo process in general preserved Israeli control over the Occupied Territories without constraining settlement or military activities in the slightest, so, too, did the Paris Economic Protocol, signed in 1995 as an annex to the Oslo II agreement, carefully preserve complete Israeli control over the Palestinian economy. Israel's insistence on the right to stop all shipment of goods for security reasons, and to hold and check those goods for as long as it wanted, all but destroyed Palestinian commerce, as did its sole right to impose closures. The economic closure, deriving its supposed legality from the Paris Protocol, is today virtually total. It prevents Palestinian goods from moving quickly, thus ruining agricultural exports, while undermining the reliability of Palestinian business people to guarantee supply to their customers. It also gives Israel control over the licensing of both industrial and commercial Palestinian enterprises, plus the authority to issue import/export permits, and stipulate which Israeli import agents, clearing/shipping agents and insurance agents must be used, thus creating high transportation, storage, insurance and clearance costs for Palestinian traders. As a result, manufacturing has been reduced to only 10 percent of the Palestinian economy. Nearly 90 percent of industrial enterprises in the Occupied Territories employ fewer than five workers each, and 70 percent of Palestinian firms have either closed or have severely reduced production (UNCTAD 2006).

Even as the Oslo peace process began, the Israeli government took an almost unexplainable decision to impose an economic closure on the West Bank. Peres had always argued that only by tangibly feeling the economic benefits of the peace process would Israelis and Palestinian be convinced of its value. Yet here, at the very outset of Oslo, Palestinians were being locked into territories that Israel had deliberately de-developed over the past quarter-century. Not only was unemployment growing and poverty rising, but upon its creation in 1994 the Palestinian Authority was required to act as Israel's enforcer, asking for or rejection permits for passage into Israel. Closure, writes Amira Hass (2002a:6), one of Israel's most respected journalists, a close observer of the peace process and a resident of the Occupied Territories for many years,

> had a very immediate advantage in the [Oslo] negotiating process underway. Particularly under Rabin and Peres, the use of closure as an instrument of economic leverage over the PA was blatant: "You arrest this one or that one, and we'll give you 500 more work permits" and "If you behave yourselves and agree to our (slow) implementation timetables, we'll allow you to export more vegetables and release from Israeli customs the heavy machinery you imported" were the unexpressed but widely understood premises underlying negotiations.

Because of hostile economic policies, the almost complete denial to Palestinian workers of access to the Israeli labor market, the effects of the Separation Barrier now being built and, most recently, the boycott of the Hamas-led Palestinian Authority, the economic situation of the Occupied Territories has reached emergency proportions. Unemployment runs to 67 percent in Gaza, 48 percent in the West Bank, and 75 percent of Palestinians, including two-thirds of the children, live in poverty, on less than $2 a day, defined by the UN as "deep poverty." More than 100,000 Palestinians out of the 125,000 who used to work in Israel, in Israeli settlements, or in joint industrial zones, have lost their jobs (UNCTAD 2006). Half the Palestinian population requires external food assistance to meet their minimal daily food needs, with 30 percent of Palestinian children under five years of age suffering from malnutrition (Christian Aid 2003, UNCTAD 2006). In the meantime, welfare payments, dependent on tax monies illegally withheld by Israel under the Paris Protocol, have fallen by $180 million.

Israel also maintains control over utilities (such as water, electricity and phone services) in the Occupied Territories, even though Israel charges exorbitant prices for these utilities, despite the low income of the Palestinians. In fact, they actually pay more for electricity than Israelis. And so, in 2004, Israel confiscated $15.8 million from humanitarian aid sent to the Palestinians for utility bills owed by Palestinian municipalities (Hever 2007a:7).

The upshot of all this is profound structural imbalances in the Palestinian economy and a high degree of artificial dependence upon Israel. Projected back over the past 40 years, the picture that emerges is one of deliberate de-development. Specially targeted has been the Palestinian infrastructure. Both the Gazan airport built with European funds and the Gazan sea port that was under construction were totally destroyed in the second Intifada, and major international investment has been totally negated by Israeli military incursions. By denying points of commercial access to the Palestinians and thereby channeling all their exports and imports through Israeli ports, economic warfare takes it steady toll.

Thus, today, 90 percent of Palestinian imports are from Israel and 88 percent of its exports go to Israel. Not only is the Palestinian economy prevented from developing, but it is unprotected from an Israeli economy 60 times its size. Since the start of the second Intifada foreign aid has been transformed from investment in infrastructure, businesses and training to humanitarian aid (Hever 2007a). That may help Palestinians survive, but it contributes little to the development of the economy. Even here Israel mounts serious obstacles. One UN official complained to me that "we don't know of another conflict area in the world where we've had these problems— even in Kosovo."

By the end of the Oslo "peace process," Palestinians in the Occupied Territories were locked into tiny, impoverished enclaves, their per capita gross national product (GNP) about one-eighth of what it had been at the beginning, seven years before. Because of the devastating assault on the Palestinian economy in the wake of the election of Hamas, the Occupied Territories occupies third place on a list of the 13 most urgent targets of international aid, all the rest being in Africa.

3. Creating "Facts on the Ground"

Israel began creating facts on the ground even as the Six Day War was still raging, when it demolished the Mughrabi Quarter in the Old City. Since then, and particularly during the three decades in which Sharon systematically and single-mindedly applied his *ta'ozim* strategy, the matrix of some 250 settlements and outposts, consolidated around seven major settlement "blocs," may well have rendered Israeli control irreversible. Sharon's ultimate goal, fragmentizing the Occupied Territories into small and disconnected "cantons," has been completed, with political implications yet to be seen.

Ironically (or not, since Labor has been actively complicit in constructing the Matrix of Control), it was with the signing of Oslo II by the Rabin government in 1995 that the Occupied Territories, whose territorial integrity Israel had promised to respect in the Oslo Agreement, were atomized into more than 70 enclaves into which more than 90 percent of the Palestinian population was confined. The West Bank itself was divided into 64 islands: Areas A, B and C, plus a large "nature preserve" in the Judean Desert (see Map 2, p. xiii). Only 18 percent (and that, remember, on only 22 percent of historic Palestine, the Occupied Territories) was put under the full control of the Palestinian Authority, and that, too, was dispersed among dozens of enclaves. Although under the Oslo agreements these enclaves were to gradually expand as Israeli withdrew from the Occupied Territories and the Palestinian Authority assumed control, Israeli refusal to implement the phases of withdrawal left the Palestinians imprisoned in these enclave-cells. What was left of their land, the 58 percent of the West Bank designated as Area C, 54 percent of East Jerusalem and 60 percent of tiny Gaza (until the "disengagement" of 2005), was further carved up and shrunken by settlements, settlement blocs, Israeli-only highways, hundreds of checkpoints, earthen obstacles to movement, military facilities and, finally, the massive Separation Barrier.

"Enclave-cells" is not simply a phrase; it conveys the reality of the restrictions on Palestinian movement that had been steadily tightened since, ironically or not, the start of the peace process. Since the early 1990s a permanent "closure" has been laid over the West Bank and Gaza, severely restricting the number of Palestinian workers allowed into Israel, hindering travel among the many enclaves and ending all access to Jerusalem, even for purposes of prayer. The closure has many physical forms: more than 300 permanent checkpoints, hundreds of semi-permanent and spontaneous "flying" checkpoints which monitor and limit Palestinian movement. Almost all the major roads of the West Bank—"bypass" roads we call them—are closed to private Palestinian vehicles, and access to virtually every Palestinian city, town and village is blocked by earthen or military obstructions.

The Separation Barrier, now being completed, has only a limited number of crossings between the West Bank and Israel, as well as between Palestinian villages and their agricultural fields; Israelis and Palestinians will use separate ones. A military order signed by Major General Yair Naveh, commander of the IDF in the Judea and Samaria region, reports Hass (*Ha'aretz*, February 22, 2006),

> forbids Palestinians from entering Israel via any route other than 11 special crossings that were allocated only to them—and they can only cross those on foot. Palestinians are not allowed

to drive inside Israel. The order also prohibits Israelis from bringing Palestinians into Israel through passages designated for Israelis only.

At the Hizma junction, which is for Israelis only, the "seam administration" of the Defense Ministry has not yet hung the signs that it already hung on the road leading from the settlement of Ma'aleh Adumim to Jerusalem. The signs are hung alongside the road and at the military checkpoint, and say, in Hebrew and Arabic, "Passage is for Israelis only. Transporting and/or movement of people who are not Israelis is forbidden through this passage."

The yellow signs explain who is an Israeli. The definition is in the major general's order, and is the standard definition used in military orders declaring "a closed military area" to Palestinians, where only Israelis are allowed to enter. "An Israeli," says the order and the sign, "is a resident of Israel, someone whose residency is in the region [meaning the occupied territory—A.H.] and is an Israeli citizen [a settler—A.H.] or one who is eligible to become an immigrant according to the Law of Return-1950 and someone who is not a resident of the region but has a valid entry permit to Israel" [a tourist—A.H.].

The Matrix extends under the earth and into the sky as well—a "vertical occupation," as the Israeli architect Eyal Weizman (2007) calls it. The settlement blocs are consciously built atop the West Bank aquifers from which Israel draws about 30 percent of its water in violation of international law which prohibits an Occupying Power from utilizing the resources of an occupied territory. Indeed, 80 percent of the water resources of the West Bank and Gaza are under Israeli control, and a full 80 percent of the water coming from the West Bank goes to Israel and its settlements. Only 20 percent is allocated to its 2.5 million Palestinian inhabitants and they receive none of the water pumped from the Jordan River. As for consumption, the settlers use six times more water per capita than Palestinians. Per capita water consumption in the West Bank for domestic and urban use (drinking, washing, consumption by public institutions, watering parks, and so on) is only 60 liters per person per day, far below the minimum water consumption of 100 liters per person per day recommended by the World Health Organization; Israelis consume 350 liters per person per day. Mekorot, the Israeli water carrier which controls all the water of the country, allocates 1,450 cubic meters of water per year to each settler, while a Palestinian receives only 83. Around 215,000 Palestinians living in 270 West Bank villages have no running water at all. The destruction of Palestinian wells and water mains, which has intensified with the construction of the wall over the main aquifers, creates months of water shortages, while the need to purchase water from Israeli tank-trucks, costing $3 during the rainy season and up to $8 in the dry months, is beyond the financial resources of the impoverished population. As a final blow, Palestinians are forbidden to collect rainwater in open reservoirs (B'tselem 2001).

As for the extension of the Matrix skyward, Israel claims control of the Palestinian airspace, including its electromagnetic communications fields, even after a peace agreement is signed.

But the Matrix truly is a matrix and must be comprehended as such, and not merely as a collection of separate elements. That's why it's crucial to grasp the significance of the settlement blocs, not simply individual settlements. For settlements alone were not sufficient for reconfiguring the country and guaranteeing that Judea, Samaria, East Jerusalem and Gaza could never be severed from Israel proper. To ensure the irreversibility of the Matrix, the settlements had to become part of the seamless fabric of Israel, indistinguishable from the Galilee, the Sharon Plain or the Negev. The "Green Line" had to be erased, not only from the maps of children's school books or the TV weather reports, not only in the public's consciousness, but from any barrier or sign on the ground. Israelis had to be able to travel from place to place, routinely visit friends, receive public or private services and decide on where they would live with no regard for any border. Through the Matrix every means possible was used to routinize the Occupation and render it invisible, so that Judea and Samaria become as normal parts of the country as the Galilee.

When Barak decided to skip over the phases of withdrawal and jump directly to final status talks at Camp David, he had to come up with Israel's bottom line. What, in fact, was Israel demanding? It was at that point that he made a subtle yet crucial tweaking of the Matrix. Instead of attempting to defend all of Israel's scattered settlements, Barak defined seven settlement "blocs" that Israel would retain under any agreement with the Palestinians. With these settlement blocs, linked into Israel proper by the massive bypass road system, including the Trans-Israel Highway passing through Israel along the West Bank, the main goals of the Matrix were realized. Judea and Samaria were irreversibly incorporated into Israel proper, while the possibility of a viable Palestinian state was permanently foreclosed.

Let's take a brief tour of the seven settlement blocs (Map 3, p. xiv) to see in detail (for the devil, again, is in the details) just how they render Israeli control permanent. We can begin with *(1) the Jordan Valley,* which has been viewed since 1967 as Israel's eastern "security border." Bordering as it does with Jordan and rising to a high plateau, the Jordan Valley gives Israel a vantage point to the east. Its genuine significance, however, is in denying the Palestinians an unsupervised border with Jordan, thus keeping it within the Israeli domain. Its water is also considered a "security" issue. How much of the Jordan Valley Israel will retain still remains to be decided. The route of the Separation Barrier removes a full 30 percent of the West Bank from the Palestinians; so, too, has a decision in 2006 to close the entire Jordan Valley to Palestinians. Israel, though, could retain only the settlements built in the valley and along the ridge or, if necessary, could even relinquish all of the Jordan Valley except the river, and still maintain full control of both the border and the water. The current construction of

the new city of Maskiot indicates that Israel sees its control
of this settlement bloc, with its 7500 settlers (as opposed to
50,000 Palestinians), as permanent.

A second settlement bloc, *(2) the "Western Samaria" bloc
centered around the city of Ariel,* controls a strategic area that
virtually divides the West Bank, seriously compromising its
territorial contiguity. Besides controlling the flow of people and
goods between the major Palestinian towns of Qalqilya, Nablus
and Ramallah, this bloc also isolates the cities of Qalqilya and
Tulkarm and restricts their urban development. The Ariel bloc
also sits atop the major aquifer of the West Bank.

The Modi'in bloc (3) connects the Western Samaria Bloc
to Jerusalem and includes some of the Palestinians' richest
agricultural land. Its anchor is the city of Modi'in which,
together with its suburbs across the Green Line (Upper Modi'in,
with its population of 30,000, is one of the largest settlements
in the West Bank), is expected to grow to a half million when
completed.

Three settlement blocs, *(4) Givat Ze'ev, (5) Ma'aleh
Adumim* and *(6) Gush Etzion, Efrat-Beitar, Illit,* comprise
"Greater Jerusalem," 97 square miles containing some 80,000
settlers which, when annexed to the Israeli-controlled city
of Jerusalem with its own 240,000 settlers, will dominate
the entire central region of the West Bank and destroy the
territorial contiguity necessary for a viable Palestinian state.
Greater Jerusalem separates the 220,000 Palestinians living in
fragmented ghettos scattered among the massive settlements in
East Jerusalem from the wider Palestinian society of the West
Bank. It also keeps West Bank Palestinians at arm's length from
Jerusalem. This is significant not only because of its historic,
religious, cultural and political importance to them, but because
tourism represents (in potential) the major Palestinian industry.
Removing Jerusalem from the Palestinian economy fatally
undermines the essential viability of a Palestinian state.

Greater Jerusalem stretches across much of the central West Bank from the Modi'in area to within twenty kilometers of the Jordan River. It effectively divides the West Bank in two, compelling Palestinians wishing to travel north–south to pass through Israeli territory, thus giving Israel control of Palestinian movement. It also cuts the natural urban link between Jerusalem and Ramallah. What's more, it fragments the Palestinian presence in the city and neutralizes it as a Palestinian urban center, not to mention its status as the Palestinian capital. Former US President Bill Clinton's formula that "Arab areas of Jerusalem are Palestinian and Jewish ones are Israeli" might have led to Israel ceding some peripheral villages and neighborhoods to the north and south of the city to the Palestinians, but not control over them. Willing, even anxious to get tens of thousands of Palestinians off their hands, Israel floated the idea of offering the Palestinians "functional autonomy," "administrative control" or "limited sovereignty" over them, and perhaps over the Haram, the Muslim and Christian Quarters of the Old City as well. Nothing, however, resembling genuine sovereignty or a Jerusalem truly integrated into a Palestinian state.

Finally, *(7) the Hebron bloc* is a salient extending from the south to the Israeli settlements in and around Hebron. It is the only settlement bloc I see as untenable. The extremely violent and fanatical settler population in Hebron (400 settlers in a city of 120,000 yet controlling 20 percent of the city including the historic Old City, the Qasba outdoor markets and the Ibrahimi Mosque), despite the large and ever-expanding settlement of Kiryat Arba connected with it, have created an unbearable situation resembling Gaza.

The threads sewing the fabric of the Matrix to that of Israel proper were the massive system of 29 highways and bypass roads which incorporated the settlements into Israel's national highway system, construction of which began during the course of the Oslo peace process when Rabin's Labor/

Meretz government was supposedly negotiating with the Palestinians over the status of the Territories. For Israelis the highways created unobstructed ribbons of fluid movement in and out of Israel; for Palestinians, whose cities and towns were completely bypassed, they represented yet another system of barriers to movement among their enclave-prisons. They also contributed measurably to the process of *nishul*. At 300 miles in length and lined with "sanitary" margins, the highways system, mainly restricted to Israeli travel only, eliminated all Palestinian homes, fields and orchards in its path, forcing the local residents to migrate eastward towards the center of the West Bank or, preferably, out of the country altogether. The thick web of bypass roads plays a key role in defining the cantons of the Palestinian bantustan.

Finally, there's the last element in the Matrix of Control, the Separation Barrier. Even before the failure at Camp David, Barak had threatened the Palestinians with unilateral separation if they failed to cooperate. In October, 2000, his government published a "Security Separation Plan" in which a proposed "barrier" would be erected between Israel and the West Bank. According to the plan, a barrier would provide physical security to Israeli citizens, including, tellingly, the settlers. But it had two other objectives—political objectives—as well: preventing Palestinians from achieving any territorial, infrastructural or political gains outside of negotiations and exacting from the Palestinians a high economic price, through closures, trade restrictions, sanctions and other means, as a way of pressuring them to submit. In what must be one of the most audacious examples of spin, Barak argued that the barrier is "essential to the Palestinian nation in order to foster its national identity and independence without being dependent on the State of Israel" (Fried 2000:14–15).

Construction of the Barrier began in June 2002. For Sharon, who initially opposed it out of fear that it would resurrect the Green Line he had spent so many years trying to erase, extended the route eastward along a convoluted path closely following the contours of Areas A and B, so that it would mark in concrete the future borders of an expanded Israel and the Palestinian bantustan. When the Barrier came up against a settlement bloc, it simply went around. Eighty percent of the settlers fall on the Israeli side of the Barrier, exactly as Barak promised.

Language, as always, is important. The Israeli government, the media and supporters of the Barrier insist vociferously on calling it a "fence," pointing out that 95 percent of it is indeed a complex of fences. In terms of its impact on the Palestinian population, however, such semantic distinctions are meaningless. The "fence" erases agricultural fields and houses within a massive 65-yard swathe extending more than 450 miles—five times longer than the Berlin Wall, which was also a mix of walls and fortified fences. Thirty-eight villages and towns find themselves completely separated from their agricultural lands, unable to farm them. The parts of the barrier which are technically a see-through "fence" include sensors, trenches, security roads, mine fields, checkpoints, terminals, watchtowers, surveillance cameras, electronic sensory devices and military patrols accompanied by trained killer dogs, certainly as formidable a barrier to movement as any wall. Some 50,000 Palestinians are trapped between the border and the wall, facing impoverishment, alienation from their land and water, and eventual transfer (UN 2005). Defenders of the Barrier note that "only" 5 percent of it consists of solid concrete walls. True, but they are 26 feet high—more than twice the height of the Berlin Wall—and they surround *all* the Palestinian cities, towns and neighborhoods along their convoluted route. The Barrier, moreover, is not linear as was the Berlin Wall. Entire cities like Qalqiliya and Tulkarm are completely encircled. About 263,000 Palestinians will be permanently confined to small encircled enclaves. The Palestinian residents of East Jerusalem have been isolated from the wider West Bank society, 55,000 of them confined in neighborhoods completely encircled by the walls, forced to use slow, humiliating and distant "terminals" to go to school, go to work, go shopping or simply visit friends. On the other side of the Barrier more than 2 million Palestinians have been enclosed within the West Bank "cantons."

From the start, many of us in the Israeli peace movement argued that the primary purpose of the Barrier was not security, the rubric under which it was sold to the public, but rather the demarcation of a political border. Its official name, the "*Separation* Barrier," underlines its essentially political character. After the International Court of Justice ruled in July, 2004, that the Barrier was totally illegal under international law, a ruling ratified by an almost unanimous General Assembly (Israel, the US, Australia and a couple of Pacific atolls being the only dissenting votes), Israel pulled it back to incorporate only 7 percent of the West Bank, although how much land the Palestinians will lose in the Jordan Valley remains to be seen. But the political-versus-security nature of the Barrier is clear to anyone looking at a map (see Map 4, p. xv). Only 20 percent of it actually follows the Green Line, the obvious route if it was indeed defensive. The rest intrudes far into the Palestinian areas, as far as twelve miles in the Ariel area. The almost exact overlap between the Barrier's route, the cantons as defined by Sharon and the settlement blocs as defined by Barak belie the claim that it is essentially a security apparatus.

Increasingly the link between the Barrier and Israel's desire to unilaterally define a "demographic border" between Israeli Jews and Palestinians has led Israeli leaders to speak candidly about its political function. Ehud Olmert, then Acting Prime Minister after Sharon's stroke, said this at the Herzliya Conference in January 2006:

> [T]here is no doubt that the most important and dramatic step we face is the determination of permanent borders of the State of Israel, to ensure the Jewish majority in the country....In order to

ensure the existence of a Jewish national homeland, we will not be able to continue ruling over the territories in which the majority of the Palestinian population lives. We must create a clear boundary as soon as possible, one which will reflect the demographic reality on the ground. Israel will maintain control over the security zones, the Jewish settlement blocs, and those places which have supreme national importance to the Jewish people, first and foremost a united Jerusalem under Israeli sovereignty.

4. Military Controls and Military Strikes

Administration, law and planning, restrictive economic policies and the creation of massive "facts on the ground" effectively control the Palestinians and their land while protecting Israel's image as a democratic country; the Matrix of Control is intended to conceal the Iron Fist of military force behind the façade of proper administration. Still, when necessary, the Matrix does rely on the presence of the military. Major operations were launched during the two Intifadas (1987–93; 2000–2004) and thereafter. Especially devastating was Operation Defensive Shield in which scores of Palestinians died and 15,000 were detained as Israel ravaged urban landscapes in its reconquest of the West Bank in March/April 2002. In Operation Rainbow some 300 houses of Palestinian refugees were demolished in the Rafah area of Gaza during one week of May 2004. Over 160 Palestinian civilians were killed in northern Gaza (over 30 of them children) in Operation Days of Penitence inaugurated in October 2004; over 500 were injured in that operation and 90 homes were demolished (Ha'aretz, January 11, 2004). Operations Summer Rains and Autumn Rains, carried out in Gaza during the last half of 2006, preceded and perhaps triggered the second Lebanon war. Since the Palestinians have no army, the death and destruction rained down upon their civilian population by these military actions were so disproportionate to any genuine security threat that they can only be described as State Terrorism.

Israel, however, can never win uncontested control over the Occupied Territories; it cannot compel the Palestinians to submit to their own incarceration. All it can aim for is pacification, a never-ending repression of the local population that can never be routinized or truly quieted, long periods of low-intensity warfare punctuated by occasional flare-ups, localized or major intifadas. Overt military operations are therefore complemented by covert ones, ceaseless and innumerable over these past 40 years. Besides its undercover *mustarabi* ("Arabic-like") army units, Israel also employs tens of thousands of collaborators, Palestinians turned unwillingly or willingly into agents of the Occupation. Here is where control comes in. Do you want a driver's license? A business license? How about a permit for work in Israel, or a permit to build a house, or a permit to travel abroad? Do you need permission for your child to receive hospital care in Israel or for your aging father to come visit you from Jordan? Has your son run foul of the law? Are you inundated by debts, can't afford even food for your family table? No problem. Everything can be arranged. All you have to do is supply us with this information or let us know what is happening in that community.

Under the guise of its own "war on terror," Israel has managed to maintain covert, low intensity warfare for four decades, at a great price to Palestinian civil society. Since 1967, more than 650,000 Palestinians have been detained, 20 percent of the total Palestinian population in the Occupied Territories (<www.miftah.org>). It is estimated that 40 percent of Palestinian men in the Occupied Territories have been arrested or detained at one time or another. During the four years of the second Intifada (September 29, 2000 to October 2004) more than 3,330 Palestinians were killed, at least 85 percent of them civilians, including about 650 children and youth, half under the age of 15 (<www.palestinemonitor.org>). And in 88 percent of the incidents in which children were killed, there was no direct confrontation with Israeli soldiers. A total of 297 Palestinians have been killed by assassination or extra-judicial executions, 180 of them intentionally targeted, the rest being "collateral damage." More than 50,000 Palestinians were injured in the second Intifada, 20 percent of them children and youth; 2,500 civilians were permanently disabled. In the first seven months of the Hamas-led Palestinian Authority (March–October 2006), almost 500 Palestinians were killed by Israelis while 19 Israelis killed by Palestinians (OCHA reports <www.ochaopt. org>). Add to that children who have been traumatized by the extreme violence to which they have been exposed: killings, military attacks, house demolitions, harassment, humiliation of their parents and teachers. According to Eyyad Seraj, head of the Palestinian Mental Health Center in Gaza, 55 percent of the young people who are suicide bombers have had their homes demolished.

The Matrix of Control, then, conceals a repressive regime intended to permanently deny the Palestinians self-determination, and their basic human rights behind a façade of proper administration, physical constraint and ostensibly justified military control. It also reconfigures the entire country, ensuring that a viable Palestinian state will never emerge and the Matrix will control Palestinian life forever. In order to link the major population centers of Israeli in the big cities and towns along the coast with the settlement blocs to the east, Sharon, in his 1977 master plan of settlements, included a "Seven Stars" plan that called for the establishment of urban centers straddling both sides of the Green Line; Modi'in is one of those "seven stars." Key to creating contiguity between Israel proper and the settlement blocs is a new highway, the Trans-Israel Highway, designed to provide a new demographic and physical spine to the country. Hugging as it does the western border of the West Bank and extending 220 miles from the Lebanese border to the Negev city of Be'er Sheva—including two long spurs across the Galilee to aid in the Judaization of

that part of the country—it will open a huge section along
the Green Line and in areas of the Galilee heavily populated
by Arabs for settlement by hundreds of thousands of Israeli
Jews, who will be resettled in some 30 new towns and cities.
With Modi'in as its center, the Trans-Israel Highway and
the matrix of bypass roads, settlement blocs and new and
expanded Israeli urban centers on both sides of the Green
Line form a new "metropolitan core-region." Metropolitan
Tel Aviv will overlap with Metropolitan Modi'in which in turn
overlaps with Metropolitan Jerusalem, thus reconfiguring the
entire Land of Israel. The north–south orientation of Israel
and the Occupied Territories upon which a solution of two
parallel states is based, is thereby permanently broken. Instead,
it is replaced by an east–west orientation in which dependent
Palestinian cantons are encompassed within an integrated
Matrix of Control extending from Tel Aviv to the Jordan
Valley. The Palestinians, now imprisoned within hundreds of
miles of concrete walls that carve their lands, cities and villages
into tiny, disconnected enclaves, now have no hope of a viable
state of their own. The Iron Wall has prevailed.

7

Concluding Dispossession:
Oslo and Unilateral Separation

Tell me what more we were supposed to do.
—Shlomo Ben-Ami, Acting Foreign Minister at Camp David
and Taba, *Ha'aretz*, September 14, 2001

In the eyes of the world, the sudden and surprise announcement that, in Oslo, the Israeli government and the PLO had agreed to direct face-to-face negotiations, followed by the signing of the Declaration of Principles on the White House lawn in September, 1993, appeared to be a major breakthrough in the conflict. Israel's opposition to Palestinian self-determination in the Occupied Territories had at last been overcome. The famous handshake of Rabin and Arafat heralded the dawn of a new era of peace in the Middle East. In fact, it is clear in hindsight, the Oslo "peace process" only represented another stage in the process of *nishul*, the sixth stage, one that sought, through diplomatic means this time, Palestinian agreement to Israeli control of the entire country. Oslo held out as an inducement the tantalizing possibility that Israel may carve out for the Palestinians a mini-state of their own. Given that the Matrix of Control continued to expand, it appeared that the Palestinians were expected to accept a kind of occupation-by-consent.

For the Oslo process did not make a fundamental break with past policy. Israel did not recognize the Palestinians as a nation

175

with legitimate claims to the land, nor their national right of self-determination. Instead, Rabin's government demanded, as a precondition for negotiations, unconditional Palestinian recognition of the State of Israel. "We demanded," writes Uri Savir (1998:74), Israel's chief negotiator during the Oslo process, "that the Palestinians accept Israel not just as a fact of life but as a legitimate political construct." Fair enough. But what did the Palestinians receive in return? Clear and explicit recognition of their right of self-determination? Hardly. In Oslo Israel merely recognized the PLO as "the representative of the Palestinian people" with which it was willing to negotiate. "We were prepared to recognize the PLO the representative of the Palestinian people," says Savir (1998:74), "but not the PLO's version as leaders of a Palestinian state." Indeed, Rabin became agitated every time Arafat "misrepresented" the Declaration of Principles as Israel's agreeing to a Palestinian state at all.

> Following a literal and legalistic interpretation of the declaration, this implied that Israel, as the official "source of authority," would grant the Palestinians limited powers...Israel tried to impose on them a security doctrine requiring everything Israel considered important to remain in its control. (Savir 1998:98, 100)

Indeed, Savir arrived at the early discussions in Oslo with clear instructions from Foreign Minister Peres: autonomy rather than independence is the prevailing concept; Jerusalem will not be included in any political arrangement; no binding international arbitration of outstanding issues; everything relating to the external security of Israel and the territories (including the settlers) must remain in Israeli hands; the settlements will remain intact; and Israel will continue to control water and other natural resources (Savir 1998:6, 39).

The Palestinians, Savir (1998:53) says, tried to "create some symmetry by making parallel demands of their own." The PLO wanted an Israeli commitment not to close Palestinian institutions in East Jerusalem; Israel agreed only to "non-PLO" institutions. The Palestinians demanded a freeze on all settlement activity; Israel refused with indignity, accompanied by a heady dose of disingenuousness, if not actual lying. "Peres shouted. Tell [them] we will not agree to freeze construction as a result of Palestinian pressure. And explain to him that in 1992 the government took a decision to halt new building" (Savir 1998:72). The Palestinians objected to calling for a halt to the Intifada while Israel continued its violent policies of occupation; in the end Arafat acquiesced and called for his people to "renounce violence." The Palestinians also sought some sort of guarantees that the Israeli-run peace process would genuinely address their needs. They suggested expanding the scope of redeployment decided by negotiation rather than solely by Israel dictates; they sought an explicit Israeli commitment to implement Security Council Resolution 242 (calling for a withdrawal from all the Occupied Territories); they sought ways to share control of the crossing between the West Bank and Jordan; they pushed for Israeli agreement to an international presence in the territories; and they raised the possibility of outside arbitration. All these proposals, however, were judged "mostly unacceptable" by Israel.

Most serious, the Israelis refused to accept the two most fundamental Palestinian demands: the right of self-determination and the refugees' Right of Return. Eventually the Palestinians had little choice but to agree to all of Israel's demands, including recognition of Israel's legitimacy as a Jewish state, although they received very little, not even a pledge that a Palestinian state would emerge at the end of the peace process. Israel had agreed to nothing that would in the slightest way reduce its control over the Occupied Territories or limit its ability to extend its settlements and infrastructure, or even to continue expropriating massive tracts of Palestinian land. Palestinian claims and wishes meant little. The Israelis insisted on their draft text of the Declaration of Principles as being the only valid one, although, says Savir (1998:37), "we agreed to insert the Palestinians' objections into the draft, in parentheses."

To make matters even worse, Rabin felt it necessary to "compensate" his unhappy military for the minor role it played in the negotiations leading up to the Declaration of Principles by allowing it to virtually take over the subsequent negotiations. In the words of Savir (1998:99):

> Rabin chose a new team of negotiators...composed mostly of military officers. When the military grumbled bitterly at having been shut out of the Oslo talks, Rabin explained that the issues discussed in Oslo had been mainly ideological and political. But he did not reject the criticism, led by Chief of Staff Ehud Barak.... That Israel's approach was dictated by the army invariably made immediate security considerations the dominant ones, so that the fundamentally political process had been subordinated to short-term military needs....The Foreign Ministry had strong misgivings about this military emphasis but did not express them publicly.

What Israeli leaders had in mind, and what ran as a common thread through both Labor and Likud conceptions of where Oslo was heading, was best articulated by Netanyahu's formula "autonomy-plus, state-minus." The Palestinians, he suggested in an interview with David Frost (Netanyahu 1997), would receive something on the order of Puerto Rico, Andorra or— where he found this model I have no idea—the Finnish island of Aland, whose Swedish-speaking inhabitants enjoyed a kind of local self-rule. But Rabin was also explicit on this score. On October 5, 1995, before a vote in the Knesset to ratify the Israel-Palestinian Interim Agreement and a month before his assassination, Rabin said: "We view the permanent solution in the framework of State of Israel, which will include most of the area of the Land of Israel as it was under the rule of the British Mandate, and alongside it a Palestinian entity that will be a home to most of the Palestinian residents living in the Gaza Strip and the West Bank. We would like this to be an entity which is less than a state, and which will independently run the lives of the Palestinians under its authority" (quoted in *Settlement Report* 5(6) of the Foundation for Middle East Peace).

As always, Israel's "security" needs and interests became the overriding engine of the peace process, which began to look to the Palestinians like a one-way road to apartheid. The closure, similar to the passbook regulations that had led to the Sharpesville uprising in South Africa, became increasingly more restrictive. Israel had discovered an even cheaper source of labor than the Palestinians, foreign workers from China, the Philippines, Thailand, Romania and West Africa, and thus used security as a reason for excluding Palestinians from the workforce. Restrictions were further tightened after the massacre of Muslim worshippers in Hebron in 1994. The 120,000 residents of the holy city of Hebron had been harassed for years by the tiny but extremely violent community of settlers that had taken control, with the backing of the government and the army, of the Ibrahimi Mosque, the sacred site of Abraham's burial. In February one of the settlers, a medical doctor named Barukh Goldstein, opened fire on Muslim worshippers in the mosque, killing 29. No steps were taken against the settlers, even though voices were raised in Israel that they should be removed. Instead, the government imposed a total two-month curfew on the Muslim parts of the city.

It is at this point, spurred by the Hebron massacre and a feeling that the Oslo process was serving only Israel's interests, that the first suicide bomb attacks take place within Israel, instigated by Hamas. That, in turn, spurred further punitive measures, then further Palestinian responses, a campaign of vilification by the right against Rabin, his assassination in November, 1995, and a few months later, partly in reaction to suicide attacks, the election Netanyau on an explicitly anti-Oslo program. He and his Foreign Minister Ariel Sharon proceeded to freeze the peace process entirely. It is at this juncture, when settlement expansion begins once more, the demolition of Palestinian homes is renewed and, in general, the Occupation is reasserted in its most brutal forms, a time when the Oslo process teeters on the brink of full collapse, that Israeli peace activists begin to reawaken from their Oslo hibernation. One expression of that was the founding of ICAHD. In the meantime, the Palestinians held their first elections for the Palestinian Authority in January, 1996. Arafat and his Fatah party won handily, although Hamas and the left-wing parties boycotted the vote. Despite the ups and downs of the peace process, 75 percent of the Palestinians supported it (Joubran 1995).

BARAK'S "GENEROUS OFFER"—AND THE SETTLEMENT BLOCS

Netanyahu pandered skillfully to old Israeli fears. His campaign had been orchestrated by none other than Bush's future Deputy Secretary of Defense Paul Wolfowitz, with the professional help of Arthur J. Finkelstein, known as the Republicans' "Godfather of Dirty Tricks." But something had happened in the brief two and a half years since the Rabin–Arafat handshake. Fear and hatred as the basis for a political program struck many Israelis as anachronistic and, in fact, hateful. When Sharon, upon departing for the Wye River negotiations, announced he would not shake Arafat's hand, he came off as petty, outmoded, even ridiculous. In May, 1999, after a bare three years in office, Netanyahu was sent packing. Ehud Barak was elected in a landslide. The public had given him a clear mandate: Get us out of the mess. Do whatever you have to do, including dismantling the settlements—*but do it!* What many miss was that Barak, an ex-Chief of Staff, had, as a Labor member of the Knesset, voted against the Oslo Accords. It was he who drove the final nail into the Oslo process by doing what Netanyahu had tried to do but failed: he reversed the paradigm shift towards peace that had survived the Hamas suicide bombings and Netanyahu's tenure, and led the Israeli public back to the old us-and-them formulation. He is best remembered for the line "There is no partner for peace." That statement, based on the contention that he made a "generous offer" to Arafat which the latter refused, closed the Israeli Jewish public, and particularly the liberals of the Labor Party, Meretz and Peace Now, to any further peace process. It is a position, as I said, that he restated recently (mid August 2007), just weeks after reclaiming the chairmanship of the Labor Party.

Barak decided to forego any process in favor of immediate final status talks. He was guided, says Robert Malley (Agha and Malley 2001), a high-level American participant in the Camp David talks, by an antipathy towards the gradual steps of Oslo, an all-or-nothing approach based on the decidedly non-peace view that Palestinians would make an historic compromise only if all other options for unappealing, and an assessment that the Israeli public would go for a far-reaching solution if it was a final one and brought quiet and normalcy. So he pushed for a go-for-broke summit—no process, no fall-back, all or nothing. Arafat balked. The process had not advanced to such a stage. The whole point of the withdrawal phases was that the Palestinians would come into the final status negotiations with a measure of parity; they would have an elected Palestinian Authority ruling 60–80 percent of the Occupied Territories. Netanyahu had withdrawn from almost nothing, and now Barak proposed no further withdrawals at all, leaving the Palestinians in effective charge of Area A (see Map 2, p. xiii), a gulag of islands scattered over only 42 percent of the West Bank and 40 percent of Gaza. Overall the Palestinian public was disillusioned with Oslo, which they were beginning to see as abject surrender to Israel, in whom they had no trust. For them, the Oslo process "read like a litany of promises deferred or unfulfilled. Six years after the agreement there were more Israeli settlements, less freedom of movement, and worse economic conditions" (Agha and Malley 2001). In Arafat's opinion it was premature to jump to final status talks; they were bound to fail.

But Barak had his way, supported by the Clinton Administration to agree. Arafat had no choice but to attend, but he did so on condition that he would not be blamed when the talks failed—which is exactly what happened. Camp David proved a disaster. Both sides proved inadequate to the task, says Malley (Agha and Malley 2001), but Israel bears the lion's share of the responsibility for the failure. Barak's all-or-nothing approach simply raised the stakes too high. The Israelis sought a final and complete peace, even though they refused to reveal their end-game. No one knew where Israel was going, including the Israelis themselves. Yet the Israeli draft agreement contained the proviso that with the parties' signatures the conflict is ended, as are all claims and grievances. In other words, that's it, no going back—but from what? What are we actually negotiating, a two-state solution (Israel denied or was vague on that point), autonomy (absolutely unacceptable to the Palestinians), or something else? The Palestinians approached the resolution of the conflict as, in fact, a process. Given that Israel wouldn't agree on an end-game, they insisted on going cautiously step by step, evaluating the merit of each proposal as they went along. And while they adhered to the two-state solution, they expected further evolution after that, unlike the Israelis who insisted that "the" solution would be it, with no further evolution.

Even if Arafat had agreed to compromises and concessions, he could not commit the entire fate of the Palestinian people to an all-or-nothing yet vague package.

If anything has destroyed the Palestinians' credibility, it has been the charge, leveled by Barak, that the Palestinians rejected a truly "generous offer." But was there ever really a "generous offer"? In an interview with the Israeli newspaper *Ha'aretz* (Shavit 2002), Barak stated candidly: "It was plain to me that there was no chance of reaching a settlement at Taba. Therefore I said there would be no negotiations and there would be no delegation and there would be no official discussions and no documentation. Nor would Americans be present in the room. The only thing that took place at Taba were non-binding contacts between senior Israelis and senior Palestinians." The 95 percent figure comes from what were called the "Clinton parameters," a proposal of actually 96 percent concessions, excluding East Jerusalem, to which both sides felt a need to respond favorably, but did so with "reservations." According to Barak, Israel's reservations filled 20 pages.

But let's say, for the sake of argument, that such an offer had been made. Would the Palestinians have been justified in rejecting it? Would it have led in fact to a just and sustainable peace, or to a Palestinian prison-state? It is only tiny details, after all, that mark the fine line between a viable, sovereign if small Palestinian state and a bantustan, between autonomy and independence. According to Benny Morris (2002a:42), these were the main elements of the "generous offer" that Clinton, with Barak's agreement, read out "slowly" to Arafat at Camp David:

- The establishment of a demilitarized Palestinian state on 92 percent of the West Bank and 100 percent of the Gaza Strip
- Some territorial compensation for the Palestinians from the pre-1967 Israeli territory
- Annexation of 8 percent of the West Bank to Israel
- Dismantling of most of the settlements and the concentration of the bulk of the settlers in the 8 percent to be annexed
- The establishment of the Palestinian capital in East Jerusalem
- Some Arab neighborhoods in East Jerusalem to become sovereign Palestinian territories and others to enjoy "functional autonomy"

- Palestinian sovereignty over half of the Old City of Jerusalem (the Muslim and Christian Quarters, but not the Armenian and Jewish Quarters)
- "Custodianship," though not sovereignty, over the Temple Mount
- A return of the refugees to the prospective Palestinian state, with no "Right of Return" to Israel proper
- A massive aid program to facilitate the refugees' rehabilitation.

The Palestinians, according to the Barak/Clinton offer, would cede just 8 percent of the West Bank in return for territorial swaps. In other words, Israel would withdraw from 92.6 percent of the combined West Bank and Gaza. Since this figure does not include East Jerusalem (except for a few peripheral Palestinian neighborhoods) or the Latrun area, which Israel does not consider occupied, Barak is really offering about an 88 percent withdrawal. That sounds generous as well, although it means that Israel will expand from its present 78 percent of the country to about 81 percent, while the Palestinians' territory shrinks from 22 percent to 19 percent. Quibbling you might say, but keep this in mind: Every square centimeter is critical for the Palestinians, who represent today about half the population of the country. If their reduced state has to accept *all* the refugees who wish to return, a traumatized, impoverished and undereducated population, is such a state viable, either socially or economically? Then put into the equation the fact that some 60 percent of Palestinians are under the age of 18, also a traumatized, impoverished and undereducated population that has lived only in conditions of conflict and violence. Could such a state offer a hopeful future to its next generations, or would it be merely an unstable regime exporting unskilled labor? These are the issues by which we must judge Barak's offer was "generous" or not.

I would argue that, given the Matrix of Control, Israel could in fact relinquish 92.6 percent of the Occupied Territories and still retain complete control, especially if we translate the "generous" figure of 92 percent into what it really means: a state on 19 percent of a small country, and that divided into two, if not more, cantons. And what about the two most defining elements of a just peace: Palestinian sovereignty in a viable state? If Barak intended to continue controlling the borders—the issue is not on Clinton's list but there has never been any indication until today that Israel has ever intended otherwise—then there is no viable Palestinian state. If the 8 percent the Palestinians must cede includes a corridor or two across the West Bank, or if Israel insists on keeping the Ma'aleh Adumim settlement with its "E-1" corridor to Jerusalem, the territorial continuity of a Palestinian state is destroyed and, again, it is not viable. If all the Palestinians water resources are included in the 8 percent Israel insists on retaining—the aquifer under the Ariel bloc and the Jordan River, for example—then their viability is withheld as well. Development experts I have spoken to claim that Jerusalem is a resource that will account for up to 40 percent of a Palestinian state's economy, since tourism is their largest potential industry. If Jerusalem is not fully integrated into the Palestinian state politically, geographically and economically, or if Israel annexes a "Greater" Jerusalem, as Barak asserted it would, then there is no viable Palestinian state, even if some part of it is declared the Palestinian capital.

Indeed, the very conception of a territorial-based "solution" is as flawed as it is misleading. Barak's generous offer did not depart in a major way from Sharon's cantonization scheme. True, he might have relinquished more territory than Sharon, but it would be sterile territory; Israel would continue to monopolize all the country's developmental potential. And if the settlement blocs that Israel would retain conform to the Sharon's grid, the basic structure around which the Matrix of control is organized, then a Palestinian state is little more than a façade for Israeli control. The significance of freedom, viability and control versus mere territory can be graphically illustrated taking the example of a prison. Imagine a blueprint of a planned prison. Looking at it, it appears as if the prisoners own the place. They have 92 percent of the territory: the living areas, the work areas, the exercise yard, the cafeteria, the visiting area. All the prison authorities have is a mere 8 percent or less: the prison walls, the cell bars, the keys to iron doors, some glass partitions, surveillance cameras and weapons. Not much in terms of territory, but enough to completely control the inmates. If these strategic points of control embedded in the Matrix of Control are not dismantled, the Palestinians will have their state, but it will be a prison-state even if they get significant land in the West Bank and Gaza.

A SECOND ATTEMPT AT *NISHUL*: UNILATERAL SEPARATION

> The system of apartheid, with two peoples occupying the same land but completely separated from each other, with Israelis totally dominate and suppressing violence by depriving Palestinians of their basic human rights. This is the policy now being followed. (Carter 2006:215)

The Oslo peace process was more than a failure. Barak's pronouncement that Israel had "no partner for peace," reinforced, it seemed, by the outbreak of the second Intifada, de-politicized the conflict and left the Israeli public disempowered. Convinced that there simply was no political solution, that the conflict was "irresolvable," Israeli Jews felt had no choice but to hunker down and wait until, someday, something would break in their favor, probably something military. That explains the apparent contradiction between the readiness of the Israelis—some 70 percent of Israelis, according to polls (*Ha'aretz*, January 18, 2005)—to "separate" from the Palestinians and their willingness to elect Ariel Sharon, whose entire political life had been dedicated to incorporating the West Bank irreversibly into Israeli proper and rendering Israeli control permanent. If not peace, at least Sharon would bring what Barak failed to do: peace and quiet through sheer military force.

For the Israeli Jewish public, bereft of a political solution, the conflict was reduced to one element only, that of personal security. A kind of deal had been struck between the people and their leaders: if you bring us personal security, if we can get on buses and go to work or play without fear of getting blown up, we will elect you. We don't care how you do it. You can establish a Palestinian state on all the territories if that will bring us peace and quiet; you can load the Palestinians on trucks on ship them all to Jordan if that will work; you can build a walls so high that birds cannot fly over it—anything. We don't care what you do as long as we are safe. We don't expect peace, but we do expect peace and quiet, personal security. Deliver, and we will continue to elect you; fail, and you are out. That is the deal. Barak failed, and the public turned to Sharon, giving him a mandate to do whatever he wanted. After the collapse of the Oslo process and the outbreak of the second Intifada, Israeli Jews had taken themselves out of the political equation.

Sharon had always been a big picture man invested with strategic military skills, great power, audacity and unlimited resources, though his schemes usually entailed rivers of bloodshed and, as in Lebanon, colossal failures. Over half a century he had, more than any other public figure except Ben Gurion, shaped Israel geographically, politically and militarily. Everything he did had a clear focus and purpose: beating the Palestinians into submission, extending Israel's sovereignty to the Jordan River and preventing the establishment of a viable Palestinian state. By the time Sharon finally achieved power in 2001, he was 73 years old, grossly overweight and in a great hurry to complete his life's work. He would complete the seventh and last stage of *nishul*. By a stroke of wild luck his rise to power coincided with that of George W. Bush, a close friend whom he had hosted on a personal trip to Israel in 1998, one of Bush's two trips abroad before he became President. Many of the neo-cons who came to power with Bush were Jews who had long voiced their view that Israel occupied a central role in the creation of American Empire, most notably in the position paper *A Clean Break* (Halper 2005b). Sharon knew them all well and, as a whole, they all shared a common agenda.

And then there was 9/11. Suddenly it all came together. Israel's and America's agendas were one in the same, the "war on terror." No longer was Israel a pet of the neo-cons in their project for American Empire; it was clear the two countries had become strategic allies. Sharon lost not a minute in exploiting 9/11 to demonize Arafat. "Arafat is our Bin Laden," he told Colin Powell immediately after the attack. He attempted, with some success, to create in the public mind, the association Arafat = Hamas = Hizbollah = Bin Laden = Taliban = Saddam Hussein = the Chechneyan rebels—and so on and so on, with the French being thrown into the pot somewhere down the line. Bin Laden contributed his bit as well, declaring in an October 2001 broadcast that "Without peace in Palestine, there will be no peace for America."

Sharon, who had long avoided a permanent solution because he believed that *nishul* would never be accepted by the US, now had a change of heart. Israel could actually win; Zionism's century-long campaign of *nishul* could finally be completed, albeit at the price of a Palestinian bantustan. But he had no time to lose. Four decisive actions would complete his life's work. First, he had to break the Palestinians' ability to resist. They had to be broken, "put in their place," all as Jabotinsky's program of the Iron Wall had dictated. Second, he had to put the final touches on the Matrix of Control, the "Separation Barrier" being the final element. Third, formal

American approval of his cantonization plan had to be secured, after which, fourth, nothing remained but to implement it. And, of course, it all had to be unilateral—or rather, bilateral, with the US as a full partner.

Stage I: Defeating the Palestinians Once and For All

A start had already been made in breaking Palestinian resistance by Sharon's visit to the Haram/Temple Mount on September 28, 2000, which triggered the second Intifada and paved his way to the Premiership. Despite Barak's accusing Arafat of "consciously turning to terror," Sharon was only the trigger and Arafat, far from being the instigator, was actually one of its targets. Frustrations had been for a long time over the Oslo "process," and fears had risen among Palestinians that Israel and the US would succeed in pressuring Arafat to sign the Camp David "agreement" formalizing Israeli control over the Occupied Territories (in the three months following Camp David, the sides met 52 times). The message of the Intifada was clear: "You do not sign Camp David." Indeed, the second Intifada took on the proportions of a full-scale struggle for independence. It spelled the final rejection by the Palestinian people of the Oslo peace process. It also afforded Arafat an opportunity to break out of the Oslo trap. Facing mass rebellion from his own people, he could insist on new frameworks of negotiations that would better advance the Palestinian cause, frameworks in which international law, human rights covenants and UN resolutions played a more significant role. Rather than leaving the process in exclusively American hands given their clear bias towards Israel, the Palestinians sought to internationalize the peace process by bringing in the Europeans, the Arab world, the UN, even the Russians.

The uprising broke Arafat out of the dead-end peace process, but he failed to capitalize on it. The "non-negotiations" of Taba soon followed, then Sharon's landslide election.

Nothing shows more starkly Sharon's intention to break Palestinian resistance than his ferocious response to the uprising, vastly disproportionate to the actual threat. In the first five days of the Intifada, before a single shot had been fired at an Israeli soldier, the army poured more than a million projectiles— from bullets to artillery shells to laser-guided missiles—into the civilian centers of the Occupied Territories. Such massive firepower against unarmed civilians from helicopter gunships, fighter planes, naval vessels, tanks, artillery and snipers, which resulted in the deaths of more than 170 Palestinians and some 7,000 wounded.

Such a massive onslaught cannot be explained by security. Sharon was reasserting Israeli authority. The "land for peace" formula of Oslo had led the Palestinians to believe they might actually wean from Israel significant parts of its ancient homeland, perhaps even "a PLO state." Worse, Oslo had given the Palestinians the feeling that they were truly "partners" in negotiations, that Israel in fact recognized them as a "side." As a first step in pacification, they had to be disabused of those notions. The challenge to Israeli hegemony had to be confronted, put down with resolute force, before "the Arabs" got it into their head that they had any legitimate claim to our land or were in fact our equal partners. Sharon was fond of saying he would beat the Palestinians "until they got the message." What was the message? *This is our land. It is our prerogative to decide if we will relinquish any parts of it, how much, to whom and under what conditions.* The Palestinians had to be shown the price for having the gall to say "no" to an Israeli dictate at Camp David. They had to be put in their place, lest Israel lose control. "Destroying the infrastructure of terrorism," the slogan of the repression campaign, actually meant destroying any resistance to the Occupation.

Israel began its unrestrained onslaught on the Palestinian areas in October 2001, a campaign that reached its climax, though certainly not its conclusion, in Operation Defensive

Shield in March, 2002. The most infamous part of the operation was the invasion and almost complete demolition of the Jenin refugee camp, where our friend the D-9 bulldozer driver Moshe Nissim just "erased and erased" for three consecutive days. But Israel reoccupied the entire West Bank in a rampage of destruction that left every Palestinian city smoldering. A fleet of D-9s, each equipped with huge hooks at the back that could be driven deep into the pavement, ripped up entire urban infra-structures as Nissim's compatriots drove them up and down the city streets. Gaza, as usual, suffered massive bombardment.

Just how divorced these wanton acts of destruction were from "security" and how much they were intended to transmit a "message" is graphically illustrated in the account of Amira Hass (*Ha'aretz*, May 6, 2002), who lives in Ramallah.

> No one deluded himself that the Palestinian Ministry of Culture, which takes up five of the eight floors of a new building in the center of El Bireh, would be spared the fate of other Palestinian Authority offices in Ramallah and other cities—that is, the nearly total destruction of its contents and particularly its high-tech equipment....On the evening of Wednesday, May 1, when the siege on Arafat's headquarters was lifted and the armored vehicles and the tanks had rumbled out, the executives and officials of the ministry who had rushed to the site did not expect to find the building the way they had left it. But what awaited them was beyond all their fears, and also shocked representatives and cultural attaches of foreign consulates, who toured the site the next day....
>
> In other offices, all the high-tech and electronic equipment had been wrecked or had vanished—computers, photocopiers, cameras, scanners, hard disks, editing equipment worth thousands of dollars, television sets....In every room of the various departments—literature, film, culture for children and youth books, discs, pamphlets and documents were piled up, soiled with urine and excrement. There are two toilets on every floor, but the soldiers urinated and defecated everywhere else in the building, in several rooms of which they had lived for about a month. They did their business on the floors, in emptied flowerpots, even in drawers they had pulled out of desks. They defecated into plastic bags, and

these were scattered in several places. Some of them had burst. Someone even managed to defecate into a photocopier....

More than anything else, it was not the destruction of the "terrorist infrastructure" but of the Palestinian civil infrastructure that stood out—houses, roads and physical infrastructure, of course, but also the institutional infrastructure such as the data banks of the government ministries. "These are the data banks developed in Palestinian Authority institutions like the Education Ministry, the Higher Education Ministry and the Health Ministry," writes Hass. "These are the data banks of the non-governmental organizations and research institutes devoted to developing a modern health system, modern agricultural, environmental protection and water conservation. These are the data banks of human rights organizations, banks and private commercial enterprises, infirmaries, and supermarkets."

Operation Defensive Shield marked the start of the dismantling of Arafat's authority to govern. His headquarters in Ramallah, the Muqatta, was leveled to the ground by the D-9s. Only a small compound, just a room or two, was spared; it was here that Arafat was imprisoned by Sharon for the last years of his life. April 9, the day the Jenin refugee camp fell to Israeli forces, was called by the Israeli newspaper *Kol Ha'ir* "the first day of apartheid." *Ha'aretz* (October 25, 2002) recognized Sharon's goal of "laying waste to the Palestinian Authority, reinstating full Israeli control of the kind that existed before the first Intifada, and reaching an imposed settlement with obedient canton administrators [or collaborators]." "Constructive destruction" was the Orwellian term the military commanders used to describe their actions.

Over time the military campaign took the form of a campaign of attrition directed against a civilian population and intended to erode the Palestinians' ability to resist the Occupation altogether. The closure was sealed hermetically, exacerbating the already chronic poverty induced by years of restrictions. A military siege was imposed and every Palestinian city, town and village subjected to frequent and prolonged curfews, and midnight raids. Earthen mounds or concrete blocks sealed every entrance and exit. The permit system was tightened and hundreds of checkpoints erected where people would be forced to wait for hours going from home to school, home to work, home to shopping, home to visit friends—and back. Harassment became so common, including the practice of preventing pregnant women or chronically sick people from reaching medical services, that a group of Israeli women organized MachsomWatch, Checkpoint Watch, to monitor the soldiers' behavior. Thousands of acres of farmland and olive groves were cleared for "security" reasons (the formal phrase was "shaving") and, during the first four years of the Intifada, some 5,000 Palestinian homes and businesses were demolished. All this induced a mass emigration of middle-class families, which B'tselem (1997), the Israeli human rights organization, called a "quiet transfer."

Stage II: Completing the Matrix of Control

The second Intifada proffered Sharon a unique opportunity to advance his plan of canonization. Despite initial reservations, the Separation Barrier represented the final element in his Matrix of Control. It was now virtually completed. Israel now had all the land, settlements and settlers it needed. Its bypass road system was almost finished and the settlement blocs defined. Settlement construction continued apace, of course. It never hurt to add additional "security nails" to the coffin of a viable Palestinian state. But so did the infrastructure of apartheid. In September 2004, the government unveiled a plan to construct an $80 million network of Palestinian-only highways, including 16 passages, bridges or tunnels that give the Palestinians "transportational" if not territorial contiguity, complementing its network of Israeli highways to the settlement blocs.

The "facts on the ground" were more or less in place. Moving from that level to a permanent political "solution" based on unilateral separation and Sharon's cantonization plan could prove tricky, however. How could Israel pursue such a plan while still pretending to negotiate with the Palestinians, as the international community expected? Since the Palestinians were not going to cooperate in their own disenfranchisement, how could cantonization be imposed without seeming to be imposed? Most important, how could Israel's plans be coordinated with the United States, whose approval was crucial. Sharon himself is absolutely clear on this point: "The unilateral steps that Israel will take in the framework of the disengagement plan will be fully coordinated with the United States," he declared at the Herzliya Conference in 2005. "We must not harm our strategic coordination with the United States."

Stage III: Getting American Approval for the Annexation of the Settlement Blocs

At this stage the international community gave Sharon a vehicle for reconciling the two-state solution with his own plan of cantonization: the Road Map announced by an extremely reluctant George W. Bush in March 2003, after some arm-twisting by Tony Blair and other members of the "Quartet"—Europe, the UN and Russia. Taken at face value, the Road Map contained some hopeful elements. Its "end-game" is far more concrete than Oslo's. Overall, it called for a negotiated agreement leading to a final and comprehensive settlement of the Israel-Palestinian conflict (by 2005), including issues of borders, Jerusalem, refugees, settlements, and a comprehensive agreement among Israel, Lebanon and Syria. The Road Map went so far as to use, for the first time in an international document, the "O" word; much to Israel's consternation it called explicitly for an end to the Occupation. It also used another key word, "viable," to describe the independent, democratic Palestinian state that would emerge side by side in peace and security with Israel. If applied conscientiously, the proviso that the Palestinian state had to be viable anticipated and foreclosed the possibility of a non-viable bantustan.

Sharon's government could not very well oppose the Road Map since the other Quartet members had cleverly inserted an unwilling Bush as the initiative's "sponsor," but it was appalled. Its pro forma acceptance of the plan was accompanied by 14 "reservations" that either made it impossible to implement or emasculated it completely (see Appendix 2). Still, everyone knew that the Road Map was a dead letter even before it was issued. What was important was to "go with the flow." Israel would accept the two-state solution that the international community obviously envisioned and would couch its various initiatives carefully within the Road Map's parameters. The goal, however, would remain the same: an expanded Israel over a dependent and truncated Palestinian mini-state.

But how could this be done? In a certain sense "separation" had been the concept of the Matrix of Control all along. As the policy of *nishul* shifted after 1948 from expulsion of Palestinians to their containment in defined enclaves, so, too, did Sharon's thinking shift to conceiving of a cantonized Palestinian state separated from a greater Israel yet posing no challenge to its control of the entire country as the most do-able form of *nishul*. If we couldn't complete 1948 and actually transfer the Arabs of the Occupied Territories out of the country, at least we could isolate and neutralize them as we did the Arabs of Israel. "Transfer" remained part of the equation—especially the qualitative, induced transfer of the Palestinian middle classes—but "separation" became the main vehicle of dispossession and permanent Israeli control—all, of course, within the parameters of the Road Map.

"The day he was elected prime minister," relates Arnon Sofer, a geographer at Haifa University and prominent proponent of separation and ethnic transfer,

> Sharon asked me to bring him a [disengagement] map I published in 2001....Look, these demographics are facts. The world is going insane. Islam is going wild. There is going to be a clash of civilizations. In the Middle East, there is going to be the highest Arab birth rate in the world. There cannot be peace....This is why I keep saying that in order to save the State of Israel, we will have to separate unilaterally, and as quickly as possible....Unilateral separation does not guarantee "peace"—it guarantees a Zionist-Jewish state with an overwhelming majority of Jews. (quoted in the *Jerusalem Post, Up Front* magazine, May 21, 2004, pp. 8–9)

Sofer's point about demography spoke powerfully to Sharon. Polls showed that this was precisely what two-thirds of the Jewish population of Israel desired. Barak himself had made his electoral slogan: "Us here, them there." Separation also dovetailed with Netanyahu's formula "autonomy-plus, state-minus." With a little creative tinkering, it could be neatly folded into the Road Map's two-state solution.

Sharon faced the same dilemma as the architects of South African apartheid: how to maintain an ethnocracy with maximal territorial claims, yet having to allow for an inassimilable national entity and also remain democratic. Guided by the same logic, he came up with the same solution: a bantustan. So as to preserve itself as a democratic "European" society, South Africa in the 1950s established ten bantustans or "homelands" for the black African majority. Located on only 13 percent of the country and bereft of vital resources, the existence of the bantustans allowed the white South African minority to claim it was a democratic state. It did not have to deny its black citizens the vote, it simply shifted their citizenship to bantustan "states" of their own where, it was claimed, they had all the rights of self-determination. "If our policy is taken to its logical conclusion as far as the black people are concerned," Connie

Mulder, the Minister of Plural Relations and Development, told the South African parliament in 1978:

> there will be not one black man with South African citizenship.... Every black man in South Africa will eventually be accommodated in some independent new state in this honourable way and there will no longer be an obligation on the Parliament to accommodate these people politically. (Wikipedia, "bantustan" entry).

The trick, Sharon saw, would be to present a credible bantustan which would fit the parameters of the Road Map's two-state solution. He was keenly aware that the international community never accepted South Africa's bantustan ruse; none of the artificial, non-viable prison-states were ever recognized—not even by the US or Israel. But Sharon believed he could succeed where South Africa failed. After all, Jewish ethnocracy (Zionism) possesses an international legitimacy that had always been denied to the Afrikaner ethnocracy expressed through apartheid.

To make this work Sharon's had only to shift slightly from the Likud's plan of autonomy over the cantons drawn around Areas A and B—42 percent of a highly truncated West Bank, plus Gaza—to a somewhat larger and more contiguous Palestinian mini-state that *looked good*, that could be sold as a two-state solution. Israel's worry over giving the Palestinians too much territory and sovereignty could be lessened if an expanded "Greater" Israel surrounded the Palestinian bantustan, much as had South Africa its own bantustans. Sharon even found a legalistic term for this system. Instead of "apartheid," former Justice Minister Amnon Rubenstein suggested "enclave-based justice" (Gorali 2003). Since none of this involved a truly viability or sovereign Palestinian state, it would clearly be unacceptable to them. Such a scheme would work only if imposed unilaterally, a workable proposition since Israel had convinced its own people, the US and many in Europe that the Palestinians, unreasonable and violent, were not in fact "partners" for peace.

"Disengagement" is what Sharon would call his new policy, and it would begin in Gaza. In April, 2004, Sharon set out for Washington to seek nothing less than formal recognition by the United States of Israel's hegemony over the entire Land of Israel between the Mediterranean and the Jordan River. He had several options in his pocket of what he would request from Bush, but the latter surprised him by giving him more than Sharon himself could have hoped for. In a letter he had prepared for Sharon, Bush began by the usual niceties and sops to the Quartet:

> Thank you for your letter setting out your disengagement plan....I remain committed to my June 24, 2002 vision of two states living side by side in peace and security as the key to peace, and to the roadmap as the route to get there....
>   The United States appreciates the risks such an undertaking represents. I therefore want to reassure you on several points.... As part of a final peace settlement, Israel must have secure and recognized borders, which should emerge from negotiations between the parties in accordance with UNSC Resolutions 242 and 338.

Bush then cut to the heart of the matter:

> In light of new realities on the ground, including already existing major Israeli populations centers [that is, Israel's major settlement blocs plus "Greater" Jerusalem], *it is unrealistic to expect that the outcome of final status negotiations will be a full and complete return to the armistice lines of 1949*, and all previous efforts to negotiate a two-state solution have reached the same conclusion. (Bush 2004; italics added)

Having recognized de facto Israel's annexation of its major settlement blocs and Greater Jerusalem, Bush then returned to the pro forma mantra dictated by the Quartet, but which has just been emptied of all content:

> It is realistic to expect that any final status agreement will only be achieved on the basis of mutually agreed changes that reflect these realities....As you know, the United States supports the establishment of a Palestinian state that is viable, contiguous,

sovereign, and independent, so that the Palestinian people can build their own future in accordance with my vision set forth in June 2002 and with the path set forth in the roadmap.

The United States understands that after Israel withdraws from Gaza and/or parts of the West Bank, and pending agreements on other arrangements, existing arrangements regarding control of airspace, territorial waters, and land passages of the West Bank and Gaza will continue.

This sharp turn in American foreign policy represented more than simply a strengthening of the traditional pro-Israel line or even a renunciation of the Road Map—supposedly Bush's own initiative. It constituted a renunciation of the very post-Second World War international system based upon the premise of the illegitimacy of the expansion of a country's territory by military force (Zunes 2004). In one fell swoop the US nullified UN Resolutions 242 and 338, the principle of "land for peace," the very basis of the two-state solution, rendering the notion of a viable Palestinian state as redundant as the Road Map itself. All previous US administrations of both parties had considered these resolutions the only working basis for Arab-Israeli peace. So, too, did the wider international community. The other three members of the Road Map Quartet (Europe, Russia and the UN) were understandably outraged at this unilateral transfer of Palestinian territory to Israel by the US, as were the Palestinians.

Yet this fundamental shift in American policy went far beyond the policies of one particular Administration. A little more than two months later, on June 23, the US House of Representatives, in an act that went almost unnoticed by the media and the public, passed Resolution 460 endorsing, by a vote of 407–9, the Sharon–Bush exchange. Although Bush's letter gave only brief nods to Palestinian aspirations of independence, the Congressional resolution edited it in a way that expressed total support for Israel at the expense of the Palestinians, eliminating any reference to a negotiated settlement or to a "viable, contiguous, sovereign, and independent Palestinian state" as specified by the Road Map. The almost unanimous vote revealed how deep bi-partisan support for Israel was in Congress. The next day the Senate passed a similar resolution (S Resolution 393) by a vote of 95–3.

Sharon, as might be expected, called the vote supporting the Bush letter one of the greatest diplomatic achievements in Israel's history. "This is a great day in the history of Israel," he told a meeting at the ruling Likud party headquarters in Tel Aviv. "The bi-partisan Congressional support for the President's letter and the State of Israel is without a doubt one of the most important diplomatic achievements for Israel since its creation." In one bold diplomatic move, then, Sharon transformed the Occupation from a temporary military situation into a permanent political fact recognized by both the executive and legislative branches of its greatest benefactor, the United States.

Stage IV: Implementation of the Cantonization Plan

In late December 2003, Sharon launched what has been called in Israel "the maneuver of the century." He unveiled a plan for "disengagement" from the Palestinians, beginning in Gaza and in an isolated corner of the West Bank. How this fit into his broader political aims was clearly laid out in his December 16, 2004, speech to the Herzliya Conference. Sharon said:

> Disengagement recognizes the demographic reality on the ground specifically, bravely and honestly. Of course it is clear to everyone that we will not be in the Gaza Strip in the final agreement. This recognition, that we will not be in Gaza, and that, even now, we have no reason to be there, does not divide the people and is not tearing us apart, as the opposing minority claim. Rather, the opposite is true. Disengagement from Gaza is uniting the people. It is uniting us in distinguishing between goals which deserve to be fought for, since they are truly in our souls—such as Jerusalem, the large settlement blocs, the security zones and maintaining Israel's character as a Jewish state—rather than goals where it is

clear to all of us that they will not be realized, and that most of the public is not ready, justifiably, to sacrifice so much for.

The thinking behind disengagement was candidly laid out by Dov Weisglass, the head of Sharon's office ("The Big Freeze," *Ha'aretz* magazine, October 8, 2004):

> *[Interviewer]: If you have American backing and you have the principle of the road map, why go to disengagement?*

> [Weisglass]: Because in the fall of 2003 we understood that everything is stuck. And even though according to the Americans' reading of the situation, the blame fell on the Palestinians and not on us, Arik [Sharon's nickname] grasped that this state of affairs would not last. That they wouldn't leave us alone, wouldn't get off our case. Time was not on our side. There was international erosion, internal erosion....

> *I still don't see how the disengagement plan helps here. What was the major importance of the plan from your point of view?*

> The disengagement plan is the preservative of the sequence principle. It is the bottle of formaldehyde within which you place the president's formula so that it will be preserved for a very lengthy period. The disengagement is actually formaldehyde. It supplies the amount of formaldehyde that's necessary so that there will not be a political process with the Palestinians.

> *Is what you are saying, then, is that you exchanged the strategy of a long-term interim agreement for a strategy of long-term interim situation?*

> The American term is to park conveniently. The disengagement plan makes it possible for Israel to park conveniently in an interim situation that distances us as far as possible from political pressure. It legitimizes our contention that there is no negotiating with the Palestinians. There is a decision here to do the minimum possible in order to maintain our political situation. The decision is proving itself. It is making it possible for the Americans to go to the seething and simmering international community and say to them, "What do you want." It also transfers the initiative to our hands. It compels the world to deal with our idea, with the scenario we wrote....

*I want to remind you that there will also be a withdrawal in the
West Bank.*

The withdrawal in Samaria is a token one. We agreed to it only so
it wouldn't be said that we concluded our obligation in Gaza....
The political process is the evacuation of settlements, it's the
return of refugees, it's the partition of Jerusalem. And all that
has now been frozen.

But why not let Sharon speak for himself? On May 24, 2005,
he addressed a gala American–Israeli Public Affairs Committee
(AIPAC) gathering in New York. Among the adulatory guests
were more than half the members of Congress, Senators and
Representatives alike. The guest of honor was no less than
Secretary of State Condoleezza Rice. At that gathering, for all
to hear, Sharon made his Likud–Labor government's position
crystal-clear: "It is thanks to disengagement," he said, "that
we can make certain that there will be no entry of Palestinian
refugees into Israel. In addition, the major Israeli population
centers in Judea and Samaria will remain an integral part of the
State of Israel and will have territorial contiguity with Israel
in any final status agreement..." (Israeli Ministry of Foreign
Affairs website <www.mfa.gov.il>, May 24, 2005).

All was going extremely well when fate intervened. Sharon
was on his way to an easy victory in the March, 2006,
elections when, on January 4, he suffered a major stroke that
incapacitated him. Ehud Olmert, Sharon's Vice-Premier and
mouthpiece, took over Sharon's political vehicle, the newly-
created Kadima party, and was elected by a very modest
plurality to succeed him as Prime Minister. Olmert took as his
government's central objective Sharon's desire to "nail down"
a permanent solution, an end of the Occupation based on the
notion of cantonization. Any major political initiative in this
direction would have to be unilateral, of course, since Israel
had nothing of meaning to offer the Palestinians. But lacking
Sharon's stature and clout, Olmert realized that in order to sell
a plan of unilateral separation to the international community

he would have to make it look attractive—he would have to give up more territory than he would like, perhaps even 85 percent of the West Bank, Gaza and sovereignty over small parts of East Jerusalem. This was the birth of his "Convergence Plan," which Olmert was invited to present before a joint session of the American Congress in May, 2006.

In the Convergence Plan, the main elements of all the major Israeli attempts to gain control over the Land of Israel while separating from its Palestinian population comes to fruition, harking back to the Allon Plan of 1967 and including Begin's notion of Palestinian "autonomy," Sharon's scheme of cantonization, the Matrix of Control, the Oslo process (and particularly Barak's version of it), Netanyahu's "autonomy-plus, state-minus" formula and Sharon's later plan of unilateral separation. In it a Greater Jerusalem and the settlement blocs—in which 80 percent of Israel's settlers live and into which the rest will be "converged"—are annexed to Israel and a Palestinian state is sandwiched between Israel's *two* eastern borders: its "demographic border" delineating the settlement blocs from the Palestinian areas, and its "security border" along the Jordan Valley. As always, the Palestinians are "given" a truncated territory with little developmental potential and only semi-sovereignty.

The one major hitch Olmert's plan encountered was its unilateralism, which contradicts the Road Map principle that a solution must be negotiated between the parties. Olmert, who is fast on his feet, came up with a quick twist: just switch from "convergence" to "realignment." In Olmert's new formulation, Israel is merely "realigning" its borders in an "interim" manner that conforms to Phase II of the Road Map. The Palestinians get their state, albeit a "transitional" state with "provisional borders." And that's where we stay forever. De facto convergence in Road Map clothing (see Map 5, p. xvi). This, of course, is the Palestinians' greatest fear, that the Road Map gets "stuck" in Phase II and never gets to

Phase III, an "independent, democratic, and viable Palestinian state." De facto for Israel means permanent. In the meantime, Olmert's Foreign Minister Tzipi Livni is working quietly with Condoleezza Rice on a plan to replace Phase I of the Road Map, which requires Israel to end violence on its part, freeze settlement activity and improve humanitarian conditions among the Palestinians, including freedom of movement and an end to house demolitions), with Phase II. If Israel can finesse a "transitional" Palestinian state while keeping its settlement blocs, Greater Jerusalem, control of the borders, Palestinian movement, air space, the electromagnetic sphere, water and the economy, plus maintaining complete military control, it has won. The Occupation, it can proclaim, is over. The two-state solution has been obtained (with a few details to work out, when the Palestinians stop being terrorists). The conflict is, from Israel's point of view—and perhaps that of the US as well—settled.

Oh yeah, the Arab League Initiative calling for a genuine two-state solution and a return of refugees on a mutually agreed-upon basis. As of this writing it does not seem to be going far. It can be viewed, in my opinion, as pap for the Arab/Muslim Street. In that Israel and the Arab world share some basic foreign policy concerns—Iran and Islamic fundamentalism in particular—the Initiative might eventually be used as a mechanism of "compromise" that could offer the Palestinians a face-saving "solution" without seriously undermining Israel's plans of *nishul* and control. This, perhaps, is the task Tony Blair will pursue as the Quartet's new Middle East envoy.

Part IV

Overcoming Oppression

8
Redeeming Israel

[W]hen 2.5 million people live in a closed-off Gaza, it's going to be a human catastrophe. Those people will become even bigger animals than they are today, with the aid of an insane fundamentalist Islam. The pressure at the border will be awful. It's going to be a terrible war. So, if we want to remain alive, we will have to kill and kill and kill. All day, every day. If we don't kill, we will cease to exist. The only thing that concerns me is how to ensure that the boys and men who are going to have to do the killing will be able to return home to their families and be normal human beings.

—Arnon Sofer, Professor of Geography at Haifa University, father of Sharon's "separation plan," quoted in the *Jerusalem Post*, *Up Front* magazine, May 21, 2004, p. 9)

The present historical moment finds us in Palestine/Israel at a fateful crossroads. From the point of view of Israel's political leadership, Israel has won its century-old conflict with the Palestinians. Surveying the landscape—physical and political alike—they can feel a great deal of satisfaction. Begin's charge to Sharon in 1977 has been fulfilled. The settlement project, part of the larger Matrix of Control, ensures permanent Israeli control over the entire Land of Israel. True, Israel has had to adjust its policy from autonomy, foreclosing a Palestinian state altogether, to autonomy-plus, state-minus, a Palestinian bantustan. But the "facts on the ground" are in place, American permission to annex the settlement blocs has been obtained while the Europeans remain passive, and the Separation Barrier effectively constitutes Israel's expanded border. All that remains is the political act that transforms the Occupation into a permanent political reality. Whether it is Olmert's convergence plan, the Livni-Rice process or some other initiative to be undertaken in the future, who cares? The status quo only serves the de facto: Israel's control will only grow and deepen. So if implementation of some peace plan is delayed for a year, a decade or another 40 years—so what? For Israel, the status quo is just as good as a peace agreement— maybe better, since Israel need make no concessions at all.

The Palestinians, now constituted as a Palestinian Authority, have been rendered irrelevant. Its "moderates" have little role but to police Israel's war against terrorism and, at some point, submit to an Israeli-dictated reality; its elected government is boycotted by the international community. Having moved in the 1980s from a one-state solution to a two-state one, it has watched as the prospective Palestinian state disappeared under the expanding grid of settlements, infrastructure and the Barrier. In light of an unspoken agreement among the Western states that control the Security Council, EU policy and global politics as a whole that Israeli hegemony and its settlement project will remain intact, if slightly modified in the interest of a "peace agreement," the Palestinians have little hope of a just and adequate solution.

But can Israel really win? Can MEASE—a Militarily-Enforced A-Symmetrical Equilibrium—really replace peace in the long term? Israel might succeed, with some creative manipulation, in preserving the status quo for the foreseeable future (even as I write these lines—August 16, 2007—*Ha'aretz* is reporting: "Israel to promote 'economic horizon' for future Palestinian state"). But assuming (as Israel does not) that national conflict, occupation and oppression cannot be normalized and that a conflict cannot truly be ended unless its underlying causes are addressed, Israel will be unable in the long term to transform its Matrix of Control into a stable, peaceful state of affairs. Gandhi once said:

How can one be compelled to accept slavery? I simply refuse to do the master's bidding. He may torture me, break my bones to atoms and even kill me. He will then have my dead body, not my obedience. Ultimately, therefore, it is I who am the victor and not he, for he has failed in getting me to do what he wanted done. Non-cooperation is directed not against...the Governors, but against the system they administer. The roots of non-cooperation lie not in hatred but in justice.

Oppressed peoples may appear weak and defeated, but they have one source of leverage: the power to say no.

For the Palestinians *are* a side to this conflict and they refuse to be sidelined. The election of Hamas did not have to do only with issues of Fatah weakness and corruption; many people voted Hamas (44 percent) who did not want an Islamic state and did not share the Hamas ideology (*New York Times*, February 14, 2006). It was an act, above all, of non-cooperation, perhaps the most powerful means of non-violent resistance the oppressed have when all other avenues to achieve their freedom and rights have been closed. It is to the international community and, yes, Israel and Fatah as well, that the Palestinians carried their message: "To hell with all of you!"

To hell with the international community who rejected the Palestinians' appeal to international law and human rights conventions. Had only the Fourth Geneva Convention been applied, Israel could never have constructed its Occupation in the first place. Even when Israel's construction of the "Separation Barrier" was ruled illegal by the International Court of Justice in The Hague and its ruling ratified by the General Assembly, nothing was done to stop it.

To hell with the United States who nullified negotiations as an avenue for redressing Palestinian rights and for enabling Israel to make its Occupation permanent. The US had never been an honest broker, but when it reclassified the Palestinian areas from "occupied" to "disputed" at the very start of the Oslo peace process it removed international law as the basis of negotiations, thus pulling the rug out from under the Palestinians. Once, due to American interference, power became the only basis of negotiations, Israel easily overwhelmed the Palestinians. Until today Palestinians have nothing to look for in negotiations. American support for Israeli unilateralism, with its frequent use of the veto (42 as of the end of 2006, in *every* case the US casting the lone veto), has effectively neutralized the UN as an avenue of redress. And to hell with the Europeans, who refuse to take a position at odds with the US.

To hell with Israel who eliminated any possibility of a viable Palestinian state by expanding its Matrix of Control deep into the Palestinian areas, making a mockery of its protestations of seeking "peace."

And to hell with Fatah who, besides its corruption, failed to effectively pursue the Palestinians' national agenda of self-determination.

Indeed, the vote for Hamas, rather than a rejection of a *just* peace, represented an emotional but also rational, intentional and powerful statement of non-cooperation in a political process that is only leading to Palestinian imprisonment. Hamas, if anything, stands for steadfastness, *sumud*, the refusal to submit, as well as active resistance to oppression. Knowing that the conflict is in the end too destabilizing for the global system to tolerate, even if it only festers, the Palestinians are saying: You can all impose upon us an apartheid system, blame us for the violence while ignoring Israeli State Terror, pursue your programs of American Empire or your notions of a "clash of civilizations." We will not submit. We will not cooperate. We will not play your rigged game. In the end, for all your power, you will come to us to sue for peace. And then we will be ready for a just peace that respects the rights of all the peoples of the region, including the Israelis. But you will not beat us. Israel may have defeated the Arab armies in only six days, yet now, after 40 years of occupation and repression, it has failed to suppress our struggle for freedom.

The Palestinians have not rejected a negotiated settlement. The need to reach national consensus *vis-à-vis* the conflict, made all the more urgent by Hamas's refusal to recognize Israel and thus by its exclusion from the political process, found expression in what was called the Prisoners' National Conciliation Document. Formulated by Palestinian prisoners in Israeli prisons of all ideological stripes, the document demonstrates that seeking a political resolution of the conflict with Israel is a goal of all the various factions—and that, in fact, a common political position can be agreed upon. The Prisoners' Document sets out the basic principles which, for Palestinians, form the foundation of any acceptable peace process:

> The Palestinian people in the homeland and in the Diaspora seek and struggle to liberate their land and remove the settlements;... to achieve their right to freedom, return and independence and to exercise their right to self-determination, including the right to establish their independent state with al-Quds al-Shareef [Jerusalem] as its capital on all territories occupied in 1967, and to secure the right of return for refugees to their homes and properties from which they were evicted, or to compensate them....All of this is based on the historical right of our people on the land of our forefathers and based on the UN Charter and international law and legitimacy....

Until Israel and the international community hear their voice, yet another element of non-cooperation—attrition—will accompany steadfastness and resistance as the Palestinians' strategy for overcoming oppression. The conflict will continue until the Israelis realize they cannot prevail by force, by their massive "facts on the ground," even by skillful international diplomacy. In the end, the cost of maintaining the Occupation will become unacceptable, if not to Israel then to the Western powers who support it at the cost of global instability and polarization. For the Palestinians possess one "weapon" that cannot be defeated: their position as gatekeepers. The

Israel-Palestine conflict has become emblematic in the Muslim world; it captures precisely the neo-colonialism, the militarily-enforced economic domination of the West and the humiliation to which the Arab and Muslim worlds are reacting. Until the Palestinians signal the wider Arab, Muslim and international communities that they have reached a satisfactory political accommodation with Israel, the conflict will continue and the "clash of civilizations" will become ever more sharp.

AN ETHNOCRACY CANNOT MAKE PEACE

At bottom, this book has argued that an ethnocracy like Israel can never come to terms with those it must oppress. Since the Occupation is only the expression of a much deeper problem of exclusivity generated by Jewish ethno-nationalism, I contend that a solution to the Israeli-Palestinian conflict will have to involve a reconceptualization of Israel as a democratic state of all its citizens before it can reach a political structure that addresses the needs of the Palestinians, both within Israel as well as in the Occupied Territories, a solution that will then permit genuine reconciliation and actually end the conflict.

But what of the Jews' right to self-determination? Why should the Palestinians have a right to a state of their own and not the Jews? Let's leave aside the problemic fact that two-thirds of the world's Jews chose to remain ethnic or religious members of the countries in which they have citizenship and not to exercise their national right for self-determination. (I was an exception: only 1 percent of American Jews, 60,000 out of 600,000, chose to settle in Israel; the vast majority religious. In fact, when I told my grandmother I was moving to Israel, she replied: "Are you crazy? Israel is no place for a Jewish boy!")

The question is not to do Jews have a right to self-determination—having immigrated to Israel, I obviously believe they do—but what exactly is the "nation" that claims self-determination? Is it the ethno-nation that claims ownership over the country, or the people, *all* the people, who inhabit it? The essential difference between the civil national of Western Europe and the tribal nationalism of Eastern Europe from whence Zionism arose is this: from the time of the American and French Revolutions, Western countries shifted their definition of "national" from a particular people to the country as a whole, represented by the state and its citizens. In 1919, when asked at the Versailles Conference how he understood the phrase "a national home for the Jewish people" as found in the Balfour Declaration, Haim Weizmann, the head of the Zionist delegation and later the first President of Israel, answered: "the country [Palestine] should be Jewish in the same way that France is French and Britain is British" (Segev 1999:117). When he said that, probably 98 percent or more of the "English" were of the traditional white "English stock" and culture. But look at what has happened to England. As a democracy it has accepted millions of immigrants from all over the world and granted them British citizenship. This has not happened without problems. Many "true" English people are upset. But it happened. "English" might still refer to a people but "Great Britain" is a country whose self-determination is defined by its citizenry and not by ethnic or religious background.

This is not the case in Eastern Europe where, as the ethnic cleansing of "Greater" Serbia demonstrates, national self-determination is determined by one's ethnicity. As an Eastern European ethnocracy Israel could not go where Britain did. The Law of Return granting automatic citizenship to Jews, together with denying Palestinian refugees the Right of Return, could not happen in Britain or France, despite the irredentist racism of Le Pen that is found in every country. For self-determination in a tribal sense is no longer sustainable, especially in a world of migration and inescapable pluralism. The Jews do have national rights of self-determination, but they have to be balanced with the rights of the 25–30 percent of Israelis who are not Jewish, not to mention the Palestinians of the West Bank. Jewish national self-determination can take the form of Cultural Zionism, infusing Israeli culture with the Hebrew language, a rich Israeli-Jewish literature, a Hebrew University, a national museum of Zionism and the like.

There's one more option. If it insists on an ethnically-based national identity yet nevertheless seeks to truly end the conflict, a Zionist Israel could suggest to the Palestinians a bi-national state in which a significant amount of ethno-national autonomy is retained within a common state framework. The one-state solution, as it is called, could work, although the history of bi-national/religious states—Lebanon, for example, or Sri Lanka or even Belgium and Canada—is not a happy one. As of this writing, Israel as a "Jewish state" is firmly committed to an ethnocratic rather than democratic or bi-national model. Weizmann was wrong. Israel cannot be compared to France or Britain. And that is the crux of the problem.

Israel must decide between an exclusively ethnic/religious form of self-determination or cultural self-determination for Jews, Palestinians and others within either a democratic or a bi-national country. And upon this choice, I would submit, genuine peace and reconciliation between Israeli Jews and Palestinians depends. Israel as a Western democracy—which is how it perceives and present itself, after all—or as a bi-national entity could find a wide range of political options to end the conflict: two democratic states, one democratic or bi-national state, a regional confederation or some other arrangement. None of these options threaten the *cultural* self-determination of Jewish Israelis. On the contrary, if Israeli Jews aspire to return to the Middle East, the hearth of their civilization, which was a cardinal principle of Zionism, then any system that helps them integrate with the peoples of the region *as a people* can only be good. If, however, Israel continues as a tribal ethnocracy asserting exclusive claim to the whole Land of Israel, conflict with the "non-Jews" of the country, including Palestinians who claim self-determination of their own, is inevitable, endemic and interminable.

Meron Benvenisti (*Ha'aretz*, August 6, 2003) wrote eloquently of a state belonging to all the inhabitants of the Land of Israel/Palestine:

> In the past year, then, I reached the conclusion that there is no choice but to think in new terms. The seemingly rational solution of two states for two nations can't work here. The model of a division into two nation-states is inapplicable. You can erect all the walls in the world here but you won't be able to overcome the fact that there is only one aquifer here and the same air and that all the streams run into the same sea. You won't be able to overcome the fact that this country will not tolerate a border in its midst. This is a country in which the Arabs are the landscape, the natives. So I am not afraid of them. I don't see myself living here without them. In my eyes, without Arabs this is a barren land....There is no choice but to think about western Palestine [the Land of Israel] as one geopolitical unit.

Interestingly, the Palestinians, who have been fighting since the First World War for a state of their own, do not link their notion of self-determination to an ethno-nationalism. Over the years they have embraced every option offered them—one state, either democratic or bi-national (which still seems the preference of the majority) or two. Only Hamas advocates for a Palestinian—or more precisely, a pan-Muslim—religious ethnocracy (a "religiocracy"?). The fact that this concept is rejected with disgust by Israel, the US, Europe and the international community that today boycotts the Hamas government should demonstrate that ethnocracies are not acceptable forms of state in the modern world. But the double-standard is intolerable. If a religio-ethnocracy is denied the Palestinians, a religio-ethnocracy should be denied the Jews as well.

ELEMENTS OF A SOLUTION

So where does all this leave us? I don't have a solution to sell. I could live with most of the solutions that have arisen over the years. It seems to be that the problem is not this technical arrangement or that, but sincerely confronting the issues underlying the conflict. What I do have to offer is an *approach* based upon those elements indispensable to *any* particular solution to the Israeli-Palestinian conflict. They would seem to be these:

1. *National expression for the two peoples.* The Israel-Palestine conflict concerns two peoples, two nations in the political sense, each of which claims the collective right of self-determination in the same country. This is what gives such compelling logic to the two-state solution, but it is an essential element in the formulation of any other approach, including a bi-national one-state solution. Within this both the collective and individual rights of all the inhabitants of Palestine/Israel must be defined and guaranteed—a requirement that will require Israel to address the underlying issue of ethnocracy.

2. *Viability.* If we go the way of the two-state solution, the Palestinian state must be viable as well as sovereign. It must control its borders and its basic resources (such as water). It must possess territorial contiguity and, above all, the ability to develop a viable economy. Given the need to resettle, educate, employ and *heal* their refugees and young people, the Palestinians' demand for a *viable* state stems not from intractability but from a sober evaluation of the enormity of the national challenge facing them.

   If a viable Palestinian state proves impossible (as my analysis of Israeli intentions, plus the extent to which the Matrix of Control has been consolidated, indicates is the case), then the requirement of a viable solution must be one that guarantees Palestinian national identity and rights,

which genuinely addresses their national claims within
Israel/Palestine and which offers them an equal share of
the country's resources and equal access to government;
that is, either a unitary democratic state, a bi-national
state or integration within a regional confederation that
allows freedom of movement and employment, as well as
protection of national rights and interests.

3. *Refugees.* Some 80 percent of the Palestinians are refugees.
A sustainable peace cannot emerge from technical
arrangements alone. Beyond self-determination and
viability lies the issue of justice. Any sustainable peace is
dependent upon the just resolution of the refugee issue. The
refugee issue does not seem especially difficult to resolve, as
even the refugees in the camps have indicated. It depends
on a package of three elements: Israel's acknowledgement
of the refugees' *Right* of Return; Israel's acknowledgement
of its responsibility in creating the refugees' plight; and
only then, technical solutions involving a mutually agreed-
upon combination of repatriation, resettlement elsewhere
and compensation.

4. *A regional dimension.* The almost exclusive focus on Israel/
Palestine has obfuscated another crucial dimension of the
conflict: its regional context. Refugees, security, water,
economic development, democratization—none of these
key issues can be effectively addressed within the narrow
confines of Israel/Palestine. Adopting a regional approach,
as we shall see, also opens new possibilities of resolving
the conflict lacking in the more narrow two-state (or even
one-state) approach.

5. *Regional security.* Israel, of course, has fundamental and
legitimate security needs. Unlike Israeli governments,
the Israeli peace camp believes that security cannot be
addressed in isolation, that Israel will not find peace and
security unless it enters into a genuine and just peace with
the Palestinians and achieves a measure of integration into

the Middle East region. The notion that security can be achieved through military means is an illusion. Israel's assertion that the security issue be resolved before any political progress can be made is as illogical as it is self-serving. We know—and the Israeli authorities know, and the Palestinians know—that terrorism is a symptom that can only be addressed as part of a broader approach to the grievances underlying the conflict. Like the US, Israel uses security concerns to advance a political agenda; in our case, to justify repressive force intended to force the Palestinians to submit to an Israeli-controlled bantustan. In fact, given the disproportional number of civilian casualties versus Israeli ones, it would appear that security for the Palestinians, though seldom discussed, is also a key part of the equation.

A RIGHTS-BASED REFRAMING

Progress towards a just peace in Israel/Palestine and the region faces two serious obstacles. One is that the Israeli public has taken itself out of the political equation, having been convinced by its leaders that there is no political solution. The other is the unwillingness of the world's governments, especially those in the West (who also control the UN), to address the conflict in an honest, constructive way. Perhaps this is inevitable, since Israel, a fellow state, belongs to the "club," whereas the Palestinians do not. Having such a powerful ally as Israel is extremely useful, while Israel itself can mobilize significant from within other states, both governmental and influential communities of support. While only the UN and governments have the mandate to actually negotiate and sign treaties, they seldom do the right thing unless prodded by us, the international civil society of non-governmental organizations (NGOs), faith-based organizations, political groups, trade unions and universities, together with activists and intellectuals. It is us who must pave the way in the absence of will on the part of both governments and the Israeli Jewish public.

But we, in turn, face formidable obstacles of our own. First of all, the emotionalism and obfuscation generated by large segments of our own international civil society which simply feeds into the power politics of governments. And then the need to replace polarized us-versus-them discourse with one that is more useful and fair. What we need is to *reframe* the conflict in terms that will lead to a just peace. That reframing cannot be based on preferring one "side" against the other; on the contrary, it will only facilitate a required win–win solution if it is inclusive of the claims, needs and rights of all the parties. The only "neutral" basis for such a reframing is universal human rights and international law.

What would a rights-based framing look like as opposed to the nationalist/security framing of Israel that I laid out in Chapter 3? Let's break it down into the same three parts: conception of rights and claims, the security component and possible solutions. (See Box 1.)

1. *Overall conception of the conflict: how to secure mutual national rights.* In contrast to the Zionist framing in which the Land of Israel belongs exclusively to the Jewish people, any constructive approach to the conflict must begin with the explicit assertion that two peoples reside in Israel/Palestine, each having a collective right to self-determination. Regardless of whether you accept Zionist claims or even Israel itself as a legitimate construct, or whether you recognize the existence of a colonized Palestinian people in its historic homeland, two national groups exist today in Palestine/Israel, and this must be our starting position. How to reconcile their mutually opposing claims to the same territory is the key to a just and lasting solution.

2. *Definition of the problem: security versus occupation and a proactive policy of expansion.*

- Security is a legitimate Israeli concern, but it is not fighting for its existence. Israel's integrity as a state is guaranteed in international law just as that of every other recognized state. The Palestinians, who have formally and repeatedly accepted the two-state solution and have explicitly accepted Israeli sovereignty over 78 percent of the country, also accept Israel's national integrity. In its Saudi Initiative of 2002, on the table until this day, the Arab League also offered Israel formal recognition, peace and regional integration in return for the Occupied Territories. This is this fundamental concession on the part of the Palestinians and the wider Arab world that must be translated into a mutually-accepted political settlement. Until such a settlement is reached, Israel may legitimately maintain its occupation and ensure its security, but only under the constraints of the Fourth Geneva Convention and other relevant laws. It cannot, however, continue to build settlements or civilian infrastructure. And while it has a right to defend its citizens, it can only do so within the constraints of proportionality; it cannot protect its own citizens while harming others. This, and the fact that it intrudes deep into Palestinian territory, is the basis upon which the International Court of Justice in The Hague ruled Israel's Separation Barrier illegal.

Israel's contention that the Palestinians are its permanent enemy must be placed within its colonial perspective. If Israel judges enmity by the refusal to accept Zionism's claims and legitimacy rather than a willingness to enter into a political settlement, then it is true: the Palestinians *are* Israel's permanent enemies. No colonial people can be expected to abrogate their own national rights, to hand over

Box 1: Reframing the Israeli–Palestinian Conflict

The Israeli Security Framing	A Rights-Based Reframing
Conception: Exclusivity	*Conception: Mutual National Rights*
• The Land of Israel belongs exclusively to the Jewish people; there is no other people that has legitimate rights or claims.	• Two peoples reside in Israel/Palestine and each has rights of self-determination.
Definition of the Problem: Security	*Definition of the Problem: A Proactive, Expansionist Occupation*
• Israel is fighting for its existence. The Arabs don't want peace; the Palestinians are our permanent enemies. • Israel's policies are based solely on concerns for security; there is no Occupation. • The underlying problem is Arab terrorism.	• The Palestinians recognize Israeli sovereignty over 78 percent of the country; the Arab world has offered Israel regional integration. • Israel pursues a proactive policy of expansion into the Occupied Territories based on settlement and control. • The problem is Israel's Occupation; Palestinian violence is a symptom of oppression. In human rights language, all attacks on civilians are prohibited, whether from non-state or state actors.
Solution: Win–Lose	*Solution: Win–Win*
• The conflict is a win–lose proposition: either we "win" or "they" do. • Since it is the victim, it is exempt from accountability for its actions. • Any solution must leave Israel in control of the entire country. If Israel allows a Palestinian state to emerge, it will necessarily be truncated, non-viable and semi-sovereign. • The answer to anti-Semitism is a militarily strong Israel aligned with the United States.	• Only a solution based on human rights and international law ensures a win–win solution. • Israel is a major regional superpower that must be held accountable for its actions. • Either a viable and truly sovereign Palestinian state must emerge, or another option which is mutually agreed-upon according to the principle of self-determination. • Anti-Semitism is a form of racism; only respect for human rights will effectively address anti-Semitism and Israel's security concerns.

most of their country, to another people, and then actually *accept* that this is right and just. Thus the Palestinians do not see the political settlement as the end of the process of anti-colonialism, but only as the beginning. Only to the degree that Israel itself de-colonizes will true integration, acceptance, normalization and reconciliation be possible.

- The Israeli claim that there is no Occupation and that the Palestinian territories are merely "disputed" is ridiculous, both empirically and because no government or international court accepts that argument. In fact, Israel's Occupation lies at the center of the conflict and therefore of the reframing. Rather than being defensive in nature, Israel's policies in the Occupied Territories are proactive, seeking territorial expansion based on settlement and control, carried out in contravention of international humanitarian law. Israel may retain its occupation under the Fourth Geneva Convention until its status is resolved by negotiations, but it is prohibited from doing anything to make its control permanent. Occupation violates Palestinian rights, both national and individual ones, and it must end by mutual agreement.
- Since all attacks on civilians are prohibited under international law, both Palestinian terrorism and Israeli state terrorism must end. International law permits both parties to employ "legitimate" forms of warfare, even armed resistance on the part of the Palestinians, but the civilian populations on both sides must be taken out of the conflict completely.

The solution: win–lose or win–win.

- A rights-based solution is a win–win one. It alone is capable of achieving a just, sustainable and genuine resolution to the conflict.
- Israel is not the weak victim in the conflict, but a major regional superpower and by far the strong party in

its dispute with the Palestinians. No just and lasting solution is possible unless Israel can be held accountable for its actions under international law, and unless the political settlement is based on mutually recognized rights. Appeals to "security" cannot be the basis for avoiding the applicability of international law.

- An apartheid-like situation of permanent Israel control over a semi-sovereign Palestinian bantustan cannot be the basis of a lasting solution. If self-determination lies at the root of a rights-based solution, then either a viable and sovereign Palestinian state must emerge alongside the state of Israel within agreed-upon borders or, if the parties desire, a single democratic state may emerge in all Israel/Palestine. Other options which violate either people's right to self-determination, be they apartheid or the elimination of Israel, are ruled out.

- Finally, a rights-based reframing would hold that the answer to anti-Semitism, a compelling concern of Zionism, is not a militarily-strong Israel embroiled in an intractable conflict that carries the danger of escalating into a genuine and irresolvable "clash of civilizations" involving Jews everywhere. Rather, it is in a world based on human rights in which anti-Semitism is opposed just like any other form of racism. Israel, however, by its own violations of human rights, undermines that struggle and thereby threatens the well-being of Jews the world over. Israel is not the ultimate protector of Jewish life; human rights are.

Reframing in human rights language enormously advances the cause of de-colonizing. It forces us, the world's elite, to confront the injustices of the global system of which we are a part, and to attain some critical distance between ourselves and our deeply-held but inherently skewed views. Through a human rights perspective we hear the other voices—voices to which we are generally deaf, of those whom Franz Fanon called "the wretched of the earth." Reframing also releases new ways of thinking, opens new possibilities inconceivable in the narrow one in which we are trapped. Going beyond the fruitless one-state/two-state debate, for example.

IMAGINING A SOLUTION: A MIDDLE EAST CONFEDERATION

Given what we've talked about in this book, it seems to me we are left with four "solutions" to the Israeli-Palestinian conflict, only one of which, a confederational approach, appears workable.

The traditional two-state solution, in which a Palestinian state emerges on all of the Occupied Territories (with minor adjustments), is today the preferred option of most of the players: the Palestinian National Authority, the Arab League, the international community (embodied in the Road Map "Quartet"), as well as perhaps a third of the Israeli public (liberal Jews and Palestinian citizens). The firm opposition of all Israeli governments to this, combined with the ever-expanding Matrix of Control, renders this option dubious at best.

An *"Israel plus-Palestine minus" two-state solution* is the one pursued by both Labor and Likud governments, and now advocated by the US as well. This option envisions a semi-sovereign, semi-viable Palestinian state arising between Israel's major settlement blocs, with the Palestinians compensated by minor territorial swaps. Israeli leaders believe that faced with military defeat, impoverishment, transfer, political isolation and its "Iron Wall" of settlements and barriers, a carefully groomed post-Arafat Palestinian leadership can be coaxed to agree. Since it constitutes little more than a sophisticated form of apartheid, I eliminate it from consideration as a sustainable solution.

A single state, either bi-national or democratic, seems the most natural and just alternative to a two-state solution rendered irrelevant by Israel. Yet, given realpolitik, it is a non-starter. As an option that entails the transformation of Israel from a Jewish state into a democratic one (with a Palestinian majority), it would be opposed totally by the Israeli Jewish population, Diaspora Jews, the US government and significant sectors of Europe. Although the one-state solution enjoys widespread popular support among Palestinians, their leadership is loath to shift to a new political program with such slight chance of success. It also poses some serious problems. Sharing a state with Israeli Jews means compromising the principle of self-determination. And the fact that Israel is so much stronger economically and institutionally than Palestinian society carries the danger that the Palestinian would become a permanent underclass even if they do possess the majority population, as in post-apartheid South Africa. In the foreseeable future, any viable solution must involve a Palestinian state, even if a single state eventually evolves by mutual consent, the Palestinians' hope and vision.

If these other options are eliminated for their various reasons, only one other option remains: a regional confederation. Less elegant than the others, more complex, more difficult to present in a soundbyte, it is also far more workable. Like the European Union, it preserves a balance between national sovereignty and the freedom to live anywhere within the region. Rather than eliminating the Occupation, it neutralizes it by compensating the Palestinians' readiness to compromise on territory in favor of the wider economic, social and geographic opportunities offered by a regional confederation. Not only is a confederational approach just and sustainable, it is win–win.

Unlike the other solutions, the confederation approach offers a "two-stage" process. It begins by recognizing that any effective solution to the Israel-Palestine conflict requires a regional perspective. Whatever particular solution prevails in Israel/Palestine, the Middle East conflict is a regional one that cannot be resolved within the narrow confines of Israel/Palestine. The refugee issue, security, water, economic development, democratization—all these are regional in scope; they cannot be crammed into little Israel/Palestine, a political and geographic unit that is simply too small. Its outlines are straightforward and transparent.

Stage 1: A Palestinian State Alongside Israel

Recognizing that Palestinian demands for self-determination represent a fundamental element of the conflict, the first stage of the confederational approach provides for the establishment of a Palestinian state. This meets the Palestinians' requirements for national sovereignty, political identity and membership in the international community. Statehood, however, does not address the crucial issue of viability. If it were only a state the Palestinians needed, they could have one tomorrow—the mini-state "offered" by Barak and Sharon. But the issue is not simply a Palestinian state. Their greatest fear is being locked into that state, into a bantustan, into a prison-state that cannot possibly address the needs of their people, now or in the future.

The "two-stage" approach offers a way out of this trap, even if the Israeli presence is reduced but not significantly eliminated. The Palestinians might be induced to accept a semi-viable state on something less than the entire Occupied Territories (with or without some territorial swaps) *on condition* that the international community guarantees the emergence of a regional confederation within a reasonable period of time (say, a decade). So while the first stage, the establishment of a Palestinian state on most of the Occupied Territories (including borders with Jordan, Syria and Egypt) addresses the issue of self-determination, the second stage, a regional confederation, would address that of viability. It would give the Palestinians a regional depth in which to meet their long-term social and economic needs.

Stage 2: A Regional Confederation Leading to a Wider Middle East Confederation

Following upon the emergence of a Palestinian state, the international community would broker a regional confederation among Israel, Palestine and Jordan; Syria and Lebanon would likely join within a fairly short time. Over time, with the entrance of Egypt and other countries of the region into the confederation, a full-blown Middle East Union might emerge.

The key element of this approach is the ability of all members of the confederation to live and work anywhere within the confederation's boundaries. That breaks the Palestinians out of their prison. Rather than burdening the small emergent state with responsibilities it cannot possibly fulfill, the confederational approach extends that burden across the entire region. It also addresses the core of the refugee issue, which is individual choice. Palestinians residing within the confederation would have the choice of becoming citizens of the Palestinian state, retaining citizenship in their current countries of residence or leaving the region entirely for a new life abroad. They could choose to return "home" to what is today Israel, but they would do so as Palestinian citizens or citizens of another member state. Israel would be under no obligation to grant them citizenship, just as Israelis living in Palestine (Jews who choose to remain in Ma'aleh Adumim or Hebron, for example, former "settlers") would retain Israeli citizenship. This addresses Israeli concerns about the integrity of their state. In such a confederation, even a major influx of Palestinian refugees into Israel would pose no problem. It is not the presence of the refugees themselves that is threatening to Israel. After all, 300,000 foreign workers and an equal number of Russian Christians reside in Israel today. The threat to Israeli sovereignty comes from the possibility of refugees claiming Israeli citizenship. By disconnecting the Right of Return from citizenship, the refugees would realize their political identity through citizenship in a Palestinian state while posing no challenge to Israeli sovereignty, thus enjoying substantive individual justice by living in any part of Palestine/Israel or the wider region they choose. And since a confederational solution does not require the dismantlement of settlements—although they will be integrated—it is not dependent upon "ending the Occupation," the main obstacle to the two-state solution. It will simply neutralize it, rendering all the walls, checkpoints, by-pass roads and segregated cities irrelevant.

A regional approach frees the Palestinians from the constraints of ethnocracy in which they can only be subordinated, alleviates the threat of apartheid and halts—even reverses—the process of displacement, *nishul*. It does not strive simply for "peace," a state of non-conflict that can be imposed and which may conceal great disparities. Instead, it restructures the relations between Israeli Jews and Palestinians, between Israel and a Palestinian state, so that the structured inequality of ethnocracy cannot reach the Palestinians, at least those living within the Palestinian state or holding Palestinian citizenship. Palestinian citizens of Israel, like other non-Jewish citizens, will continue to suffer subordination in the "Jewish" state, but with the pressures of the Arab-Israeli conflict resolved, a second process, the democratization of Israel, will be able to proceed. It will not be an easy process. The transformation of Israel from a Jewish state to a state of all its citizens, from ethnocracy to democracy, will not, I fear, be as willing and conscious as the transition from the South African ethnocracy under apartheid to majority rule. On the contrary, as forces for democracy—the Palestinian citizens of Israel, the Jewish left, the "ethnic Russians" and other non-Jewish immigrants—press for structural change, and as the Arab minority in particular

reaches that demographic threshold where it can challenge
Jewish rule (as is beginning to happen), we can expect harsh
repressive measures on the part of the authorities. Eventually
Israel will be forced to make the transition to democracy; there
are simply too few Jews who chose to live there and too many
"non-Jewish" citizens to prevent it. The process will not be
completed, however, until a comprehensive political solution
is implemented.

The two-stage or two-state-plus regional solution will
encounter opposition. Israel, perceiving itself as a kind of
Singapore, has no desire to integrate into the Middle East
region, relinquish its control over the entire country or, to say
the least, accommodate Palestinian refugees. But it does offer
the Israeli people, willing, unlike its governments, to truly
disengage from the Occupation, a way out of an untenable
situation. The autocratic regimes of the region might resist such
a project out of fear of the democratization it would entail,
but the advantages of an end to the conflict in the region are
obvious. International pressures and economic inducements,
combined with a strong civil society initiative, should persuade
the region's countries to participate. And for the Palestinians
there are only advantages. The two-stage approach offers
them much more than the two-state solution, and is far more
achievable than a single state.

Although such a Union sounds like a pipedream in the
present context of intense conflict, the infrastructure already
exists. If the Palestinians achieve their goal of self-determination,
I believe they will, as the gatekeepers of the process, signal the
Arab and Muslim worlds that normalization is now possible.
The readiness to integrate Israel into the region, reflected in
the Arab League Initiative, will also some to the fore. Israel,
too, has its gatekeeper role, especially in regards to the US.
Common foreign policy concerns and dependence on the US
for the foreseeable future could unite the region if the Israeli-
Palestinian conflict can just be overcome.

REDEEMING ISRAEL

Ethnocracy is a downward spiral. It goes far beyond a political system privileging one particular group; by its very nature it contains the seeds of oppression. Jews were a tiny minority in Russia (numbering fewer than 1 million in a population of 30 million when the Pale of Settlement was created in 1792), but nevertheless were subject to extreme restrictions and were never considered Russian. Imagine the degree of violence and impunity required to carve a Jewish state out of a country with a settled population of 1.25 million inhabitants living in more than 1,000 cities, towns and villages in 1948. Violence: "Ben-Gurion was right. If he had not done what he did, a state would not have come into being. That has to be clear. It is impossible to evade it. Without the uprooting of the Palestinians, a Jewish state would not have arisen here." And impunity: "I don't think that the expulsions of 1948 were war crimes. You can't make an omelet without breaking eggs" (Morris 2004).

But politics and demography alone cannot explain the often superfluous cruelty an ethnocracy displays towards those it excludes. As in the Russian Pale where Jewish boys were taken from families at age twelve and impressed into the Russian army for 31 years, in Israel the suffering and humiliation we rain on the Palestinians take on a life of their own beyond rational fears of the Other. Why was Salim and Arabiya's home demolished? I learned a lot following the threads leading from that act. About house demolitions as acts of collective punishment and means of alienating Palestinians from their land and confining them to tiny enclaves. About the role of house demolitions in the wider process of *nishul*, both in the Occupied Territories and within Israel. About Zionism, ethnocracy and the exclusivist concepts of which the house demolition policy is merely one expression. The demolition of the Shawamreh house on that "black day" in Anata taught me much, but I still lacked answer to the question "why *that* house," and more to the point, why four times (so far)? The political and even racist rationale behind house demolitions dissipates when so much effort is expended on one particular home. Is it Sharon's "message" that is so important: we will not countenance *any* challenge to our dictates and policies? Was it a way to warn Palestinians not to cooperate with ICAHD (though thousands of houses are rebuilt and re-demolished with no connection to us)? Or is the reason simply that an oppressive system knows no bounds, that cruelty and impunity are part and parcel of any system which makes such elementary human acts as building a home for one's family illegal?

Why do Israeli settlements pour their raw sewage into the fields of Palestinian farmers (Christison and Christison 2005)? Why do pregnant women die at checkpoints, why are Palestinian children terrorized on their way to school, why have more than a million olive and fruit trees been uprooted, why are entire Bedouin villages demolished in the Negev (homes of Arab citizens of Israel who serve in the army), why do 70 percent of the Palestinians live in deep poverty, why, why, why…? The Israeli philosopher Adi Ophir devoted a whole book, *The Order of Evils* (2005), to an examination of how the Occupation systematically produces evils, including superfluous cruelty.

Given the history of the past 60 years which seems to have no end, I would extend that analysis to ethnocracy in general. Besides physical extermination, perhaps the greatest evil is the extermination of a people's culture, society and identity, which, in fact, *are* considered forms of genocide, as is *nishul*, dispossession. In his book *Sacred Landscape*, Meron Benvenisti describes in detail the process of Judaizing the landscape of Palestine, creating a "Hebrew map" of the country. Already in the 1920s, when the Jewish National Fund set up a committee to determine Jewish names for all new settlements and their environs, Arab place names began to be replaced by Jewish ones. Jews working for the British during the Mandatory Period, either as employees of the survey department or within the British army, lobbied hard for Hebrew designations of sites, and when that failed they produced their own Hebrew maps which proved invaluable to the Hagana in the 1948 war. With the establishment of the state, although the Hebrew map had by then became official, there were still too many Arabic names for comfort. Ben Gurion convened the Committee for the Designation of Place-Names in the Negev Region in July, 1949. Laying out their terms of reference, he wrote: "We are obliged to remove the Arabic names for reasons of state. Just as we do not recognize the Arabs' political proprietorship of the land, so also do we not recognize their spiritual proprietorship and their names" (Benvenisti 2000:14).

Zionism was a national liberation movement that became— and remains—a colonial regime. All colonial regimes are ethnocracies by nature, yet not all colonial ethnocracies, cruel, exploitative and exclusionary as they were, were genocidal. There were acts of genocide to be sure; the Belgium Congo, for example, was one of the worst cases. But even here there was no attempt to drive the indigenous population out of the country and eradicate its historical presence. Apartheid South Africa tried to carve a European country out of a populated black African territory, but it, too, talked of "separate development," not of erasing the Africans spiritual proprietorship and names. We are left, as Zionism's legacy, with ethnic cleansing, not the physical killing of Milošević's Greater Serbia, perhaps, but something just a little less evil: the driving from their homes and preventing the return of more than 700,000 innocent people, a crime that is ongoing after 60 years; imposing a repressive Occupation on almost 4 million Palestinians of the West Bank, East Jerusalem and Gaza, a crime lasting now 40 years; and the reduction of the Arab remnants in Israel to second-class status and displacement.

For Israel, which is still pursuing *nishul* with full vigor on both sides of the Green Line, more than mere peace is needed to redeem its soul. Even a just peace, which does not appear imminent, will only open the processes, no less important, of acknowledgement, contrition, restorative justice and reconciliation with the Palestinians. In a review of Pappe's book *The Ethnic Cleansing of Palestine* (2006), the reviewer takes the usual tack: we are the victims, they are the perpetrators. "Pappe makes one egregious mistake," Seth Frantzman writes (*Jerusalem Post*, August 17, 2007). "He never bothers to ask the same question of the Arabs he does of the Jews: What about their lists, their intelligence reports and their ethnic cleansing plans?" That won't work anymore. After 60 years, indeed, a full century and more, we know what the Zionist concept was; we know what it still is in Israel as well as in the Occupied Territories. We know Israel is not the innocent victim; we know we carry the lion's share of the responsibility; we know our policies and actions were proactive, not defensive; we know we have always been the strong party in the conflict; and we know—although we still can't admit it—that we carried out, and still carry out, serious crimes against humanity.

No, we must go way beyond peace to redemption. We must redeem our country from its colonial past and present not only to enable us to finally normalize our existence and find our place in the Middle East, but for our own sakes. We need to reconceptualize Israel as a country which celebrates the heritage of all its citizens, which promotes a cultural Zionism while making room for other its cultures, which develops an *Israeli* pluralism that may or may not morph into something new, and which is committed to human rights. The road is long and we haven't even discovered it yet.

9
What About Terrorism?

Neither Jewish ethics nor Jewish tradition can disqualify terrorism as a means of combat.
> —Former Prime Minister Yitzhak Shamir,
> *Journal of the LEHI, the Stern Gang*, Summer, 1943

Woman of Violence: Memories of a Young Terrorist, 1945–1948.
> —Title of the autobiography of Geula Cohen,
> former Knesset member and leader of the Tehiya party

But what about terrorism? Many people feel something is wrong with Israel's occupation policies but are held back from criticizing Israel by the phenomenon of terrorism, presented in the Israeli framing as the basis of the conflict, an independent variable having to do with "Arabs" and "Islam" rather than with a political conflict for which Israel carries much responsibility. Indeed, the Israeli framing makes sense to many because it dovetails with the post-9/11 preoccupation with terrorism. It is an issue we must confront.

Terrorism is truly a frightful and immoral thing. It targets the innocent and, by its very nature, violates the most fundamental human right of all: the right to life. As Amnesty International notes:

> A fundamental principle of international humanitarian law is that parties involved in a conflict must at all times distinguish between civilians and combatants, and between civilian objects and military objectives. It is not permitted to target civilians, that is, people who are not members of the armed forces of either side. This principle, known as the Principle of Distinction, is

codified in the four Geneva Conventions of 1949 and their two Additional Protocols of 1977. The Principle of Distinction is a fundamental rule of customary international humanitarian law, binding on all parties to armed conflicts, whether international or non-international. (Amnesty International 2002b)

For me, the issue is simple: non-combatants, innocent civilians, cannot be killed, harmed or made to fear for their lives in any way. Any act or policy that does so, be it of a state or non-state actor, is terrorism, and as such is illegal, immoral and prohibited. Interestingly enough, my common-sense approach corresponds with that of Benjamin Netanyahu (1995), certainly a figure no one could accuse as being a naïve peacenik, who defines terrorism as "the deliberate and systematic murder, maiming and menacing of civilians to inspire fear for political purposes."

Governments, however, don't like such a straightforward approach; in fact, there is no internationally agreed-upon definition of terrorism. For international law gives oppressed peoples the right to resist, including armed resistance, in particular in conditions of colonialism under which the Occupation could easily be classified. And who, pray tell, would they be resisting? States for the most part. And since states claim for themselves an exclusive monopoly over the right to use of force, they make a clear distinction between their harming of civilian populations and "terrorism," which by their definition can only be perpetrated by non-state actors. The trick in relieving themselves of responsibility, used often by Netanyahu and the neo-cons in Washington, is to insert *intention* into the equation. It may be true that Israel has killed three times more Palestinian civilians than Israelis have been killed, or that the US has killed far more innocent civilians in Iraq and Afghanistan than insurgents, but "intention" is what makes all the difference. States do not *intend* to kill civilians; they die regrettably but unavoidably as "collateral damage." Non-state actors are terrorists, no matter what their cause, because, states argue, they intend to kill civilians, and even if they attack military targets as the "insurgents" in Iraq do, their use of force as non-state actors is by definition illegal and illegitimate. They are "terrorists" no matter what. So states such as Israel and the US cannot be culpable of terrorism; only their victims, Palestinian resistance groups and the Iraqi insurgents, are. Get it?

Inserting intention into a consideration of terrorism strikes me as mere self-serving sophistry. I go back to what I (and Netanyahu at face value) said before: Terrorism is the killing, harming or intimidation of civilians. Period. What does it matter if the perpetrators are states or non-states, except to let states off the hook? And they have a big hook to be let off of. It turns out that states have a far more deadly record of terrorism than do the non-state actors whom we normally accuse of such crimes. In his book *Death by Government*, R. J. Rummel (1994:13) claims that

> during the first eighty-cight years of this [twentieth] century, almost 170 million men, women and children have been shot, beaten, tortured, knifed, burned, starved, frozen, crushed or worked to death; buried alive, drowned, hung, bombed or killed in any other of the myriad ways governments have inflicted death on unarmed, helpless citizens and foreigners. The dead could conceivably be nearly 360 million people.

And that doesn't include Zaire, Bosnia, Somalia, Sudan, Rwanda, Saddam Hussein's reign, the impact of UN sanctions on the Iraqi civilian population and other state-sponsored murder that occurred after Rummel compiled his figures. It also does not account for all the forms of State Terrorism that do not result in death: torture, imprisonment, repression, house demolitions, induced starvation, intimidation and all the rest. "Terrorism from below," that committed by non-state actors, while horrible, pales in comparison to the "terrorism from above" of states. With the exception of 2001, terrorists have claimed fewer than 1,000 victims per year worldwide, while the killing of civilians by states reaches into the millions. "Just to give perspective on this incredible murder by government," Rummel writes (1994:15), "if all these dead were laid head to toe, assuming each to be an average of 5 feet tall, they would circle the earth ten times. Also, this democide murdered six times more people than died in combat in all the foreign and internal wars of the century."

Now we see why governments go to such lengths to separate themselves from non-state actors. Is a prime minister or president responsible for unleashing deadly force upon an entire people exempt from being labeled a terrorist merely because he or she is the leader of a state, or because he or she did not "intend" to harm civilians? No, it seems to me that we must stick with the blanket definition of terrorism that covers both state and non-state actions: *all* violent or intimidating acts against civilians are prohibited.

By this account, the Palestinians have a right to resist, including armed resistance to Israeli occupation, but not to attack Israeli civilians. There have been horrific attacks by Palestinians on Israeli Jews going back to pre-state days, which explain why it is easy to convince the Jewish public that peace is impossible. But the story does not end there. Since the Palestinians have never had more than token armed groups, certainly nothing approaching an army, Zionism's campaign of dispossession was by definition conducted against a civilian population. It was never an equal contest, even in the realm of terrorism. The *Yishuv* was an urbanized, industrial European society with access to far greater economic resources than the indigenous Arabs. It had a quasi-state governmental structure fully engaged in international diplomacy versus a fragmented, feudal and locally-oriented society. And its members had gained valuable military experience serving with the British Army in the Second World War, including the ability to import and manufacture arms. Only it was capable of planning and executing the systematic campaign of ethnic cleansing described by Pappe. But even the specific acts of terrorism were organized into effective campaigns—according to Begin's Irgun, political violence and terrorism were "legitimate tools in the Jewish national struggle for the Land of Israel" (Perliger and Weinberg 2003)—in marked contrast to the sporadic attacks of the Arabs. Just a few examples will convey the scope and planning of Jewish terrorism, beginning with the "eye for an eye" operations begun around April 1936 with the outbreak of the Arab Revolt (or "the riots" as we call them):

- On November 25, 1940, a Jewish militia blew up a ship in Haifa with its civilian passengers still on board
- The Irgun bombed King David Hotel in Jerusalem, headquarters of the British civil and military administration, killing 91 people, 17 of them Jews (July 22, 1946)
- Hostages were taken to put pressure on a government: the Irgun kidnapped and killed two British sergeants after the British authorities refused to cancel the death sentence of two of their comrades in Akko prison
- The Irgun bombed the British Embassy in Rome (October 31, 1946)
- Twenty letter-bombs were sent to British politicians from Italy (June, 1947)
- The Irgun carried out the Deir Yassin massacre, condemned but also assisted by the Hagana incident (April 9, 1948)
- The Stern Gang assassinated the UN Middle East mediator Count Bernadotte in September 1948
- Hundreds of other attacks occurred which involved bombs being placed in Arab markets and cafes, in cinemas, railway stations, government offices and other public spaces; landmines being placed on roads and exploded by remote control; bombs being thrown into passing cars and into Arab crowds; bombs being placed in trucks and cars and being detonated near buildings; and Arab houses and hotels being blown up.

The terrorist nature of the right-wing Jewish militias before the establishment of the state was recognized by contemporary observers, including Jewish leaders in Israel and abroad. On December 2, 1948, 26 prominent Jews in the US, including Albert Einstein, Hannah Arendt, Sidney Hook and Harry Orlinsky (a well-known professor at the Jewish Theological Seminary), published a letter in the *New York Times* protesting Menachem Begin's visit. It reads in part:

> Among the most disturbing political phenomena of our times is the emergence in the newly created state of Israel of the "Freedom Party" (*Tnuat Haherut*), a political party closely akin in its organization, methods, political philosophy and social appeal to the Nazi and Fascist parties. It was formed out of the membership and following of the former Irgun Zvai Leumi, a terrorist, right-wing, chauvinist organization in Palestine.
>
> The current visit of Menachem Begin, leader of this party, to the United States is obviously calculated to give the impression of American support for his party in the coming Israeli elections, and to cement political ties with conservative Zionist elements in the United States....
>
> This is the unmistakable stamp of a Fascist party for whom terrorism (against Jews, Arabs, and British alike), and misrepresentation are means, and a "Leader State" is the goal.
>
> In the light of the foregoing considerations, it is imperative that the truth about Mr. Begin and his movement be made known in this country. It is all the more tragic that the top leadership of American Zionism has refused to campaign against Begin's efforts, or even to expose to its own constituents the dangers to Israel from support to Begin.
>
> [signed]
>
> Isidore Abramowitz, Hannah Arendt, Abraham Brick, Rabbi Jessurun Cardozo, Albert Einstein, Herman Eisen, M.D., Hayim Fineman, M. Gallen, M.D., H.H. Harris, Zelig S. Harris, Sidney Hook, Fred Karush, Bruria Kaufman, Irma L. Lindheim, Nachman Maisel, Seymour Melman, Myer D. Mendelson, M.D., Harry M. Oslinsky, Samuel Pitlick, Fritz Rohrlich, Louis P. Rocker, Ruth Sagis, Itzhak Sankowsky, I.J. Shoenberg, Samuel Shuman, M. Singer, Irma Wolfe, Stefan Wolfe

I am not bringing this up in order to portray all Zionists or
Israelis as terrorists or to minimize Palestinian responsibility
for both sporadic and systematic attacks on civilians over many
decades. The point is that as pre-state militias (and Palestinian
resistance groups are still at that stage) both the Jews and
the Arabs resorted to terrorism, both finding it an effective,
even decisive, strategy for creating desired political realities.
"Already in the early stages of the revolt," as Begin called the
Irgun's violent actions against the British and the Arabs, "we
achieved an important strategic objective: we succeeded in
nullifying the local Arab factor."

> For twenty years the Arabs has held the military and political
> initiative....The Hebrew Revolt put an end to this shameful and
> dangerous phase....The Arabs soon forgot the "child of death"
> and began to respect and even admire the Jewish "jeddah"
> [grandmother]. This last was an indirect result, but of great
> practical significance. The Arabs lost the military initiative....
> I had occasion, in the early days of the revolt, to see for myself
> the psychological effect among the Arabs of our surprise attacks.
> (Begin 1951 (1977):87–88)

Even more important, the Jewish resort to terrorism did not
end in 1948; it was merely transformed into a policy of state
and integrated into Israel's official military. The forcible de-
Arabization and Judaization of the Land of Israel/Palestine;
the massive demolition of Palestinian homes from 1948 until
today, both in Israel and the Occupied Territories; a 40-year
(and counting) war against civilians in order to maintain an
occupation in perpetuity; repeated and unrestrained military
attacks on Lebanon, including the remote-control massacre of
Sabra and Shatilla; a decades-long campaign of assassinating
Palestinian leaders, leaving the Palestinians bereft of effective
political leadership—these and other policies and actions
discussed earlier constitute State Terrorism. If we want to
use such a loaded and imprecise word as "terrorism" (the US
Army once counted 109 definitions), we cannot be misled into

applying the term only to non-state actors, letting states off the hook simply because, as states, they claim sole legitimacy over the use of force. The terminology, like so much of the language used in the Israeli-Palestinian conflict ("fence" or "wall," settlement" or "community," "occupied" land or "disputed," "stealing" or "redeeming," "Palestinians" or "Arabs," "Palestine" or "the Land of Israel"), is self-serving and deceiving. If in popular use "terrorist" refers only to non-state actors, then it makes perfect sense that only the Palestinians are the terrorists—and therefore the bad guys—and the Israelis are not. This perception does fit reality. With the resources to control the media, indeed, our very language, and having an army of "experts" in international law at their disposal, it is easy for Israel not only to avoid accountability but to blame the victim, casting the Palestinians as the problem, not Israel's oppression of them. Even if, on occasion, states are held accountable—in 2004, after all, the International Court of Justice in The Hague did rule that Israel's Wall was illegal and must be dismantled—they normally have the political clout to avoid actually complying with the verdict.

STATE TERRORISM AND ACCOUNTABILITY

The only way out of oppression is to unambiguously "name the thing" and demand accountability on the part of the oppressors. Language is a key. Orwellian language, in which Israel specializes, is designed to obfuscate and deflect responsibility, as our anonymous expert on international law explained to us earlier. If we can get the international community to debate what "occupation" actually means instead of enforcing the Fourth Geneva Convention, we buy years of unhindered oppression. If we succeed in tying terrorism to intention, the powerful states will be the ones to determine whose intention is terroristic and whose isn't—with theirs being in the latter category, of course. We need a better language, one which will enable us to hold states and not only non-state actors accountable for their actions. And that language already exists, the language of human rights. Thus, Amnesty International never uses the term "terrorism," which it finds unhelpful, although it has tackled the problem head-on through reports extremely critical of both Palestinian and Israeli attacks on civilians. "Attacks on civilians are not permitted under any internationally recognized standard of law, whether they are committed in the context of a struggle against military occupation or any other context," Amnesty International (2002b) states flatly and unambiguously. "Not only are they considered murder under general principles of law in every national legal system, they are contrary to fundamental principles of humanity which are reflected in international humanitarian law."

The Fourth Geneva Convention Relative to the Protection of Persons in Time of War, a foundation stone of international law which applies to occupations but whose applicability to its Occupation Israel denies, also asserts the principle of protecting civilians unambiguously. Article 3 reads:

> [For] Persons taking no active part in the hostilities, including members of armed forces who have laid down their arms...the following acts are and shall remain prohibited at any time and in any place whatsoever: violence to life and person, in particular murder of all kinds, mutilation, cruel treatment and torture;...and outrages upon personal dignity, in particular humiliating and degrading treatment.

A human rights approach to the issue of terrorism is useful because it is precise and inclusive. It condemns all forms of terror from whatever source, whether "from above" (State Terror) or "from below" (non-state terror), thereby extending accountability to countries. During the second Intifada more than 1,000 Israeli civilians were killed, including 113 children and youths, and around 6,000 injured. Some 3,500 Palestinians died in Israeli attacks, 85 percent of them civilians including

650 children or youth. More than 29,000 were injured (Palestinian Red Crescent Society; *Palestine Monitor*). *All* are victims of terrorism.

Now it's all well and good to nail down what terrorism means and to draw up rules that eliminate it as a legitimate means of warfare or struggle, but something else is needed: ways of resolving conflicts so that terrorism is unnecessary. This should not be an issue for states, since they have no business engaging in terrorism in the first place. Governments possess the requisite power, authority and *responsibility* to avoid the degree of oppression that would spawn terrorism. They have a responsibility to their citizens to maintain law, order and security, but within the parameters of human rights and international law which, crucially, protect citizens from their own governments should they become oppressive. And if they don't respect the fundamental rights of their own people or of peoples they control, international law requires the other states to bring to trial, under the principle of "universal jurisdiction," those responsible for human rights violations. Persons suspected of genocide, war crimes in international or localized armed conflict, grave breaches of the Geneva Conventions and, in general, "crimes against humanity"—systematic campaigns of murder, extermination, enslavement, deportation, imprisonment or other severe deprivation of physical liberty in violation of fundamental rules of international law, torture, rape and other sexual violence, persecution, enforced disappearance, apartheid and other inhumane acts—all must face prosecution. And if a state is unwilling to take legal measures against its own suspected violators of human rights, other states must do so (Amnesty International 1999b).

Interestingly enough, Israel was one the first states to invoke the principle of universal jurisdiction when, immediately upon its founding, it called on the world's nations to relentlessly pursue and prosecute Nazi war criminals. Yet it displays a firm unwillingness to apply international law to its own occupation. Israel refuses to try its own officials, soldiers or citizens accused of human rights violations or, worse, war crimes or crimes against humanity. It also refuses to allow accused Israelis to be extradited, or to cooperate with other international courts. This is intolerable, the International Court of Justice declared in its advisory ruling on the legality of the Wall. "Given the character and the importance of the rights and obligations involved," the Justices wrote,

> the Court is of the view that all States are under an obligation not to recognize the illegal situation resulting from the construction of the wall in the Occupied Palestinian Territory, including in and around East Jerusalem. They are also under an obligation not to render aid or assistance in maintaining the situation created by such construction. It is also for all States, while respecting the United Nations Charter and international law, to see to it that any impediment, resulting from the construction of the wall, to the exercise by the Palestinian people of its right to self-determination is brought to an end. In addition, all the States parties to the Geneva Convention relative to the Protection of Civilian Persons in Time of War of 12 August 1949 are under an obligation, while respecting the United Nations Charter and international law, to ensure compliance by Israel with international humanitarian law as embodied in that Convention. (ICJ ruling, July 9, 2004, article 159)

So international mechanisms exist to ensure that states do not depart from internationally agreed-upon norms, although we know well that they are painfully weak. Still, there have been significant gains. In 1998 the international community approved the Rome Statutes that established, in 2002, an International Criminal Court (ICC) in which individual offenders could be brought to trial if their own countries refuse to try them. (Note: 145 states have signed on to the ICC; the US, China, India and Israel are among the few to refuse to do so.) Pinochet, Milošević, Charles Taylor of Liberia, accused war criminals from the Rwanda genocide—the record of bringing war criminals to trial is limited and mixed, but more and more concern over accountability is entering the considerations of world leaders. Many of these cases came to trial only because civil society groups pressed for them, governments being notoriously reluctant to try "their own," probably because of the skeletons they all have in their national closets. Thus, even as laws, covenants and institutions emerge to strengthen the implementation of human rights norms and international humanitarian law, we, the people, still have a crucial role to play in monitoring the activities of states and pressing for accountability when the international system falters.

In Israel accountability is coming completely from civil society, since the government does all it can to avoid it. Take the case of Major General Doron Almog, a former commander of the Israel armed forces in Gaza who ordered the wanton destruction of 59 homes of Palestinian civilians in the Rafah refugee camp in January 2002, an act of collective punishment in which a pregnant mother of ten, Noha Shukri Al-Makadma, was killed (Salim and Arabiya's rebuilt home is dedicated to her and Rachel Corrie). He also ordered the dropping of a one-ton bomb in a densely populated Gaza City neighborhood which killed 15 people and injured 150. Learning that he was to travel to London, Yesh Gvul, an Israeli organization of reservist soldiers who refuse to serve in the Occupied Territories, initiated a warrant for his arrest when he stepped off the plane. Almog was tipped off, however, and evaded arrest by remaining on the El Al plane, which promptly returned him to Israel. Although the Scotland Yard agents should have boarded the plane to arrest him—an airliner parked at Heathrow has no extra-judicial rights—apparent collusion between the Israeli Embassy and British officials allowed him to escape.

Soon after, the former Chief of Staff during the second Intifada, Moshe Ya'alon, went into hiding in New Zealand when a local court issued a warrant for his arrest for his part in the assassination of a leading Hamas figure, Salah Shehadeh, who was killed by the same one-ton bomb Almog ordered dropped on his house in the crowded Gaza neighborhood. He escaped trial only because the Attorney General of New Zealand canceled the warrant. Many other officers and even simple soldiers who routinely committed war crimes (such as the one who killed British cameraman James Miller at point blank range in Gaza) are reportedly expressing fears of travelling abroad lest they face arrest. The head of the Building Inspectors unit of the Jerusalem municipality wrote to the mayor demanding the municipality support him if charges are brought against him for house demolitions, even after he retires.

And then there's Salim and Arabiya's demolished home. In February, 2007, Salim appeared for the second time before the Israeli Supreme Court asking that the 15-year demolition order on their home be rescinded—a permanent order under which the family has had its home demolished four times. They also petitioned the Court to instruct the authorities to issue them a building permit. The hearing, which I attended, did not go well. Salim's lawyer, retained by ICAHD, expected a negative ruling to be issued within a week, after which the Civil Administration could—and would—demolish the home for the fifth time. The interweaving of the particulars of their case with Israel and international law is instructive and revealing. Briefly, Salim and Arabiya's lawyer argued that:

- The Fourth Geneva Convention forbids an Occupying Power to extend its law and administration to an occupied territory, rendering the very process of granting or denying permits to Palestinians, not to mention Israel's policy of house demolitions, patently illegal under international humanitarian law.
- Trying to prove the good faith of the Shawamrehs in repeatedly seeking a permit and the bad faith of the Civil Administration in repeatedly refusing it for differing and sundry seasons, their lawyer pointed out that the

family had applied for a permit three times (each time at a cost of $5,000), encouraged each time to do so by Civil Administration officials. Especially egregious was the declaration, published in a major Israeli newspaper, that the Shawamrehs would be granted a permit if they provided what the Civil Administration, in the third application, claimed were two missing signatures on their deed of ownership. Despite lengthy contact between the lawyer and the Civil Administration, the latter would not reveal which exact signatures were required, and when pressed then claimed they lost the Shawamreh file.

- Resigned to the reality that the Israeli courts do admit international law, the Shawamrehs' lawyer questioned the very legality of the master plan under which demolitions are done, a British-era plan called RJ-5 enacted in *1942*. A plan that has never been revised over the past 65 years despite significant changes in demography and land use cannot, he argued, be considered a just, legal or binding document. Its effect is clearly to deny the Shawamrehs and thousands of other Palestinian families their fundamental right to actualizing their property rights and to secure housing.

- Finally, the legality of repeatedly demolishing the Shawamreh home under the original "perpetual" demolition order was questioned, especially since such a practice is illegal in Israel itself and is not applied to Israeli settlements in the Occupied Territories.

The Supreme Court, as in the past, would have none of it. In his response, Justice Eliezer Rivlin, speaking for the other judges, refused to allow any consideration of international law. Remaining solely within the narrow confines of Israel law, he also refused to address the issue of the validity of RJ-5 or the procedures of the Civil Administration. What this entire case boils down to, he said, was a request to retroactively approve an illegal house, something the Court cannot do.

ICAHD is now planning to take Salim and Arabiya's case to international courts, arguing that universal jurisdiction applies since the Shawamrehs have plainly exhausted all avenues of redress in the Israeli court and administrative systems over the past 15 years and cannot obtain justice. By coincidence, on the very day the Supreme Court held its hearing on the case, Chilean judge and human rights expert Juan Guzman, who had taken Pinochet to trial in Spain, was visiting Israel/Palestine at ICAHD's invitation. Salim and I ran directly from the Supreme Court building to consult with him, taking him with us to Salim and Arabiya's home in Anata. Then and there we agreed to take the case to an international court, most likely a Spanish one, since the Spaniard system is the most open to cases of universal jurisdiction. We circulated our intentions among the media, and the following story appeared in the *Jerusalem Post* (February 7, 2007):

PINOCHET JUDGE VISITS TO SEE IF OFFICIALS CULPABLE FOR HOUSE DEMOLITIONS

The judge who indicted former Chilean dictator Augusto Pinochet is in Israel this week to study the feasibility of international legal action against Israeli decision-makers responsible for the demolition of Palestinian homes. In Chile, Juan Guzman is famous for his efforts to bring Pinochet to justice for the dictator's involvement in the kidnapping, torture and killing of those who opposed his regime. He arrived in Israel on Thursday for a weeklong visit at the invitation of the Israel Committee Against House Demolitions (ICAHD), which has solicited his legal opinion, and that of others as it works to build an international legal case against Israelis involved in the demolition of Palestinian homes....

As a jurist committed to human rights, Guzman said, he was interested in the issue of house demolitions and had come to study the issue. "I came to see with my own eyes what I have read and heard about," Guzman told *The Jerusalem Post*....Still, Guzman said, irrespective of the feasibility of an international case, it was clear to him that Israel's practice of demolishing Palestinian homes was a "violation of human rights." Such practice was against a number of international laws and agreements including the 1998 Rome Statute of the International Criminal Court, he said. It is always preferable to settle the matter in a local court, Guzman said. "But if you cannot find justice in the country where the human rights are violated, then you would have to go [seek justice] in a country with universal criminal laws," said Guzman.

But Halper said that his organization had chosen that route, in part because it believed that legal options in Israel with respect to preventing home demolitions had been exhausted. He added that ICAHD had trouble recognizing the court's jurisdiction within the West Bank and east Jerusalem. "One of the major ways of forcing Israel to respect human rights is by forcing it to be accountable to human rights. The only way to do that is to target the people who are responsible," he said.

The threat to take the Shawamreh case abroad may be having its effect. The Supreme Court should have issued its ruling within a week; as of this writing six months later it still has not done so. But the plans have been made. The only question is one of time: once the ruling comes down, will we be able to get some kind of international court order to stop the demolition, or will the home be demolished immediately?

ALTERNATIVES TO TERRORISM AS A WAY OUT OF OPPRESSION

So much for holding states accountable. But what of non-state groups? Terrorism—like human rights—has been called the weapon of the powerless. What can oppressed peoples do when they lack the military and political power to struggle against repressive states? Here they face a dilemma. On the one hand, international law recognizes the right to resist oppression, even violently. But it does not permit *anyone*, including rebels, insurgents, freedom fighters or liberation organizations, to attack civilian populations. Since in many cases grassroots insurgencies cannot mount effective challenges to the armed forces of states, what option exists other than terrorism?

First of all, we cannot fall into the trap of de-politicizing groups that engage in terrorism. As horrific as terrorist attacks are, the only way to counter them is to understand the political and economic conditions that engendered them. This does not mean accepting the legitimacy of each and every group engaged in terrorism; the "civilizational" terrorism of groups like al-Qaida who see themselves as engaged in a life-or-death struggle against the non-Muslim and mainstream Muslim worlds will remain intractable and essentially irresolvable. Such violent campaigns must be opposed, even militarily. The international community has every right to demand that oppressed peoples renounce terrorism as a weapon of resistance, but it cannot expect them to sit passively and endure oppression forever. Assuming, as we must, that terrorism is a symptom and not an independent variable, that it is a cry of suffering rather than of some "clash of civilizations" or good versus evil, then we must provide alternative means of achieving freedom and rights to terrorism—and hopefully to any kind of armed struggle.

The international community, for example, may demand the end to Palestinian terrorism, which many Palestinians, like other oppressed peoples, consider acts of resistance, especially since they find themselves the victims of state terrorism to which the international community does not seem to object. But that will work only if it makes available to them alternative, effective avenues for throwing off the Occupation and securing their rights to self-determination. Two legitimate avenues of redress jump out at us, both denied to the Palestinians. One is genuine negotiations based on international law or the application of existing international laws, such as the Fourth Geneva Convention, which would cause the collapse of the Occupation under the weight of its own illegality.

We've already seen how Israel and the United States undermined the Oslo negotiations by basing them on power politics rather than on international law. If the motive was to perpetuate Israeli control and frustrate Palestinian national aspirations, this was the way to go. Since every element of the occupation was illegal, negotiations based on international law would force Israel to relinquish its Occupation. If, however, the Palestinians had to negotiate each centimeter of territory with an overwhelming superior occupying power, they would lose—which is, of course, precisely what happened. The very fact that over seven years of negotiations the Palestinians eked out of Israel control over only 18 percent of 22 percent of the country (Area A—see Map 2, p. xiii), and that Israel doubled its settler population from 200,000 to 400,000, makes it crystal-clear that negotiations would not lead to Palestinian rights. The tremendous strengthening of the Occupation in the six years since Oslo ended, combined with the destructive force of Israel's campaign of repression and Israeli vetoes over which Palestinian leaders it will sit with or not, makes the prospects of future negotiations nil.

OK, then there's a second legitimate avenue open to the Palestinians instead of resistance and terrorism: international law. If only the Fourth Geneva Convention, among many pieces of international law, would be applied to the Occupied Territories, imagine how it would boost Palestinian perceptions that they, too, have a position of power from which they could effectively fight the Occupation:

- Article 27 reads: "Protected persons are entitled, in all circumstances, to respect for their persons, their honour, their family rights, their religious convictions and practices, and their manners and customs. They shall at all times be humanely treated, and shall be protected especially against all acts of violence or threats thereof and against insults and public curiosity."
- Article 32 forbids assassinations, and any brutalization of the civilian population.

- Article 33 prohibiting pillage would obtain to Israel's extensive use of West Bank and Gazan water resources, especially as they are denied the local population.
- Article 39 stipulates: "Protected persons [residents of occupied lands] who, as a result of the war, have lost their gainful employment, shall be granted the opportunity to find paid employment," and thereby prohibits the imposition of a permanent "closure" on the Occupied Territories, such as Israel has done since 1993.
- Article 49 forbids deportations and any "forcible transfers," which would include such common practices as revoking Jerusalem IDs or banning Palestinians from returning from work, study or travel abroad. It also stipulates that "The Occupying Power shall not…transfer parts of its own civilian population into territories it occupies"—a clear ban on settlements.
- Article 53—"Any destruction by the Occupying Power of real or personal property belonging individually or collectively to private persons…is prohibited"—outlaws house demolitions.
- Article 64 forbids changes in the local legal system that, among other things, alienate the local population from its land and property, as Israel has done through massive expropriations.
- Article 146 holds accountable individuals who have committed "grave breaches" of the Convention. According to Article 147, this includes many acts routinely practiced under the Occupation, such as: willful killing, torture or inhuman treatment, willfully causing great suffering or serious injury, unlawful deportation, taking of hostages and extensive destruction and appropriation of property.
- Indeed, according to Article 8 of the Fourth Geneva Convention, the PLO had no right in the first place to abrogate their rights and suspend the applicability of

the Convention, since "Protected persons may in no circumstances renounce in part or in entirety the rights secured to them by the present Convention." Since virtually every element of Israel's occupation violates a provision of the Fourth Geneva Convention, it would only take its application to the Occupied Territories for the Occupation to be dismantled.

Adherence to human rights and international humanitarian law seems to me the key to international peace in general and the just resolution of the Israeli-Palestinian conflict in particular. This means holding both state and non-state violators accountable for their actions. The mechanisms exist, yet they are controlled by states, and asking governments to police themselves is a self-defeating proposition. On the contrary, states seem to be the problem. Since, as Rummel demonstrates, governments are responsible for the overwhelming majority of violence and deaths, it is far more important to hold them accountable to international law than groups we vilify as "terrorists." For the symptoms of suffering that give rise to terrorism—but even more important the suffering billions of people endure daily without resorting to violence or terrorism—have their roots in the intolerable conditions created by states. Until such a time as international enforcement agencies such as the UN, the ICJ, the ICC, international criminal tribunals and national courts operating under the principle of universal jurisdiction can effectively sanction them, monitoring and demands for implementation rests with us, the people, international civil society.

10
Where Do We Go From Here?

When the people lead, the leaders follow.

We refuse to be enemies.

—Slogans of the critical Israeli peace movement

What if the Occupation actually wins? What if, in the light of day, in the glare of the mass media, an entire people is literally imprisoned behind 26-foot concrete walls? What if, on the southern border of Europe, with the active support of the American government, a new bantustan emerges and the world is confronted with a new apartheid state? The Israeli-Palestinian conflict long ago ceased being a localized spat between two peoples in a far-away corner of the Middle East. It is a global conflict whose consequences reverberate far and wide.

For the Arab and wider Muslims peoples, it epitomizes, together with Iraq, Western neo-colonialism and American Empire, as Bin Laden's broadcasts plainly reveal. In a place where Western policy and weapons have denied Arabs their rights and, for the last 40 years, have supported an ever-more repressive occupation, the conflict represents the Clash of Civilizations from the Muslim point of view, the Occupation being not Israeli but American-European-Israeli. Its destabilizing impact on the entire global system is beginning to be appreciated. The Iraq Study Group headed by former Secretary of State James Baker has said it clearly: "The United States cannot attain its goals in the Middle East unless it deals directly with the Arab-Israeli conflict and regional instability. [That means] a two-state solution for Israel and Palestine" (Baker and Hamilton 2006:7).

The stakes, though, are much higher. Israel-Palestine, as in biblical times, lies on a critical fault-line of history, and the battle being fought there today will largely determine where our world is headed. Fundamentalist Christians, the "Christian Zionists" who run much of American policy today, frame this as Armageddon, the battle of battles inaugurating the end of the world and the Second Coming of Christ. I prefer a Lord of the Rings analogy. The Occupation is Mordor, the fortress of those powerful and violent forces that have always ruled our planet—realpolitik, domination, militarism, exploitation, exclusivity. From the heart of the Holy Land no less, it casts a Great Darkness over our earth. Standing opposed to Occupation Mordor are all of us, the varied and wonderful peoples who make up the international civil society, the little Frodos crying out: "Human rights! Human rights!"

The battle has already been joined. If we lose, if the Occupation prevails, the progressive forces of the world, those struggling for a new age in which human rights, international law, cultural pluralism, economic development, inclusivity, justice and peace rule, will be set back to square one. The human-centric values we advocate, whether based in human rights or religion or our particular cultural traditions, will be rendered hollow. If the Occupation prevails—and all the powers-that-be have united to ensure it will—not only will the Palestinians have lost but every person throughout the world aspiring to a better future will lose as well. The effect will be chilling. And for Jews as well, so many of whom have thrown their support behind Israel's occupation policies. Armageddon may usher in salvation, but only for the few. In the view of the Christian *Zionists*, those who so fervently support Israel as a vehicle of redemption, the Jews die in Armageddon; only a few who accept Christ will survive. If the Mordor of the Occupation prevails, all the values that define modern Jewry in the Diaspora, a commitment to human rights and social justice, will have been sacrificed to the Occupation (Halper 2007). This struggle has brought me full circle. Now an "Israeli in Palestine," I see my own people coopted by Israel's security framing and disempowered. They have not joined Mordor's army, but their leaders have, and they have turned Israeli young people—those soldiers at the checkpoints, those sent to evacuate the Shawamreh family from its home before demolishing it, those who serve "security" blindly—into unthinking Orcs. Israel's aggressive marketing of military systems developed from its years of occupation and conflict, including "counterinsurgency" weapons and tactics to be used in support of oppressive states and against their own people, has forced me to join up with forces outside Israel in this decisive struggle.

So where do we go from here, we Hobbits of the world? Since the resolution of the Israeli-Palestinian conflict is so intertwined with the global struggle for political, social and economic justice, I would glean from what I've said in this book and suggest focusing on four strategic elements: a global vision; a just peace in the Middle East based upon a regional approach; an international strategy of advocacy; and, in the end, perhaps an element more important to me than to you: redeeming Israel.

A Global, Regional, Local and Personal Vision

For me, as an old 1960s radical who has seen my generation turn into the most selfish, unfeeling and destructive in history, the most inspiring and hopeful development of the past 20 years or so has been the emergence of a strong international civil society, thousands of peace and human rights organizations, NGOs working on issues of development, churches and other faith-based organizations, political groups, trade unions, universities who, together with activists, intellectuals and concerned people everywhere, form the progressive, non-violent global army confronting Mordor in Israel/Palestine and elsewhere. We used to be called simply "the people," but with the rise of economic globalization dominated by Big Business and Big Government, we have necessary reconceived ourselves as a more organized source for change than in the past. Social forums, and in particular the World Social Forum held in Porto Alegre, Brazil, and now other locations, represent the most visible expression of international civil society, sometimes drawing 100,000 grassroots organizations, activists and thinkers. 'We are diverse," declares the Social Movements' Manifesto (Fisher and Ponniah 2003:346):

> women and men, adults and youth, indigenous peoples, rural and urban, workers and unemployed, homeless, the elderly, students, migrants, professionals, peoples of every creed, colour and sexual orientation. The expression of this diversity is our strength and our unity. We are a global solidarity movement, united in our determination to flight against the concentration of wealth, the proliferation of poverty and inequalities, and the destruction of our earth. We are living and constructing alternative systems, and using creative ways to promote them. We are building a grand alliance from our struggles and resistance against a system based on sexism, racism and violence, which privileges the interests of capital and patriarchy over the needs and aspirations of people.

True, with one superpower in the world aggressively advancing a predatory form of capitalism (and little Israel, its "strategic ally" and the world's third or fourth largest exporter of arms playing its modest role), the scope and power of the forces of injustice are exponentially greater than they were a generation ago. But we also have a more varied and powerful arsenal at our disposal. The internet and other forms of communication give us unlimited access to information and possibilities of organization; together with mass transportation, physically meeting in regional or world forums is possible for us, where once only the privileged could do so.

We have new political instruments at our disposal as well. Against the will of states jealously safeguarding their sovereignty and privileged access to violence, a vibrant world of human rights has emerged since the Second World War, based on the Universal Declaration of Human Rights and the Geneva Conventions. Dozens of human rights covenants detailing people's collective and individual rights have been codified and passed into international law over the past 60 years, and dozens more are in the pipeline. Enforcement, as we have seen, is still weak, but we now have an expanding array of institutions of implementation: an International Court of Justice, a brand new International Criminal Court, international tribunals empowered to monitor and ensure compliance and empowered national court systems, together with a High Commissioner for Human Rights who holds the rank of Under Secretary-General of the UN. Even when enforcement proves impossible—as in Israel's violations of the Fourth Geneva Convention or its outright defiance of the ICJ ruling that the Wall is illegal and must be dismantled—the "politics of shame" comes into play. It was this that forced the world's governments to grudgingly approve the Universal Declaration (Drinan 2001, Korey 1998), and it is this, given that the concept of human rights has passed a critical threshold in the public's consciousness, that constrains and concerns Israel even if it doesn't actually halt its illegal practices.

When I am out doing my international advocacy, I stress to my audiences that they don't have to be Israel-Palestine wonks to be concerned with our struggle; I try to impart to them the global significance of winning the fight over Israel's Occupation, the tremendous surge of hope that Palestinian freedom would inject into the world's neo-colonized peoples and, in general, the greater security that Israelis and Palestinians will enjoy once occupation and ethnocracy are replaced—like the end of apartheid in South Africa, an uplifting event which would radiate powerfully outward. This global vision should inspire and inform our efforts to win a world based on human rights no matter how local and parochial our issue may seem.

The Israeli-Palestinian conflict, I reiterate, cannot be resolved in isolation. Just as the conflict is global, so is its resolution global and regional, not merely local. Efforts to find a just and workable peace in Israel/Palestine have floundered because issues of regional scope—conflict resolution, refugees, security, water, economic development, democratization, the integration of Israel into the region and eventually the emergence of a peaceful and prosperous Middle East—cannot be crammed into little Israel/Palestine. It may still be too early to advocate for the Middle East confederation I proposed; we're all stuck in the one-state/two-state paradigm. But as that option recedes, mainly because of Israeli intransigence and the permanency of its settlement enterprise, a regional approach will sooner or later emerge. When it does, my confederational approach is in the pot to be considered.

The eventual resolution of the Israel-Palestine conflict will not be merely the result of some technical arrangements. Justice is an irreplaceable element of the equation. True peace cannot come about without justice. That is why Israel's attempt to impose "peace" on the Palestinians, that is, an absence of overt conflict, a kind of industrial quiet, without resolving the repression and suffering concealed behind it, is futile.

AN INTERNATIONAL STRATEGY OF ADVOCACY

OK. We have compelling analyses of the ideological and political causes of the conflict. We understand the policies and structures that maintain it, particularly the Matrix of Control. And we have identified the underlying issues of ethnocracy that must be addressed in order to achieve a just peace, even identifying the elements required of any workable solution. The next step, then, is to ask: How can we translate our analyses and proposals into policy? Since we the people are not elected and have only certain limited types of clout (like civil disobedience, protesting, boycotting, turning to the courts and influencing public opinion), how can we develop an effective program of advocacy designed to prod the decision-makers into realizing a just peace? Now that I have an explanation of why Salim and Arabiya's house was demolished four times and what its deeper meanings are, how can I prevent the fifth demolition?

A first step, I think, is offering a clear and compelling reframing of the conflict. The rights-based reframing that I presented earlier in answer to Israel's security framing is one contribution, but many other reframings are possible as well, depending of the audiences we wish to reach. We at ICAHD have developed, for example, a Jewish reframing that reminds Jewish communities abroad how much human and civil rights define modern Jewry and question whether the policies of an ethnocracy with an occupation can truly form the center of their communal life. We have a Christian reframing—mainstream Protestant as well as Evangelical—that shows how human rights dovetails with Christian values and counters the claims of Christian Zionism. We've developed an American reframing showing how support for Israel's Occupation is undermining the American role in the world, and a European reframing that does the same while stressing the connection between human rights, the Holocaust and the acceptability—even the duty—of criticizing Israel, even while supporting its existence. Our women's reframing stresses the unique experience of women and girls under Occupation. Reframings empower because they impart alternative approaches leading to unconsidered solutions. Now that you've got the idea, develop reframings of your own and send them to us at <info@icahd.org>.

Then we must mobilize civil society and, if possible, find supporters in our governments as well. What is called for, in my opinion, is a concentric framework, beginning with a limited number of strategic Big Picture "meta-campaigns" focusing on the nature and structure of the Occupation, human rights violations, Israeli accountability, the international community's responsibility towards the Palestinians and the danger of an impending apartheid. Highlighting larger political processes such as the steady progression of the Israeli government towards the establishment of an apartheid regime prevents us from missing important opportunities to make our voices heard. When, for instance, Jimmy Carter published his book *Palestine: Peace Not Apartheid* in 2006—an event we all knew about well in advance—most of the activists were so preoccupied with their particular campaigns that few either exploited the debate we knew would ensue or effectively supported Carter.

ICAHD, for instance, is currently developing two meta-campaigns in response to what we consider the most pressing political process of the moment: an anti-apartheid campaign and a campaign to mark 60 years of 1948.

The anti-apartheid campaign has a double focus: resistance to any attempt to unilaterally impose an apartheid regime over Israel-Palestine; and a continued call for a complete end to the Occupation. It is therefore organized in two phases: a campaign which warns against the possibility that Israel will try to impose an apartheid regime over Palestine, hoping to prevent that eventuality; and, if and when an apartheid regime is in fact announced, when Israel officially announces the implementation of a variation of its "Convergence Plan" or a "transitional" Palestinian state is established, a full-fledged anti-apartheid campaign.

So as to give you a glimpse into our approach to international advocacy, let me lay out briefly some of the major elements of this campaign.

Phase I: Until an Apartheid Plan is Implemented

- **A civil society call.** The anti-apartheid campaign will be launched with a Call from the Palestinian civil society, joined by Israeli groups and finally by international ones, calling for international support and action. A draft of the Call is presented below (Box 2). It presents in concise form the issue of apartheid, stresses the urgency of the situation and demands international intervention based on the civil society call of Palestinian NGOs of July 2005. As it is circulated among Palestinian and Israeli NGOs and activist groups, it will be modified in a way that balances a substantive campaign squarely addressing the issues before us and a language that permits the maximum mobilization of international organizations.

- **Development of effective informational materials and their dissemination.** Among the most basic materials needed are:

  —**Apartheid in Israel-Palestine?** A basic brief flyer or brochure in different languages raising the issue and possibility of apartheid in Israel-Palestine in an open-ended manner that makes the case forcibly yet leaves the reader to draw his/her own intentions. The piece will include facts, maps, quotes, a concise definition of apartheid, an explanation of why the Israeli case applies, references to the International Convention on the Suppression and Punishment of the Crime of Apartheid, the Fourth Geneva Convention and other relevant documents, as well as reference to supporting statements of parliamentary, church, human rights or other respected voices. The material will also be translated into a PowerPoint presentation and short video formats.

  —**Reframings** of the conflict "pitching" our case in terms of the worldviews and language of the different groups we are attempting to influence.

Box 2: A Call of Civil Society to Prevent the Imposition of an Apartheid Regime by Israel Over the (Occupied) Palestinian Territories

We, representatives of Palestinian, Israeli and international civil societies, call upon governments, international organizations and individuals of conscience to raise their voices against the threatened imposition of a permanent apartheid regime of Israel over Palestine, a plan spelled out in detail by Prime Minister Olmert and his Foreign Minister Tzipi Livni, and agreed-upon by Condoleezza Rice in the name of the Bush Administration. We call on you to join with us to end the Occupation totally before all hopes of a just peace in Palestine-Israel are dashed forever.

With explicit American approval, Israel is poised to unilaterally annex its massive West Bank settlement blocs containing 87 percent of its settlers. It will then declare the Wall, extending far into Palestinian territory, as its new "demographic" border. The Jordan Valley, Israel's "security" border, will become its *second* eastern border, sandwiching the Palestinians into tiny, impoverished and disconnected enclaves—a non-viable bantustan, a prison-state.

This physical "separation" of Jewish and Palestinian populations in which Israel establishes a permanent regime of domination constitutes nothing less than apartheid. Israel will permanently control 82–85 percent of Palestine-Israel, including all the borders. Palestinian freedom of movement will be severely limited. Palestine's economy, bereft of its richest agricultural lands and sources of water, unable to transport its goods, will be left de-developed and dependent upon Israel. Palestine will lose its historic, religious, cultural, political and economic capital, Jerusalem. Even the country's airspace and communication spheres will be controlled by Israel. So as to avoid the impression that its actions are in fact unilateral, Israel will declare the borders "provisional," but this means, in reality, the transformation of a temporary military state of Occupation into a permanent regime, effectively depriving the Palestinians of their fundamental rights of self-determination.

The international community cannot remain silent. It is inconceivable that, only a few years after the fall of both the Berlin Wall and South African apartheid, the international community would permit an entire people to be literally imprisoned and a new apartheid regime to emerge before our eyes.

We of the Palestinian, Israeli and international civil societies call upon the international community to take immediate and effective steps:

▶

1. Reaffirm the Palestinian people's inalienable right to self-determination as guaranteed in international law.
2. End totally Israeli occupation and colonization of all Arab lands, and dismantle the Wall.
3. Find a just and mutually agreed-upon solution to the refugee issues that complies with international law and UN Resolution 194 regarding the rights of Palestinian refugees.
4. Guarantee to the Arab-Palestinian citizens of Israel the fundamental right to full equality.
5. Ensure the integrity and security of all the states in the region.

For the sake of justice and genuine peace in Palestine/Israel, we call upon you to join with us in initiating a worldwide Campaign to Prevent Israeli Apartheid.

- **Intensifying boycott, divestment and sanctions campaigns.** (See ICAHD's position paper and statement, Appendix 4.)
- **Legal initiatives.** Developing a strategy for bringing to international courts cases of Israeli army officers, policymakers and civil servants involved in human rights violations, and publicizing them.
- **Lobbying.** While confronting the political establishment is important, we should also engage with it. Each country's activist community should develop a program of lobbying its leaders, both official and others (church leaders, opinion-makers, intellectuals, and so on), as well as lobbying and currying relations with university teachers and students, trade unions, religious groups and other significant members of the civil society.
- **Additional activities:**
    - **Development of an on-line resource pool** of visuals (photos, film-clips, access to films, PowerPoint presentations, and so on), maps, brochures, documents and reports.
    - **Organizing speaking tours** for Israeli and Palestinian activists. Anti-apartheid activists from South Africa

might also be recruited to help in strategizing, mobilizing and speaking.

—**Developing exhibits** on issues related to *nishul*, house demolitions and women's experiences under Occupation, as well as artistic exhibits.

—**Theatrical performances.** A number of powerful theater pieces exist and could be mounted locally: "My Name is Rachel Corrie," "Territories," and others.

—**Learning and solidarity activities in Palestine-Israel.** Expanding the wide variety of activities "on the ground" offered by Palestinian and Israeli organizations, such as critical tours of the Occupied Territories, conferences, workshops and resistance activities. These experiences are powerful ways of bringing target groups—activists, parliamentary delegations, journalists, faculty and students, community leaders and others—into contact with the realities, issues and people involved. They should be employed as effective means of persuasion.

Stage II: When Apartheid is Declared, a Full-Fledged Anti-Apartheid Campaign

The steps suggested above are intended to call public attention to the coming plan of apartheid, to make it an issue *before* it happens, and in that way prime public opinion for our strong response. For in all likelihood an apartheid regime *will be* declared (though not by that name, of course) in the near future. We must be ready, primed for a strong response that redefines the conflict from one of occupation to one of apartheid.

Planned responses within the framework of a major campaign include the following:

- **Worldwide ads.** When apartheid becomes a reality, we should have ads already prepared and monies raised to take out large ads in our major newspapers proclaiming the establishment of a new apartheid regime, explaining in bullet form why it is an apartheid regime, and calling for protests and resistance activities. We should have materials ready for press conferences, key journalists identified and primed, protests planned and have ready any other measures we think effective. But we must be ready: if we merely respond after the fact, our voice will be lost.

- **Major gatherings and demonstrations.** Gatherings and demonstrations are ideal ways of mobilizing our supporters; they give focus and urgency to our efforts to organize. They also give tangible expression to our campaign. May 2008 stands out as a crucial date, the 60th anniversary of 1948.

- **Major conference/protest gatherings on the issue of implementation of international law**, to be held either in Geneva (the Swiss government being responsible for convening the High Contracting Parties of the Fourth Geneva Convention) or in Jerusalem (alternating between Israeli and Palestinian areas). Such a conference, with a strong protest/demand component, would focus attention on the critical problem of implementing international humanitarian law and human rights conventions, with specific demands to apply international law in order to end 40 years of occupation.

The second major meta-campaign being developed by ICAHD is called **60 Years Later: Marking 1948.** A central concept underlying the year-long campaign is the overarching policy and process described in this book: displacement and dispossession, *nishul*, taking place on both sides of the Green Line. The theme of the 60th anniversary of 1948, however, must be inclusive as well as clear and uncompromising. Since Israeli Jews today constitute a national group, as do the Palestinians, a theme must be formulated which encompasses the rights of both peoples and paves the way for a just resolution of the conflict. Toward this end, a tri-lateral theme is suggested: End the Occupation. Stop *nishul*. Self-determination for both peoples. This captures the essence of the conflict yet leaves open the particular solution which the peoples will eventually negotiate. (I won't go into more detail here.)

Within these meta-campaigns all the ongoing campaigns focusing on particular issues can be placed: campaigns for boycott, divestment and sanctions (BDS), Stop the Wall, campaigns against house demolitions, against the demolition of the caves in the South Hebron Hills, against arms sales to Israel; campaigns to suspend the EU Association Agreements with Israel, in support of Palestinian farmers, of refugee rights, and so on. Each of these campaigns is important, but without Big Picture meta-campaigns in which to frame them, the public is liable to lose the forest for the trees.

REDEEMING ISRAEL

Israel sits atop a seething poltergeist and the phantoms are clearly stirring. The delusion, or hope that the Land of Israel was the Jews' exclusive patrimony, "a land without people for a people without a land," has turned into a violent nightmare, even after 60 years of systematic attempts to erase all traces of its Muslim, Christian, Palestinian and Bedouin character. It is a self-defeating enterprise. The more we Israeli Jews try to "Judaize" Palestine, the more we destroy it. Currently we are engaged in burying it under massive Los Angeles-scale highways, dense blocks of fortress-like "neighborhoods," *kibbutzim*-cum-shopping malls and, still, under national parks like the "City of David" in the Silwan area of East Jerusalem. The more we assert our singular claims, the more we discover that a country like Israel-Palestine can never "belong" to a particular people.

I am an Israeli in Palestine, but I am also an Israeli. Sometimes I get glimpses of what could be if "the situation" did not foreclose all options. When I take my granddaughter to play on Saturday in the public park near my house, I encounter dozens of Palestinian families picnicking alongside Jewish families, many of them religious and certainly not "leftist" in their views. All our relations on the swings and the slides, where there is sometimes great crowding and competition among impatient kids, are normal; no more or less cordial than in any other public place. In those moments the stupidity of the conflict strikes me. All the suffering, for what? For the settlements? So that 25 percent of the world's Jews can have a state of their own? We're trapped in a tribal paradigm that neither serves the interests of the Jews of Israel—most of whom have long since become Israelis with no need whatsoever for a "Jewish" state—nor fits the global reality of the twenty-first century, our walls versus the internet. There's got to be an alternative, an *Israeli* alternative.

"When we enter our land," said Yitzhak Epstein in "The Hidden Question" (1905 (2004)) more than a century ago, "we must rid ourselves of all thoughts of conquest and uprooting....We need to refrain from every ugly enterprise, from every suspect step and from every action that has a tinge of injustice." He then poses "the question of questions": "How can we establish ourselves in the Land of Israel without sinning against justice and without harming anyone?" His answer of *1905*, had it been heeded, might have avoided the terrible and ongoing conflict in which we are now embroiled:

> Our approach to land purchase must be a direct expression of our general attitude to the Arab people. The principles that must guide our actions when we settle amidst or near this people are:
>
> A. The Hebrew people, first and foremost among all peoples in the teaching of justice and law, absolute equality, and human

brotherhood, respects not only the individual rights of every person, but also the national rights of every people and tribe.

B. The people Israel, as it aspire to rebirth, is a partner in thought and in deed to all the peoples who are stirring to life; it honors and respects their aspirations, and when it comes to contact with them, it cultivates their national recognition.

We must, therefore, enter into a covenant with the Arabs and conclude an agreement that will be of great value to both sides and to all humankind...because its outcome is the rebirth of two ancient Semitic peoples, talented and full of potential, who complement each other....We need, therefore, to study the psyche of our neighbors and to understand its differences.

Was the conflict between the Jews and Arabs inevitable? Imagine what could have happened if Epstein had been listened to. What, if instead of pressing an exclusive claim to the country, the Zionist movement had said to the Arabs: "We want to come home to the Land of Israel, which we consider as our national homeland. We want to revitalize our national life, our language, our culture; we want to build national institutions like universities and theaters. But we recognize and acknowledge your presence in this country as well, your national aspirations, your claims to the land of Syria/Palestine. Let's sit down and try to find a way to accommodate our separate yet mutual national interests."

Epstein's alternative vision is as relevant today as it was a hundred years ago. *Everything* he warned of—colonial condescension towards the "primitive Arabs," stealing the land of the peasants, ignoring Palestinian nationalism and its national claims, exclusivity, employing violence against the those who stand in our way, using foreign governments to press our claims against the will of the local population—are sins, avoidable sins, *colonial* sins, for which we are all paying until this today. True, the early Zionists were "complete illiterates in anything concerning the Arabs" and had little knowledge of the country. True, they were caught in an Eastern European tribal form of nationalism that led them to press an exclusive claim to the land, foreclosing any possible accommodation with the local Arab population. True, Arab, and particularly Palestinian, nationalism was still in its infancy, a generation behind that of the Jews—though clear expressions of it were certainly in evidence. But there *were* voices in the *Yishuv* that advocated a non-colonial Jewish national movement in Palestine, what became known as "Cultural Zionism."

The critical voices were there, and they were not marginal ones. They included some of the most renowned names in the Zionist pantheon: Ahad Ha'am, Albert Antebe, Martin Buber, Judah Magnes, Henrietta Szold, Gershom Scholem, Ernst Simon, Hugo Bergmann, Moshe Smilansky, David Yellin and Eliahu Eliaschar, to mention just a few. But they were not heeded because Cultural Zionism's nemesis, the hard-headed, "pragmatic," territorial, exclusivist Political Zionism of Ben Gurion and Jabotinsky thought, as it does right down to the present day, that it can win, that it can dispossess its rival claimants to the Land and create a purely Jewish space. If there is any consistent policy that characterizes the mainstream Zionist movement from its earliest pre-Zionist days in the 1880s until today, it is a complete disregard for the national existence and rights of the Palestinians, combined with efforts to bypass them and secure the Land of Israel for the Jews through both colonial powers and rival Arab leaders in the surrounding countries.

The chickens have come home to roost. Political Zionism has exhausted itself. It may have succeeded beyond the wildest dreams of the Zionist "pioneers." After all, Israel has in-gathered millions of Jews, has become a prosperous state, a formidable military power and a respected member of the international community. But it has failed to achieve accommodation, justice, peace and reconciliation with the Palestinian people. That might not be of prime importance to most Israelis, but it means interminable conflict and, even if we "win" every round, it becomes a Jewish state that, as Ahad

Ha'am feared, has nothing "Jewish" about it, a state rooted in oppression, violence and *nishul* from its inception on. Political Zionism *had* to fail morally and systemically, since it could accommodate itself to the other people living in the land. It can no longer point a way of the present conflict.

That terrible conflict that has pitted us against the Arabs since modern Jewish settlement began in 1882 might never have had to happen if, in the early stages of Zionism, Cultural Zionism had prevailed over an exclusive ethno-nationalism. Cultural Zionists argued that the Jewish people needed only a cultural space where it could develop and flourish. They understood the pluralistic nature of pre-state Palestinian society and the necessity of acknowledging the Palestinian presence. In their efforts to revive Jewish culture and place it on a par with other contemporary cultures, the Land of Israel assumed a central importance, but as a national home, not yet a political state. They questioned early on the sustainability of an ethnocracy living in permanent fear, alienation and conflict with the very people with whom it shares its country.

Had they taken control of the Zionist movement instead of Ben Gurion and Jabotinsky, the Jewish-Arab conflict might still have happened. After all, even "good" nations fight. But the conflict was not inevitable, and the Cultural Zionists, rejecting national exclusivity, could have found a solution. The tragedy is that now we have to do precisely what Epstein proscribed after a delay of a century, when it is so much more difficult. Restorative justice is much harder to swallow than finding the just path on the way. Just witness Israel's absolute unwillingness to deal with the issue of the refugees, perhaps the core of the conflict for the Palestinians. Not only can we not contemplate allowing their return to Israel—though that right is categorically enshrined in international law—we cannot even acknowledge that right or the role we played in driving the refugees from the country, critical to any process of reconciliation, because to do so would undermine the very concept of exclusivity upon which Political Zionism and the state of Israel are founded.

The time might be ripe for a return to a New Cultural Zionism capable of acknowledging and dealing with the bi-nationalism that, like it or not, defines Palestine/Israel today. Even in a bi-national state a New Cultural Zionism would preserve a vibrant Israeli culture, a powerful economy and strong national institutions while opening up possibilities of integration, development and reconciliation closed to ethnocracy. This vision lies at the root of this book. If it comes about finally, after long and bitter struggle, it will finally resolve the seeming contradiction in my being an Israeli in Palestine.

My life's work at this political moment is situated on the side of Israelis, Palestinians and good people everywhere working to end the Occupation and to get on the promises of a just peace in our region. I really don't understand why this should be controversial. I don't mind being attacked and denigrated by people who disagree with me, although I would wish they could enter into dialogue rather than seeing *me* as the problem. My greatest source of disappointment, however, are those who *do* agree with me, and especially the majority of Jews who share my principles, my overall vision and even (in their honest moments when no one else is around) my analysis, but are unwilling to stand up for justice. These are the liberals, the "good people," the "moderate" local clergy, including a rabbi, who criticized Martin Luther King's coming to Birmingham to further civil rights in the city. "I must make two honest confessions to you, my Christian and Jewish brothers," he wrote in his *Letter from Birmingham Jail*:

> First, I must confess that over the past few years I have been gravely disappointed with the white moderate. I have almost reached the regrettable conclusion that the Negro's great stumbling block in his stride toward freedom is not the White Citizen's Councilor or the Ku Klux Klanner, but the white moderate, who is more devoted to "order" than to justice; who prefers a negative peace

which is the absence of tension to a positive peace which is the presence of justice; who constantly says: "I agree with you in the goal you seek, but I cannot agree with your methods of direct action;" who paternalistically believes he can set the timetable for another man's freedom; who lives by a mythical concept of time and who constantly advises the Negro to wait for a "more convenient season." Shallow understanding from people of good will is more frustrating than absolute misunderstanding from people of ill will. Lukewarm acceptance is much more bewildering than outright rejection.

So, until Israelis, Palestinians and good people everywhere come together to ensure that no more Palestinian homes are demolished, Salim and I will refuse to be enemies and will continue our struggle. We're going out to "wipe up" some humus this week in a little place near the Old City, where we'll talk about our next round of rebuilding. An orthodox Jew living in the US, an 80-year-old Holocaust survivor who is extremely distraught at what Israel does in the name of the Jews, in *his* name, donated $1.5 million to ICAHD to build a home for every Palestinian family whose home is demolished in this 40th year of the Occupation, about 300 homes. Salim, a construction engineer, is our field coordinator responsible for talking to the families and supervising the building. I know what he's going to say as we lick the humus off our fingers. Salim's going to lean over, pick at my shirt as if he's confiding in me his greatest secret, and say: "You know, what's good for the Arabs is good for the Jews." I can't argue with that.

POSTSCRIPT

Just before this book went to print, at the end of November 2007, Israel, the Palestinians and representatives of 49 other countries, including Saudi Arabia and Syria, met under American auspices in Annapolis. The meeting (downgraded from a "regional summit") went well. By mid-December the two sides will begin negotiating the final status issues, with the intention of signing a peace agreement before the end of 2008, before President Bush leaves office. Signs that some progress might be made on the Israeli-Syrian front were also encouraging.

The problem, however, is not *how* to reach peace. The two-state solution has been readily available for the past 20, if not 40 years. The problem remains one of good faith. Is Israel genuinely willing to end the conflict by permitting the establishment of a viable and truly sovereign Palestinian state or, as has been the case in the past, is it trying to finesse permanent control over the entire Land of Israel under the guise of a two-state solution? On the one hand, cracks are appearing in Israel's ability either to sustain its Occupation or to create a Palestinian Bantustan. "If the day comes when the two-state solution collapses, and we face a South African-style struggle for equal voting rights (also for the Palestinians in the territories)," Olmert said plainly after the Annapolis conference, "then, as soon as that happens, the State of Israel is finished" (*Ha'aretz*, November 29, 2007). On the other hand, the Olmert government is already throwing up insurmountable obstacles to a negotiated peace. It is now requiring the Palestinians to recognize Israel as a "Jewish state," something both the Palestinian Authority and Israel's own Palestinian citizens refuse outright. It is conditioning its agreement to abide by the first phase of the Road Map, which calls for a freeze on settlement building, on agreement that such a freeze does not apply to the Jerusalem area or the settlement blocs. And it is demanding "security before a political settlement," meaning it may negotiate a solution but will delay implementation until it is satisfied that absolute security has been achieved—an impossible demand. Nor is the Olmert government strong enough to negotiate a settlement. Just before the Annapolis meeting the Knesset passed a law requiring an unattainable two-thirds majority for any change in the status of Jerusalem.

The overriding question for Israeli governments, then, is not how to reach peace, but how to transform its occupation into a permanent political fact without seeming to descend into apartheid. If that cannot be achieved in the time-frame established by Annapolis, well, the tried-and-true policy of maintaining the status quo indefinitely remains an effective default position.

Appendix 1
House Demolitions in the Occupied Territories since 1967

Year	No. of Demolitions
1967	6,317
1968	140
1969	301
1970	191
1971	2,231
1972	35
1973	34
1974	61
1975	77
1976	24
1977	1
1978	2
1979	18
1980	30
1981	24
1982	35
1983	12
1984	2
1985	44
1986	49
1987	104
1988	587
1989	567
1990	306
1991	307
1992	193
1993	130
1994	153
1995	69
1996	168
1997	257
1998	180
1999	142
2000–04 (Intifada)	4,747 (2,781 military) (1,966 administrative)
2005	290
2006	319
Total	**18,147**

These are figures for Palestinian homes. If approximately 120,000 Druze and Arabs were expelled from the Syria Golan Heights in 1967 and their villages (134 in number) were completely demolished, that makes about 20,000 additional demolished homes, assuming six people per family unit.

SOURCES

The following sources are by year. In years without sources, the figures were arrived at through interviewing Israeli government or military personnel, or by collecting Palestinian testimonies.

1967: United Nations General Assembly (1967). "Report of the Secretary-General under General Assembly Resolution 2252 (ES-V) and Security Council resolution 237 (1967)." Retrieved September 25, 2006 from <www.domino.un.org>. Thomas Aboud (2000) "The Moroccan Quarter: A History of the Present." Jerusalem: Jerusalem Quarterly. Retrieved September 25, 2006 from <www.jerusalemquarterly.org>. Palestine Remembered (n.d.) "Imwas," "Bayt Nuba," "Yalu." Retrieved September 25, 2006 from <www.palestineremembered.com>. The UN Report refers to 850 houses demolished in Qalqilya and 360 in Beit Awa. It also states that the Beit Mersim (Beit Marsam) was entirely demolished and had an original population of approximately 500. We averaged just over eight people per house to arrive at the figure of 60 houses for this village. Also quoted in the report is the demolition of 18 houses in Surif. Aboud's articles states that 135 houses were demolished in the Moroccan Quarter of Jerusalem's Old City. The villages of 'Imwas, Yalu and Beit Nuba were entirely demolished in 1967. The website "Palestine Remembered" cites the 1931 British census listing 224 houses in 'Imwas, 245 in Yalu and 226 in Beit Nuba. According to the 1961 Jordanian census, the population of the towns increased by 91 percent, 70 percent and 43 percent. An extremely conservative estimate would be a 10 percent increase in the amount of housing by the 1961 census, adding a total of 69 more houses for a three-village-total of 764. This total does not include the numbers from the Jordan Valley villages of Nuseirat, Jiftlik, and Arajish, all of which were leveled.

1967–82: United Nations General Assembly (1984). "Report of the Secretary-General, Living Conditions of the Palestinian People in the Occupied Palestinian Territories." Retrieved September 25, 2006 from <www.domino.un.org>. This is the source for all statistics on demolitions between 1967 and 1982. In the actual report these are listed as punitive demolitions because all demolitions were classified as "Collective Punishment."

1971: Human Rights Watch (2004). *Razing Rafah.* New York: Human Rights Watch. Jeff Halper (2005) *Obstacles to Peace* (third edition). Jerusalem: PalMap. This number is from a mass demolition that took place in the Gaza Strip in August. It happens that Ariel Sharon was the leader of that mission.

1983: Ronny Talmor (1989). *Demolition and Sealing of Houses as a Punitive Measure in the West Bank and Gaza Strip During the Intifada.* Jerusalem: B'tselem. This report is the source for the data on punitive demolitions from 1983 to 1986.

1987: B'tselem (2005). "Statistics on Demolition of Houses as Punishment 1987–2005." Retrieved September 25, 2006 from <www.btselem.org>. All the statistics on punitive house demolitions from 1987 to 2005 come from this source. B'tselem (2006). "Statistics on Demolition of Houses Built Without Permits." Retrieved September 25, 2006 from <www.btselem.org>. All the statistics on administrative demolitions between 1987 and 1993 come from this source.

1994: Meir Margalit (2006) *Discrimination in the Heart of the Holy City.* Jerusalem: IPCC. Also personal communication with Dr. Margalit, field researcher for ICAHD. B'tselem (2006). "Statistics on Demolition of Houses Built Without Permits." Retrieved September 25, 2006 from <www.btselem.org> . UN Office for the Coordination of Humanitarian Affairs (2005–06). Weekly Humanitarian Briefings Nos 86–178. All statistics about administrative house demolitions between 1994 and 2006 come from these sources.

2000–04: B'tselem (2006). "Statistics on Houses Demolished for Alleged Military Purposes." Retrieved September 25, 2006 from <www.btselem. org>. UN Office for the Coordination of Humanitarian Affairs (2005–06). Weekly Humanitarian Briefings Nos 86–178.

Appendix 2
The Road Map, and Israel's 14 Reservations

This abridged version of the Road Map sets out the initiative's goals and what is required of each of the parties.

GOALS

Quartet

1. To resolve the Israel-Palestinian conflict through a negotiated settlement leading to a final and comprehensive settlement of the Israel-Palestinian conflict by 2005.
2. To end the occupation.
3. To see the emergence of an independent, democratic Palestinian state side by side in peace and security with Israel and its other neighbors.
4. To address Israel's strategic goals of security and regional integration.

MECHANISMS

Quartet

- Goals and process based on terms of reference of the Madrid Conference and the principle of land for peace, UNSCRs 242, 338 and 1397, agreements previously reached by the parties, and the Arab initiative proposed by Saudi Crown Prince Abdullah, as endorsed by the Arab Summit in Beirut.
- A performance-based plan with clear phases and benchmarks to be agreed upon (including their interpretation) in advance of the process.
- Supervision by the Quartet—although the United States is bidding for a leadership role. According to the American plan, the US will head the supervising mechanism of the Road Map's implementation, helped by the other members of the Quartet. (The US government recently announced that a special unit would be

set up in the CIA to monitor the implementation process.) The supervising mechanism will further include four committees: a Security Committee that will deal with reforms in the Palestinian Authority (PA) security apparatus, renewed security coordination and monitoring of Palestinian activity against terror, as well as the Israeli withdrawals from PA areas. A Special Operations Committee will deal with the settlement freeze, evacuation of the illegal outposts, a cessation of the incitement and the reopening of Palestinian institutions in East Jerusalem. A Humanitarian Committee will try to alleviate the suffering of the Palestinian residents of the Occupied Territories and address the policies behind it (such as the closure). A fourth committee will deal with reforms in the Palestinian Authority.

PHASES OF IMPLEMENTATION

PHASE I: October 2002 to May 2003 (Transformation/Elections)
FIRST STAGE: October–December 2002 (three months)

Quartet Requirements

- Quartet develops detailed Road Map, in consultation with the parties, to be adopted at December Quartet/Ad Hoc Liaison Committee (AHLC) meeting.
- AHLC Ministerial launches major donor assistance effort.
- In coordination with Quartet, implementation of US rebuilding, training and resumed security cooperation plan in collaboration with outside oversight board (US-Egypt-Jordan).

Palestinian Requirements

- Appointment of new Palestinian Cabinet, establishment of empowered Prime Minister, including any necessary Palestinian legal reforms for this purpose.
- Palestinian Legislative Council (PLC) appoints Commission charged with drafting of Palestinian constitution for Palestinian statehood.
- PA establishes independent Election Commission. PLC reviews and revises election law.
- Palestinian leadership issues unequivocal statement reiterating Israel's right to exist in peace and security and calling for an immediate end to the armed Intifada and all acts of violence against

Israelis anywhere. All Palestinian institutions end incitement against Israel.

- Palestinian security organizations are consolidated into three services reporting to an empowered Interior Minister.

Israeli Requirements

- Government of Israel (GOI) facilitates travel of Palestinian officials for PLC sessions, internationally supervised security retraining, and other PA business without restriction.
- GOI implements recommendations of the Bertini report to improve humanitarian conditions, including lifting curfews and easing movement between Palestinian areas.
- GOI ends actions undermining trust, including attacks in civilian areas, and confiscation/demolition of Palestinian homes/property, deportations, as a punitive measure or to facilitate Israeli construction.
- GOI immediately resumes monthly revenue clearance process in accordance with agreed transparency monitoring mechanism. GOI transfers all arrears of withheld revenues to Palestinian Ministry of Finance by end of December 2002, according to specific timeline.
- GOI dismantles settlement outposts erected since establishment of the present Israeli government and in contravention of current Israeli government guidelines.

Joint Palestinian-Israeli Requirements

- Restructured/retrained Palestinian security forces and IDF counterparts begin phased resumption of security cooperation and other undertakings as agreed in the Tenet work plan, including regular senior-level meetings, with the participation of US security officials.

Requirements of Arab States

- Arab states move decisively to cut off public/private funding of extremist groups, channel financial support for Palestinians through Palestinian Ministry of Finance.

PHASE I: SECOND STAGE: January to May 2003 (five months)

(Goals: For the next five months: An end to terror and violence, normalization of Palestinian life and establishment of Palestinian institutions. Israel withdraws from the PA areas, and the status quo from before the Intifada is restored, in accordance with progress in the security cooperation, according to the Tenet work plan. A settlement freeze is announced, according to the Mitchell plan.)

Quartet Requirements

- Quartet monitoring mechanism established.

Palestinian Requirements

- Continued Palestinian political reform to ensure powers of PLC, Prime Minister, and Cabinet.
- Independent Commission circulates draft Palestinian constitution, based on strong parliamentary democracy, for public comment/ debate.
- Devolution of power to local authorities through revised Municipalities Law.
- Palestinian performance on agreed judicial, administrative, and economic benchmarks, as determined by Task Force.
- Constitution drafting Commission proposes draft document for submission after elections to new PLC for approval.
- Palestinians hold free, open, and fair elections for PLC.
- The Palestinians begin focused efforts to dismantle the terrorist infrastructure, implement security cooperation, collect illegal weapons and disarm militant groups in the first stage of the program.

Israeli Requirements

- As comprehensive security performance moves forward, IDF withdraws progressively from areas occupied since September 28, 2000. Withdrawal to be completed before holding of Palestinian elections. Palestinian security forces redeploy to areas vacated by IDF.
- GOI facilitates Task Force election assistance, registration of voters, movement of candidates and voting officials.
- GOI reopens East Jerusalem Chamber of Commerce and other closed Palestinian economic institutions in East Jerusalem.
- GOI freezes all settlement activity consistent with the Mitchell report, including natural growth of settlements. Israel is required to make a top priority out of freezing projects that disrupt Palestinian territorial contiguity, including in the Jerusalem area.

Joint Palestinian-Israeli Requirements

- Palestinians and Israelis conclude a new security agreement building upon Tenet work plan, including an effective security mechanism and an end to violence, terrorism, and incitement implemented through a restructured and effective Palestinian security service.

Requirements of Arab States

- Regional support: Upon completion of security steps and IDF withdrawal to September 28, 2000 positions, Egypt and Jordan return ambassadors to Israel.

PHASE II: June 2003 to December 2003 (Transition) (six months)

(Goal: A transition phase, for the purpose of establishing a Palestinian state inside temporary borders according to a new constitution. The Quartet will convene an international conference, in consultation with the parties (in the early draft it required their consent), to be followed by the start of Israeli-Palestinian dialogue about the establishment of the interim state. Still under discussion is to what extent the Quartet will act to win the new Palestinian state acceptance in the UN.)

- Progress into Phase II will be based upon the consensus judgment of the Quartet of whether conditions are appropriate to proceed, taking into account performance of both parties. That judgment is facilitated by establishment of a permanent monitoring mechanism on the ground.

Phase II starts after Palestinian elections and ends with possible creation of a Palestinian state with provisional borders by end of 2003.

Quartet Requirements

- International Conference: Convened by the Quartet, in agreement with the parties, immediately after the successful conclusion of Palestinian elections to support Palestinian economic recovery and launch negotiations between Israelis and Palestinians on the possibility of a state with provisional borders. Such a meeting would be inclusive, based on the goal of a comprehensive Middle East peace (including between Israel and Syria, and Israel and Lebanon), and based on the principles described in the preamble to this document.

- Conclusion of transitional understanding and creation of state with provisional borders by end of 2003. Enhanced international role in monitoring transition.

Palestinian Requirements

- Newly elected PLC finalizes and approves new constitution for democratic, independent Palestinian state.
- Continued implementation of security cooperation, complete collection of illegal weapons, disarm militant groups, according to Phase I security agreement.

Israeli Requirements

- Further action on settlements simultaneous with establishment of Palestinian state with provisional borders.

Joint Palestinian-Israeli Requirements

- Israeli-Palestinian negotiations aimed at creation of a state with provisional borders.
- Implementation of prior agreements, to enhance maximum territorial contiguity.
- Conclusion of transitional understanding and creation of state with provisional borders by end of 2003.

Requirements of Arab States

- Other pre-Intifada Arab links to Israel restored (trade offices, and so on).
- Revival of "multilateral talks" (regional water, environmental, economic development, refugee, arms control issues).

PHASE III: 2004 to 2005 (Statehood)

(Goals: A permanent arrangement. The purpose of the agreement is an end to the Israeli-Palestinian conflict. In early 2004, a second international conference is convened, to welcome the new state with its temporary borders and to formally launch the negotiations for a final status agreement.)

- Progress into Phase III is based on the judgment of the Quartet, taking into account actions of all parties and Quartet monitoring.

Quartet Requirements

- Second International Conference: Convened by the Quartet, with agreement of the parties, at beginning of 2004 to endorse agreement reached on state with provisional borders and to launch negotiations between Israel and Palestine toward a final, permanent status resolution in 2005, including on borders, Jerusalem, refugees and settlements; and to support progress toward a comprehensive Middle East settlement between Israel and Lebanon and Syria, to be achieved as soon as possible.

Palestinian Requirements

- Continued comprehensive, effective progress on the reform agenda laid out by the Task Force in preparation for final status agreement.

Israeli Requirements

- None.

Joint Palestinian-Israeli Requirements

- Continued sustained, effective security cooperation based on security agreements reached by end of Phase I and other prior agreements.
- The text also has a special section on Jerusalem. It says that a negotiated settlement of Jerusalem's status will take into account "the political and religious concerns of both sides and will protect the religious interests of Jews, Christians and Muslims throughout the world."

Requirements of Arab States

- Arab state acceptance of normal relations with Israel and security for all the states of the region, consistent with Beirut Arab Summit initiative.

ISRAEL'S 14 "RESERVATIONS"

1. The maintenance of "calm" is a condition for the commencement and continuation of the process. The Palestinians must disarm and dismantle the existing security organizations and "terrorist organizations" (Hamas,

Islamic Jihad, the Popular Front, the Democratic Front, and the al-Aqsa Brigades), implement new security reforms and act to combat terror, violence and incitement. (Israel is not required to crease violence or end incitement against Palestinians.)

2. Progress between phases will be conditional on the full implementation of the previous phase. Performance benchmarks and not time-lines will be the only reference points.

3. The emergence of a new leadership in the Palestinian Authority.

4. Monitoring progress will be solely under American management.

5. The character of the provisional Palestinian state will be determined through negotiations between the Palestinian Authority and Israel. The provisional state will have provisional borders and "certain aspects of sovereignty." It will be fully demilitarized without the authority to undertake defense alliances or military cooperation. Israel will control the entry and exit of all persons and cargo, as well as its air space and electromagnetic space.

6. The Palestinians must declare Israel's right to exist as a Jewish state and waive the refugees' Right of Return.

7. The end of the process will end all claims and not only end the conflict.

8. A settlement will be reached through agreement between the two parties in accordance to Bush's June 24 address.

9. Neither the Road Map nor the Quartet will enter into final status issues. Among the issues *not* to be discussed are settlement, the status of the PA, and all other issues relating to the final settlement.

10. Removal of all terms of reference except UN Resolutions 242 and 338, and those only as an "outline" of a settlement, which will be arrived at autonomously between the parties.

11. Continued reform in the Palestinian Authority, including a transitional Constitution. (Israel has no Constitution.)

12. Redeployment of Israel forces to the September 2000 lines will be subject to security considerations and calm.

13. Subject to security concerns, Israel will work towards the restoration of normalcy to Palestinian life—without reference to US Bertini report.

14. Arab states will condemn terrorism. No link will be made between the Palestinian track and negotiating tracks with other Arab states.

Appendix 3
Letter From US President George W. Bush to Prime Minister Ariel Sharon (April 14, 2004)

His Excellency
Ariel Sharon
Prime Minister of Israel

Dear Mr. Prime Minister,

Thank you for your letter setting out your disengagement plan.

The United States remains hopeful and determined to find a way forward toward a resolution of the Israeli-Palestinian dispute. I remain committed to my June 24, 2002 vision of two states living side by side in peace and security as the key to peace, and to the roadmap as the route to get there.

We welcome the disengagement plan you have prepared, under which Israel would withdraw certain military installations and all settlements from Gaza, and withdraw certain military installations and settlements in the West Bank. These steps described in the plan will mark real progress toward realizing my June 24, 2002 vision, and make a real contribution towards peace. We also understand that, in this context, Israel believes it is important to bring new opportunities to the Negev and the Galilee. We are hopeful that steps pursuant to this plan, consistent with my vision, will remind all states and parties of their own obligations under the roadmap.

The United States appreciates the risks such an undertaking represents. I therefore want to reassure you on several points.

First, the United States remains committed to my vision and to its implementation as described in the roadmap. The United States will do its utmost to prevent any attempt by anyone to impose any other plan. Under the roadmap, Palestinians must undertake an immediate cessation of armed activity and all acts of violence against Israelis anywhere, and all official Palestinian institutions must end incitement against Israel.

The Palestinian leadership must act decisively against terror, including sustained, targeted, and effective operations to stop terrorism and dismantle terrorist capabilities and infrastructure. Palestinians must undertake a comprehensive and fundamental political reform that includes a strong parliamentary democracy and an empowered prime minister.

Second, there will be no security for Israelis or Palestinians until they and all states, in the region and beyond, join together to fight terrorism and dismantle terrorist organizations. The United States reiterates its steadfast commitment to Israel's security, including secure, defensible borders, and to preserve and strengthen Israel's capability to deter and defend itself, by itself, against any threat or possible combination of threats.

Third, Israel will retain its right to defend itself against terrorism, including to take actions against terrorist organizations. The United States will lead efforts, working together with Jordan, Egypt, and others in the international community, to build the capacity and will of Palestinian institutions to fight terrorism, dismantle terrorist organizations, and prevent the areas from which Israel has withdrawn from posing a threat that would have to be addressed by any other means. The United States understands that after Israel withdraws from Gaza and/or parts of the West Bank, and pending agreements on other arrangements, existing arrangements regarding control of airspace, territorial waters, and land passages of the West Bank and Gaza will continue.

The United States is strongly committed to Israel's security and well-being as a Jewish state. It seems clear that an agreed, just, fair and realistic framework for a solution to the Palestinian refugee issue as part of any final status agreement will need to be found through the establishment of a Palestinian state, and the settling of Palestinian refugees there, rather than in Israel.

As part of a final peace settlement, Israel must have secure and recognized borders, which should emerge from negotiations between the parties in accordance with UNSC Resolutions 242 and 338. In light of new realities on the ground, including already existing major Israeli populations centers, it is unrealistic to expect that the outcome of final status negotiations will be a full and complete return to the armistice lines of 1949, and all previous efforts to negotiate a two-state solution have reached the same conclusion. It is realistic to expect that any final status agreement will only be achieved on the basis of mutually agreed changes that reflect these realities.

I know that, as you state in your letter, you are aware that certain responsibilities face the State of Israel. Among these, your government has stated that the barrier being erected by Israel should be a security rather than political barrier, should be temporary rather than permanent, and therefore not prejudice any final status issues including final borders, and its route should take into account, consistent with security needs, its impact on Palestinians not engaged in terrorist activities.

As you know, the United States supports the establishment of a Palestinian state that is viable, contiguous, sovereign, and independent, so that the Palestinian people can build their own future in accordance with my vision set forth in June 2002 and with the path set forth in the roadmap. The United States will join with others in the international community to foster the development of democratic political institutions and new leadership committed to those institutions, the reconstruction of civic institutions, the growth of a free and prosperous economy, and the building of capable security institutions dedicated to maintaining law and order and dismantling terrorist organizations.

A peace settlement negotiated between Israelis and Palestinians would be a great boon not only to those peoples but to the peoples of the entire region. Accordingly, the United States believes that all states in the region have special responsibilities: to support the building of the institutions of a Palestinian state; to fight terrorism, and cut off all forms of assistance to individuals and groups engaged in terrorism; and to begin now to move toward more normal relations with the State of Israel. These actions would be true contributions to building peace in the region.

Mr. Prime Minister, you have described a bold and historic initiative that can make an important contribution to peace. I commend your efforts and your courageous decision which I support. As a close friend and ally, the United States intends to work closely with you to help make it a success.

Sincerely,

George W. Bush

Appendix 4
The Case for Sanctions Against Israel: ICAHD's Position on Boycott, Divestment and Sanctions

In line with the principles just discussed, economic sanctions against Israel are not invoked against Israel per se, but against Israel *until the Occupation ends*. With this proviso it is Israel's policy of occupation that is targeted, its status as an Occupying Power, not Israel itself. When South Africa ended its system of apartheid, sanctions ceased and it fully rejoined the international community. When apartheid ended, so did the boycott of its sports teams, one of the most potent measures employed to impress on the South African government its international isolation. The divestment campaign currently directed against Caterpillar has gained considerable momentum among the international public, effectively educating people about Israel's policy of demolishing Palestinian homes. It has generated calls for other sanctions, such as the Presbyterian Church's initiative to divest from companies profiting from the Occupation. The European Parliament has also called for trade sanctions on Israel given Israel's violation of the "Association Agreements" that prohibit the sale of settlement products under the "Made in Israel" label. The US Congress should take similar steps, since Israel's use of American weapons against civilian populations violates the human rights provisions of the Arms Control Exports Act. The boycott of California grapes in the 1960s played a key role in gaining employment rights for migrant workers. The current boycott of settlement products is intended to express moral opposition to the very presence of settlements while making it economically and politically difficult for Israel to maintain them.

Once it builds momentum, there is probably no more effective means for civil society to effectively pursue justice than a campaign of sanctions. Its power derives less from its economic impact—although, with time, that too can be decisive—than from the moral outrage that impels it. Sanctions themselves seriously affected the South African economy. Following massive protests inside South Africa and escalating international pressure in mid 1984, some 200 US companies and more than 60 British ones withdrew from the country and international lenders cut off Pretoria's access to foreign capital. US Congressional pressure played a crucial role as well, an element totally lacking *vis-à-vis* the Israel-Palestine conflict, which makes the possibility of actually imposing sanctions on Israel that more difficult. In 1986 Congress—*with a Republican-controlled Senate*—passed the Comprehensive Anti-Apartheid Act over the Reagan's veto. The Act banned new US investment in South Africa, sales to the police and military and new bank loans.

Although the Act was not strictly enforced by the Reagan and Bush Administrations, although European governments found ways of quietly doing business with Pretoria (while Israel, by the way, was helping South African businesses bypass sanctions by peddling their products in the US and Europe under a "Made in Israel" label, as well as by continued involvement in military development in South Africa, including nuclear), it did generate a climate—moral and economic—that made it increasingly difficult to maintain business-as-usual with the apartheid regime. The moral dimension led to a delegitimization of the very apartheid system that left no room for "reform." Carried over to Israel's Occupation, the moral element in a larger political condemnation of Israel's policies could delegitimize the Occupation to the point where only its complete end is acceptable. A campaign of sanctions which highlights the moral unacceptability of Israel's Occupation could have a great impact, eventually impelling governments to impose economic sanctions while creating a climate difficult for businesses (beginning with Caterpillar) to continue function.

It is not only the political unacceptability of Israel's Occupation which makes the call for sanction urgent and obligatory, it is the massive violations of Palestinian human rights, of international law and of numerous UN resolutions that the Occupation entails. If Israel as the Occupying Power is not held accountable for the intolerable situation within its ability, indeed, within its *responsibility* to end, the entire international system of justice is rendered meaningless and empty. And that is what makes the Occupation an international issue. If Israel succeeds in defying the Fourth Geneva Convention and making its Occupation permanent, if an entire population is literally locked behind walls and its right of self-determination trampled, then the ability of human rights to win out over an international order founded on power politics and militarism is jeopardized. We all have a stake in ending the Occupation; the implications of occupation actually prevailing and a new apartheid regime emerging are chilling. Since the Palestinians do not have the power to shake off the Occupation on their own and the Israelis will not, only international pressure will effectively achieve a just peace. A campaign of sanctions represents one of the most efficacious measures.

ICAHD supports a campaign for selective sanctions. This approach is no less principled and focused than a call for total sanctions, but it targets

Israel's Occupation rather than Israel itself. A campaign of selective sanctions can be effective if the choice of targets is strategic: refusing to sell arms to Israel that would be used to perpetuate the Occupation, especially in attacks on civilian populations, for example, or banning Israeli sports teams from competing in international tournaments, especially potent in the South African case. (Israel is currently the European basketball champion and is scheduled to play in the football/soccer World Cup.) These and other selected measures could have a great impact upon Israel, as well as the ability to mobilize international opposition to the Occupation. Yet, with strong civil society advocacy, they also have a reasonable chance, over time, of being adopted.

ICAHD, then, supports in principle a multi-tiered campaign of sanctions against Israel *until the Occupation ends*. We believe that a selective campaign is most effective and we would incorporate into that campaigns that other organizations have already launched. ICAHD supports the initiative of churches throughout the world to begin to raise their moral voices—and tentatively flex their financial and political muscle—in support of selective boycott, divestment and sanctions (BDS). The Anglican Church voted in 2006 to divest its shares in Caterpillar and others, amounting to some $64 million in stocks. Over the last few years the Presbyterian Church of the US has moved steadily, despite tremendous pressures exerted upon it by the organized Jewish community, to divest in "multinational corporations that provide products or services to...the Israeli police or military to support and maintain the occupation,...that have established facilities or operations on occupied land,...that provide services or products for the establishment, expansion or maintenance of Israeli settlements,...that provide products or services to Israeli *or Palestinian* organizations/groups that support or facilitate violent acts against innocent civilians,...that provide products or services that support or facilitate the construction of the Separation Barrier" (<www.pcusa. org/mrti/engagement.htm>). We certainly support the campaign against Caterpillar whose bulldozers demolish thousands of Palestinian homes.

We join with the Jewish Voice for Peace (JVP) in the US whose statement in support of the Presbyterians says in part:

> At JVP, we fully support selective divestment from companies that profit from Israel's occupation of the West Bank, Gaza, and East Jerusalem. This includes American companies like Caterpillar who profit from the wholesale destruction of Palestinian homes and orchards. It also includes Israeli companies who depend on settlements for materials or labor or who produce military equipment used to violate Palestinian human rights.
>
> We believe that general divestment from Israel is an unwise strategy at this time. We believe that economic measures targeted specifically at the occupation and the Israeli military complex that

sustains it are much more likely to produce results. However, we absolutely reject the accusation that general divestment or boycott campaigns are inherently anti-Semitic. The Israeli government is a government like any other, and condemning its abuse of state power, as many of its own citizens do quite vigorously, is in no way the same as attacking the Jewish people. Further, it is crucial not only to criticize the immoral and illegal acts of the Israeli government, but to back up that criticism with action.

We also note with satisfaction the many Jewish and Israeli organizations who support the idea of selective sanctions on Israel: European Jews for a Just Peace (a coalition of 16 Jewish groups from eight European countries); New Profile (Israel); Not in My Name (US); Matzpun (Israel/International); Jews Against the Occupation (NYC Chapter); the petition of South African government minister Ronnie Kasrils and legislator Max Ozinsky, which has gathered more than 500 signatories from South African Jews; Jewish Voices Against the Occupation (US); Jewish Women for Justice in Israel and Palestine (US); Gush Shalom (Israel); Jews for Global Justice (US); and Visions of Peace With Justice (US), among others.

ICAHD's statement on BDS is shown in Box 3.

Box 3: Sanctions Against the Israeli Occupation: It's Time

After years of diplomatic and political efforts aimed at inducing Israel to end its Occupation, while watching it grow ever stronger and more permanent, ICAHD supports a multi-tiered campaign of strategic, selective sanctions against Israel *until the Occupation ends*; that is, a campaign targeting Israel's Occupation rather than Israel per se. We believe that in most cases merely enforcing existing laws, international as well as domestic, would render the Occupation untenable and would pull Israel back into compliance with human rights covenants. We also favor selective divestment and boycott as tools of moral and economic pressure.

Since sanctions are a powerful, non-violent, popular means of resisting the Occupation, a campaign of sanctions seems to us the next logical step in international efforts to end the Occupation. While it will develop over time, ICAHD supports the following elements at this time:

- Sales or transfer of arms to Israel conditional upon their use in ways that do not perpetuate the Occupation or violate human rights and international humanitarian law, violations

▶

that would end if governments enforced existing laws and
regulations regarding the use of weapons in contravention of
human rights
- Trade sanctions on Israel due to its violation of the "Association
  Agreements" it has signed with the European Union that
  prohibit the sale of settlement products under the "Made in
  Israel" label, as well as for violations of their human rights
  provisions
- Divestment from companies that profit from involvement
  in the Occupation. In this vein ICAHD supports initiatives
  like that of the Presbyterian Church of the US which targets
  companies contributing materially to the Occupation and
  certainly the campaign against Caterpillar whose bulldozers
  demolish thousands of Palestinian homes
- Boycott of settlement products and of companies that provide
  housing to the settlements or which play a major role in
  perpetuating the Occupation
- Holding individuals, be they policy-makers, military personnel
  carrying out orders or others, personally accountable for
  human rights violations, including trial before international
  courts and bans on travel to other countries.

ICAHD calls on the international community—governments,
trade unions, university communities, faith-based organizations
as well as the broad civil society—to do all that is possible to
hold Israel accountable for its Occupation policies and actions,
thereby hastening the end of this tragedy. While we also call on the
Palestinian Authority to adhere to human rights conventions, our
support for selective sanctions against Israel's Occupation policies
focuses properly on Israel which alone has the power to end the
Occupation and is alone the violator of international law regarding
the responsibilities of an Occupying Power.

Bibliography

Abu Hussein, Hussein, and Fiona McKay. 2003. *Access Denied: Palestinian Land Rights in Israel.* London: Zed Books.

Abu-Zayyad, Ziad. 1997. Land: The Core of the Conflict. *Palestine-Israel Journal* 4(2):13–16.

Aburish, Said K. 1998. *Arafat: From Defender to Dictator.* London: Bloomsbury.

Agha, Hussein, and Robert Malley. 2001. Camp David: A Tragedy of Errors. *New York Review of Books* 48(13).

Ahad Ha'am 1891 (2004) Truth from *Eretz Israel.* In Adam Shatz (ed.) *Prophets Outcast: A Century of Dissident Jewish Writing about Zionism and Israel.* New York: Nation Books, pp. 32–33.

Amnesty International. 1999a. *Demolition and Dispossession: The Destruction of Palestinian Homes* (December).

—— 1999b. *Universal Jurisdiction: 14 Principles on the Effective Exercise of Universal Jurisdiction.* London: Amnesty International (May).

—— 2002a. *Shielded from Scrutiny: IDF Violations in Jenin and Nablus.* London: Amnesty International (November).

—— 2002b. *Without Distinction: Attacks on Civilians by Palestinian Armed Groups.* London: Amnesty International (July).

—— 2004. *Under the Rubble: House Demolition and Destruction of Land and Property.* London: Amnesty International (May).

Baker, James, and Lee Hamilton. 2006. *The Iraq Study Group Report.* Washington: Government Press Office.

Bazbaz, Marwan. 1997. Settlement in the West Bank and the Gaza Strip. *Palestine-Israel Journal* 4(2):31–36.

Begin, Menachem. 1951 (1977). *The Revolt.* New York: Dell.

Beinin, Joel. 2004. No More Tears: Benny Morris and the Road Back from Liberal Zionism. *Middle East Report* 240:38–45.

Beit-Hallahmi, Benjamin. 1987. *Israeli Connection: Who Israel Arms and Why.* New York: Pantheon Books.

—— 1992. *Original Sins: Reflections on the History of Zionism and Israel.* London: Pluto Press.

Ben Ami, Shlomo. 2001. End of a Journey. *Ha'aretz,* September 13.

Ben-Eliezer, Uri. 1995. A Nation-in-Arms: State, Nation and Militarism in Israel's First Years. *Comparative Studies in Society and History* 37(2):264–285.

Benvenisti, Eyal. 1989. *Legal Dualism: The Absorption of the Occupied Territories into Israel.* Jerusalem. Jerusalem Post Press (West Bank Data Project).

—— 2004. *The International Law of Occupation.* Princeton: Princeton University Press.

Benvenisti, Meron. 1996. *Intimate Enemies: Jews and Arabs in a Shared Land*. Berkeley: University of California Press.

—— 2000. *Sacred Landscape: The Buried History of the Holy Land Since 1948*. Berkeley: University of California Press.

Benvenisti, Meron, and Shlomo Khayat. 1988. *The West Bank and Gaza Atlas*. Jerusalem: Jerusalem Post.

Bimkom. 2005. *A Planning Snare: Planning Policy and House Demolitions in East Jerusalem*. Jerusalem: Bimkom (February) (Hebrew).

Bishara, Azmi, Sara Scalenghe, Steve Rothman, and Joel Beinin. 1996. On Palestinians in the Israeli Knesset: Interview with Azmi Bishara. *Middle East Report* 201:27–30.

Bishara, Marwan. 2001. *Palestine/Israel: Peace or Apartheid*. London: Zed Books.

Bollens, Scott. 2000. *On Narrow Ground: Urban Policy and Ethnic Conflict in Jerusalem and Belfast*. Albany: SUNY Press.

Boyle, Francis. 2003. *Palestine, Palestinians and International Law*. Atlanta: Clarity Press.

B'tselem. 1997. *The Quiet Deportation: Revocation of Residency of East Jerusalem Palestinians*. Jerusalem: B'tselem.

—— 1998. *The Quiet Deportation Continues*. Jerusalem: B'tselem

—— 2001. *Not Even a Drop: Water Crisis in Palestinian Villages*. Jerusalem: B'tselem (July).

—— 2002. *Land Grab: Israel's Settlement Policy in the West Bank*. Jerusalem. B'tselem (May).

—— 2004a. *Through No Fault of Their Own: Israel's Punitive House Demolitions in the al-Aqsa Intifada*. Jerusalem: B'tselem (November).

—— 2004b. *Demolition for Alleged Military Purposes: Destruction of Houses and Property on the Rafah-Egyptian Border*. Jerusalem: B'tselem.

Bush, George W. 2004. Letter from US President George W. Bush to Prime Minister Ariel Sharon, April 14 <www.mfa.gov.il/MFA/Peace+Process/Reference+Documents/Exchange+of+letters+Sharon-Bush+14-Apr-2004.htm>

Campbell, Elizabeth. 1998. "Maximum Territory, Minimum Population"—Jerusalem: The Laboratory for the Policies of Zionist Colonization. *News From Within* 13(11):8–13.

Carey, Roane (ed.). 2001. *The New Intifada: Resisting Israel's Apartheid*. New York: The Verso Press.

Carey, Roane, and Jonathan Shanon (eds.). 2002. *The Other Israel: Voice of Refusal and Dissent*. New York: The New Press.

Carter, Jimmy. 2006. *Palestine: Peace Not Apartheid*. New York: Simon and Schuster.

Cheshin, Amir S., Bill Hutman, and Avi Melamed. 1999. *Separate and Unequal: The Inside Story of Israeli Rule in East Jerusalem*. Cambridge: Harvard University Press.

Chomsky, Noam. 1983. *Fateful Triangle: The United States, Israel and the Palestinians*. Boston: South End Press.

Christian Aid. 2003. *Losing Ground: Israel, Poverty and the Palestinians*. London: Christian Aid.

—— 2004. *Facts on the Ground: The End of the Two-State Solution?* London: Christian Aid.

Christison, Kathleen, and Bill Christison. 2005. Polluting Palestine: The Settlements and Their Sewage. *Counterpunch* <www.counterpunch.org>, September 24.

Colton, Joel. 1987. *Leon Blum: Humanist in Politics*. Durham: Duke University Press.

Cohen, Shaul Ephraim. 1993. *The Politics of Planting: Israeli-Palestinian Competition for Control of Land in the Jerusalem Periphery*. Chicago: University of Chicago Press.

Davis, Uri. 2003. *Apartheid Israel: Possibilities for the Struggle Within*. London: Zed Books.

de Jong, Jan. 2000. Israel's Greater Jerusalem Engulfs the West Bank's Core. *Jerusalem Quarterly File* 10.

Dershowitz, Alan. 2003. *The Case For Israel*. Hoboken: Wiley.

Drinan, Robert. 2001. *The Mobilization of Shame*. New Haven: Yale University Press.

Eliashar, E. 1997. *To Live with Palestinians*. Jerusalem: Misgav (Hebrew).

Eldar, Akiva, and Idit Zartal. 2004. *Masters of the Land: The Settlers and the State of Israel 1967–2004*. Or Yehuda: Kinneret (Hebrew).

Elon, Amos. 1971. *Israel: Founders and Sons*. New York: Holt, Rinehart and Winston.

Epstein, Yitzhak. 1905 (2004). The Hidden Question. In Adam Shatz (ed.) *Prophets Outcast: A Century of Dissident Jewish Writing about Zionism and Israel*. New York: Nation Books, pp. 35–52.

Eqbal, Ahmad. 2002. Straight Talk on Terrorism. *Monthly Review* (January).

Falah, Ghazi. 1996. The 1948 Israeli-Palestinian War and its Aftermath: The Transformation and De-Signification of Palestine's Cultural Landscape. *Annals of the Association of American Geographers* 86(2):256–285.

Falk, Richard. 2000. *Human Rights Horizons: The Pursuit of Justice in a Globalizing World*. New York: Routledge.

Finkelstein, Norman. 2003. *Image and Reality of the Israel-Palestine Conflict*. London: Verso.

—— 2005. *Beyond Chutzpah: On the Misuse of Anti-Semitism and the Abuse of History*. Berkeley: University of California Press.

—— 2006. Should Dershowitz Target Himself for Assassination? *Counterpunch* <www.counterpunch.org>, August 12.

Fisher, William, and Thomas Ponniah (eds.). 2003. *Another World is Possible: Popular Alternatives to Globalization at the World Social Forum*. Nova Scotia: Fernwood.

Flapan, Simcha. 1979. *Zionism and the Palestinians*. London: Croom Helm.

—— 1987. *The Birth of Israel: Myths and Realities*. New York: Pantheon.

Fried, Efrat. 2000. Us Here, Them There: Barak's Plan of "Unilateral Separation." *News From Within* 14(8):14–16.

Fulghum, Robert. 1988. *All I Really Need to Know I Learned in Kindergarten*. New York: Random House.

Gatto, John Taylor. 1992. *Dumbing Us Down: The Hidden Curriculum of Compulsory Education*. Philadelphia: New Society Publishers.

Gorali, Moshe. 2003. Legality is in the Eye of the Beholder. *Ha'aretz*, September 26.

Gorenberg, Gershom. 2002. The Collaborator. *New York Times*, August 18, at sec. 6, p. 34.

—— 2006. *The Accidental Empire: Israel and the Birth of the Settlements, 1967–1977*. New York: Henry Holt.

Gorny, Yosef. 1987. *Zionism and the Arabs, 1882–1948*. Oxford: Oxford University Press.

Grossman, David. 1988. *The Yellow Wind*. New York: Farrar, Straus and Giroux.

Habitat International Coalition and Adalah-Legal Center for Arab Minority Rights in Israel. 2006. Statement to the UN Commission on Human Rights, March 2.

Halper, Jeff. 1991. *Between Redemption and Revival: The Jews of Jerusalem in the Nineteenth Century*. Boulder: Westview.

—— 1998. Israel's War on Palestinians: The Campaign of House Demolitions. *Tikkun* 13(5):56–59.

—— 2000a. The Road to Apartheid: The Trans-Israel Highway. *News From Within* 16(5):1–7.

—— 2000b. Barak Threatens a Separation Barrier. *News From Within* 16(5):8–9.

—— 2000c. The 94 Percent Solution: A Matrix of Control. *Middle East Report*, Fall.

—— 2002. The Three Jerusalems: Planning and Colonial Control. *Jerusalem Quarterly File* 15:6–17.

—— 2004. Paralysis Over Palestine: Questions of Strategy. *Journal of Palestine Studies* 34(2):55–69.

—— 2005a. Israel in a Middle East Union: A "Two-stage" Approach to the Conflict. *Tikkun* 20(1):17–21.

—— 2005b. Israel as an Extension of American Empire. In *Challenging Christian Zionism: Politics, Theology and the Israeli-Palestine Conflict.* Jerusalem: Sabeel.

—— 2007. A Prophetic Judaism of Human Rights: Rene Cassin and Resistance to the Israeli Occupation. In Murray Polner and Stefen Merken (eds.) *Peace, Justice, and Jews: Reclaiming Our Tradition.* New York: Bunim and Bannigan, pp. 276–282.

Hass, Amira. 2000. Don't Shoot Till You Can See They're Over the Age of 12. *Ha'aretz*, November 20.

—— 2002a. Israel's Closure Policy. *Journal of Palestine Studies* 23(3):5–20.

—— 2002b. Someone Even Managed to Defecate Into the Photocopier. *Ha'aretz*, June 5.

Hever, Shir. 2005a. *The Economy of the Occupation (Part 1): Foreign Aid to the Occupied Palestinian Territories and Israel.* Jerusalem and Beit Sahour: Alternative Information Centre.

—— 2005b. *The Economy of the Occupation (Part 3): Divide and Conquer: Inequality and Discrimination.* Jerusalem and Beit Sahour: Alternative Information Centre.

—— 2007a. *The Economy of the Occupation (# 11–12): The Separation Wall in East Jerusalem: Economic Consequences.* Jerusalem and Beit Sahour: Alternative Information Centre.

—— 2007b. Occupation or Aid. Paper presented at the United Nations Seminar on Assistance to the Palestinian People <www.aic.org>.

Human Rights Watch. 2004. *Razing Rafah: Mass Home Demolitions in the Gaza Strip* (October).

Huxley, Elspeth. 1959. *The Flame Trees of Thika.* London: Chatto and Windus.

Israeli Committee Against House Demolitions. 2004. *A Destructive Policy: House Demolitions in East Jerusalem: Facts, Intents and Implications* (December) (Hebrew).

Israeli Ministry of Foreign Affairs. 1998. *Population of Israel – General Trends and Indicators.* <www.israel-mfa.gov.il/MFA/Archive/Communiques/1998/POPULATION%20OF%20ISRAEL-%20GENERAL%20TRENDS%20AND%20INDICATOR>

Jabotinsky, Vladimir. 1923 (1937). O Zheleznoi Stene. *Rassvyet*, 4 November 1923 (Russian). Published in English as The Iron Wall: We and the Arabs. *Jewish Herald* (South Africa), 26 November 1937.

Jiryis, Sabri. 1976. *The Arabs in Israel.* New York: Monthly Review Press.

Joubran, Salam. 1995. Support for the Peace Process is Growing. *Davar Rishon*, December 24.

Kaminer, Reuven. 1995. *Politics of Protest: The Israeli Peace Movement and the Palestinian Intifada.* Brighton: Sussex Academic Press.

Kaminker, Sarah. 1995. East Jerusalem: A Case Study in Political Planning. *Palestine-Israel Journal* 2(2):59–66.

Khalidi, Rashid. 1997. *Palestinian Identity: The Construction of Modern National Consciousness.* New York: Columbia University Press.

Khalidi, Walid. 1971. *From Haven to Conquest. Readings in Zionism and the Palestine Problem until 1948.* Beirut: Institute for Palestine Studies.

—— 1992. *All That Remains: The Palestinian Villages Occupied and Depopulated by Israel in 1948.* Washington: Institute for Palestine Studies.

Kimmerling, Baruch. 1976. *Land, Conflict and Nation Building: A Sociological Study of the Territorial Factors in the Jewish-Arab Conflict.* Jerusalem: Hebrew University (mimeo).

—— 1983. *Zionism and Territory.* Berkeley: Institute of International Studies.

—— 2001. *The Invention and Decline of Israeliness: State, Culture and Military in Israel.* Berkeley: University of California Press.

—— 2003. *Politicide: Ariel Sharon's War Against the Palestinians.* London: Verso.

Kolatt, Israel. 1983. The Zionist Movement and the Arabs. In Shmuel Almog (ed.) *Zionism and the Arabs.* Jerusalem: Zalman Shazar Center, pp. 1–34.

Korey, William. 1998. *NGOs and the Universal Declaration of Human Rights.* New York: St. Martin's Press.

Kretzmer, David. 2002. *The Occupation of Justice: The Supreme Court of Israel and the Occupied Territories.* New York: SUNY Press.

Lustick, I. 1980. *Arabs in the Jewish State. Israel's Control of a National Minority.* Austin: University of Texas Press.

—— 1996. To Build and to Be Built By: Israel and the Hidden Logic of the Iron Wall. *Israel Studies* 1(1):196–223.

Magid, Aaron. 2007. Israeli Youth More "Israeli" Less "Jewish." *Jerusalem Post,* July 24.

Makovskey, David. 2003. Taba Mythchief. *The National Interest,* Spring:119–129.

Mansour, Atallah. 1997. Arab Lands in Israel: A Festering Wound. *Palestine-Israel Journal* 4(2):25–30.

Maoz, Ze'ev. 2006. Israel's Nonstrategy of Peace. *Tikkun* 21(5):49–50.

Margalit, Meir. 2006a. *Discrimination in the Holy City.* Jerusalem: International Peace and Cooperation Center.

—— 2006b. *No Place Like Home: House Demolitions in East Jerusalem.* Jerusalem: ICAHD.

Masalha, Nur. 1992. *Expulsion of the Palestinians: The Concept of "Transfer" in Zionist Political Thought, 1882–1948*. Washington: Institute for Palestine Studies.

Matar, Ibrahim. 1997. The Quiet War: Land Expropriation in the Occupied Territories. *Palestine-Israel Journal* 4(2):40–45.

McGreal, Chris. 2003. Sharon Trying to Regionalize Palestinian Conflict by Striking Syria. *Guardian*, October 9.

Moratinos, Miguel. 2001. "Non-Paper" on the Taba Negotiations. *Ha'aretz*, February 14.

Morris, Benny. 1999. *Righteous Victims: A History of the Arab-Israeli Conflict, 1881–1999*. New York: Knopf.

—— 2002a. Camp David and After: An Exchange (1. An Interview with Ehud Barak). *New York Review of Books* 49(10):42–45.

—— 2002b. A New Exodus for the Middle East? *Guardian*, October 3.

—— 2004. *The Birth of the Palestinian Refugee Problem Revisited, 1947–1949*. Cambridge: Cambridge University Press.

Netanyahu, Benjamin. 1995. *Fighting Terrorism: How Democracies can Defeat Domestic and International Terrorists*. New York: Farrar, Straus and Giroux.

—— 2007. Interview conducted by David Frost, February 28 <www.mfa.gov.il/MFA/Archive/Speeches/ISRAELI%20PM%20BENJAMIN%20NETANYAHU%20WITH%20DAVID%20FROST%20-%202>

Ophir, Adi. 2005. *The Order of Evils: Toward an Ontology of Morals*. Cambridge: MIT Press.

Oren, Michael. 2002. *Six Days of War: June 1967 and the Making of the Modern Middle East*. Oxford: Oxford University Press.

Pacheco, Allegra. 1989. Occupying an Uprising: The Geneva Law and Israeli Administrative Detention Policy During the First Year of the Palestinian General Uprising. *Columbia Human Rights Law Review* 21.

Palestinian Center for Human Rights. 2003. *Demolition of Palestinian Houses by Israeli Occupying Forces as a Means of Punishment and Determent* (June) <www.pchrgaza.org/Library/alaqsaintifada.htm>.

Palestinian Central Bureau of Statistics. 2007. Labor Force Survey Results. Ramallah: PCBS.

Palestine Monitor <www.palestinemonitor.org>.

Pappe, Ilan. 1988. *The Making of the Arab-Israeli Conflict, 1948–1951*. London: Macmillan.

—— 2006. *The Ethnic Cleansing of Palestine*. Oxford: One World Publications.

—— 2004. The Geneva Bubble. *London Review of Books* 26(1):23–28.

Peri, Yoram. 2006. *Generals in the Cabinet Room: How the Military Shapes Israeli Policy.* Washington: United States Institute of Peace Press.

Perliger, Arie, and Leonard Weinberg. 2003. Jewish Self Defense and Terrorist Groups Prior to the Establishment of the State of Israel: Roots and Traditions. *Totalitarian Movements & Political Religions* 4(3):91–118.

Perry, Yaakov. 1999. *Strike First.* Tel Aviv: Keshet (Hebrew).

Reinhart, Tanya. 2002. *Israel/Palestine How to End the War of 1948.* New York: Seven Stories Press.

Roy, Sara. 1987. The Gaza Strip: A Case of Economic De-development. *Journal of Palestine Studies* 17(1):56–88.

Rummel, R.J. 1994. *Death by Government.* New Brunswick: Transaction Books.

Sachar, Howard M. 1963. *The Course of Modern Jewish History.* New York: Dell.

—— 1981. *A History of Israel: From the Rise of Zionism to Our Time.* New York: Knopf.

Sa'di, Ahmad. 2003. The Koenig Report and Israeli Policy Towards the Palestinian Minority, 1965–1976: Old Wine in New Bottles. *Arab Studies Quarterly* 25(3):51–62.

Said, Edward. 1979. *The Question of Palestine.* New York: Vintage Books.

—— 2001. *The End of the Peace Process: Oslo And After.* New York: Vintage Books.

Savir, Uri. 1998. *The Process.* New York: Vintage.

Schueftan, Dan. 2003. Voice of Palestine: The New Ideology of Israeli Arabs. *Azure* 14:73–106.

Segev, Tom. 1986. *1949: The First Israelis.* New York: The Free Press.

—— 1999. *One Palestine, Complete. Jews and Arabs Under the British Mandate.* New York: Henry Holt.

Shalhoub-Kevorkian, Nadera. 2007. House Demolition: A Palestinian Feminist Perspective. *"...Not Only Was the House Lost": A Photo Essay.* Jerusalem: The Jerusalem Link and ICAHD.

Shapira, Anita. 1992. *Land and Power: The Zionist Resort to Force, 1881–1948.* Oxford: Oxford University Press.

Shatz, Adam. (ed.). 2004. *Prophets Outcast: A Century of Dissident Jewish Writing about Zionism and Israel.* New York: Nation Books.

Shavit, Ari. 2002. Eyes Wide Shut. *Ha'aretz Magazine,* September 6.

—— 2004a. Survival of the Fittest. *Ha'aretz Magazine,* January 9.

—— 2004b. The Big Freeze. *Ha'aretz Magazine,* October 8.

Shehadeh, Raja. 1997. Land and Occupation: A Legal Review. *Palestine-Israel Journal* 4(2):25–30.

Shlaim, Avi. 1988. *Collusion Across the Jordan.* Oxford: Clarendon.

—— 2000. *The Iron Wall: Israel and the Arab World.* New York: Norton.

—— 2001. Israel and the Arab Coalition in 1948. In Eugene R. Rogen and Avi Shlaim (eds.) *The War for Palestine: Rewriting the History of 1948.* Cambridge: Cambridge University Press, pp. 79–103.

Silberstein, Laurence. 1999. *The Postzionism Debates: Knowledge and Power in Israeli Culture.* New York: Routledge.

Smooha, Sami, and T. Hanf. 1992. The Diverse Modes of Conflict-Regulation in Deeply Divided Societies. In A.D. Smith (ed.) *Ethnicity and Nationalism.* New York: E.J. Brill.

Sternhell, Zeev. 1998. *The Founding Myths of Israel: Nationalism, Socialism and the Making of the Jewish State.* Princeton: Princeton University Press.

Tekiner, Roselle. 1990. Israel's Two-Tiered Citizenship Law Bars Non-Jews from 93 percent of its Lands. *Washington Report on Middle Eastern Affairs* 190:20.

Teveth, Shabtai. 1985. *Ben-Gurion and the Palestinian Arabs, from Peace to War.* Oxford: Oxford University Press.

UN (United Nations). 2005. *The Humanitarian Impact of the West Bank Barrier on Palestinian Communities.* Jerusalem: OCHA.

UNCTAD (United Nations Conference on Trade and Development). 2006. *The Palestinian War-torn Economy: Aid, Development and State Formation.* New York: United Nations.

UNRWA (United Nations Relief and Works Agency). 2006. *Prolonged Crisis in the Occupied Palestinian Territory: Recent Socio-Economic Impacts on Refugees and Non-Refugees.* Gaza: UNRWA.

Uris, Leon. 1958. *Exodus.* New York: Doubleday.

Weissbrod, Rachel. 1999. Exodus as a Zionist Melodrama. *Israel Studies* 4(1):129–152.

Weizman, Eyal. 2003. Ariel Sharon and the Geometry of Occupation (part 1). *Open Democracy* <www.opendemocracy.net/conflict/article_1474.jsp>.

—— 2004. Strategic Points, Flexible Lines, Tense Surfaces and Political Volumes: Ariel Sharon and the Geometry of Occupation. *Philosophical Forum* 35(2):221–244.

—— 2006. *The Art of War* <www.frieze.com/feature_single.asp?f=1165>.

—— 2007. *Hollow Land: Israel's Architecure of Occupation.* London: Verso.

World Bank. 2004. *Four Years— Intifada, Closures and Palestinian Economic Crisis.* Washington: World Bank.

—— 2005. *West Bank and Gaza Update.* Washington: World Bank (November).

Yiftachel, Oren. 1999a. "Ethnocracy": The Politics of Judaizing Israel/ Palestine. *Constellations* 6:364–391.

—— 1999b. Judaize and Divide: Shaping Spaces in the Israeli Ethnocracy. *News From Within* 15(11):13–20.

Zunes, Stephen. 2004. *Congress to Sharon: Take All You Want* <www. anti-war.com>.

—— 2006. *The Real Lobby: The Military-Industrial Complex.* FPIF <www.fpif.org/fpiftxt/3270>.

Further Resources

Al-Haq: <alhaq.org>
Alternative Information Center: <www.alternativenews.org>
Arab Association for Human Rights: <www.hra.com>
Ariga: <www.ariga.com>
Badil: <www.badil.org>
Bat Shalom: <www.batshalom.org>
B'tselem: <www.btselem.org>
Christian Peacemaker Team: <www.prairienet.org>
Coalition of Women for Peace: <www.coalitionof women4peace.org>
The Electronic Intifada: <electronicintifada.net>
Foundation for Middle East Peace: <www.fmep.orgt>
Gush Shalom: <www.gush-shalom.org>
Ha'aretz newspaper: <www.haaretzdaily.com>
Hebrew website: <mahsom.org>
Indymedia: <www.indymedia.org.il>
The Israeli Committee Against House Demolitions (ICAHD): <www.
   icahd.org>
Jerusalem Center for Social and Economic Rights: <www.jcser.org/
   english>
Jerusalem Center for Women: <www.j-c-w.org>
Jerusalem Media and Communication Center: <www.jmcc.org>
Jerusalem Report: <www.jrep.com>
Jewish Voice For Peace: <www.jewishvoiceforpeace.org>
LAW: <www.law@lawsociety.org>
New Profile: <www.newprofile.org>
Palestine Monitor: <www.palestinemonitor.org>
Palestinian Center for Human Rights (PCHR): <www.pchrgaza.org>
Palestinian Hydrology Group (PHG): <www.phg.org>
The Palestinian Initiative for the Promotion of Global Dialogue and
   Democracy: <ww.miftah.org>
PalMap: Palestine Mapping Center <www.palmap.org>
PENGON: <www.pengon.org>, <www.stopthewall.org>
PASSIA: <www.passia.org>
Rabbis for Human Rights: <www.rhr.israel.net>
Sabeel: <www.sabeel.org>
Ta'ayush: <taayush.tripod.com>
US Campaign Against the Occupation <www.endtheoccupation.org>
Yesh Gvul: <yeshgvul.org>

Index

Compiled by Sue Carlton